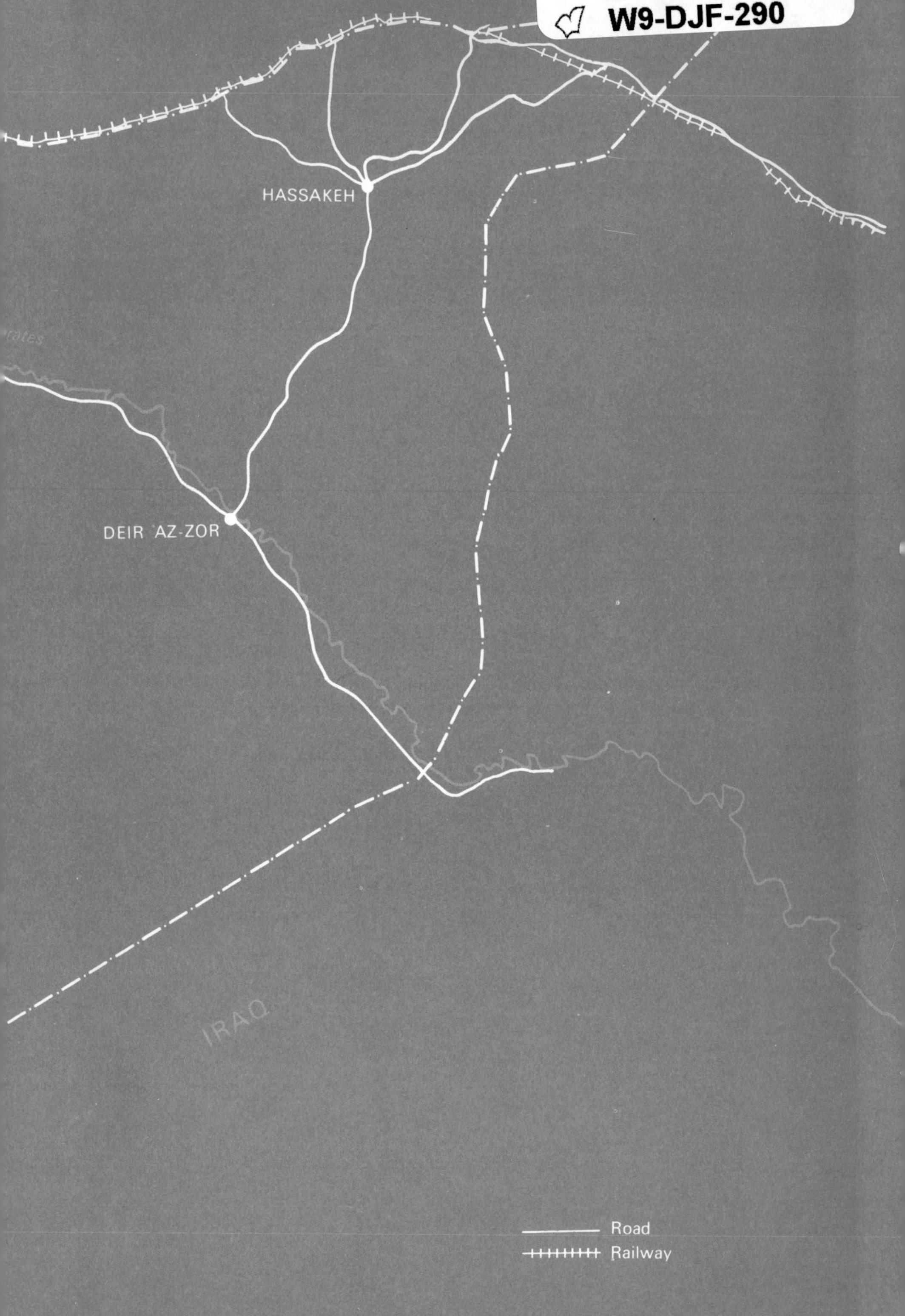
HASSAKEH
DEIR 'AZ-ZOR
IRAQ
Road
Railway

15.50
EMM

THE SHILOAH CENTER FOR MIDDLE EASTERN AND AFRICAN STUDIES
THE MONOGRAPH SERIES

SYRIA UNDER THE BA'TH 1963–66

THE ARMY—PARTY SYMBIOSIS

The Shiloah Center for Middle Eastern and African Studies
Tel Aviv University

The Shiloah Center is, with the Department of Middle Eastern and African History, a part of the School of History at Tel Aviv University. Its main purpose is to contribute, by research and documentation, to the dissemination of knowledge and understanding of the modern history and current affairs of the Middle East and Africa. Emphasis is laid on fields where Israeli scholarship is in a position to make a special contribution and on subjects relevant to the needs of society and the teaching requirements of the University.

The Monograph Series

The studies published in this series are the work of the Research Associates and Visiting Research Associates at the Shiloah Center. The views expressed in these publications are entirely those of the authors.

URIEL DANN / IRAQ UNDER QASSEM

DAVID KIMCHE / THE AFRO-ASIAN MOVEMENT

ITAMAR RABINOVICH / SYRIA UNDER THE BA'TH 1963–66

ARYEH YODFAT/ARAB POLITICS IN THE SOVIET MIRROR

SYRIA UNDER THE BA'TH 1963–66

THE ARMY-PARTY SYMBIOSIS

Itamar Rabinovich

ISRAEL UNIVERSITIES PRESS, Jerusalem

HALSTED PRESS
A Division of JOHN WILEY & SONS, INC., New York

ISRAEL UNIVERSITIES PRESS
is a publishing division of the
ISRAEL PROGRAM FOR SCIENTIFIC TRANSLATIONS, LTD.
P. O. Box 7145, Jerusalem, Israel

IUP Cat. No. 36079
ISBN 0 7065 1266 9

Manufactured by Keter Press, Jerusalem, Israel

To the memory of
G.E. von Grunebaum

CONTENTS

FOREWORD

For a good many years Syrian politics have been widely regarded as obscure and incomprehensible to outsiders. In Western countries contact with Syria has been slight and information skimpy; Syria has undergone a series of internal upheavals, which have enhanced the image of her as a hotbed of fanaticism and irrationality. The puzzlement has been compounded by the odyssey of the Ba'th. Before 1963 it had been a familiar landmark in the Arab world, as the party of Michel 'Aflaq and Salah al-Bitar, embodying the aspirations of a rising intelligentsia—in several Arab states— for unity, democracy, and social reform. Once in power, the party soon changed its shape and colour, and many observers were taken by surprise. 'Aflaq and Bitar lost their prominence and eventually disappeared from the scene altogether; unknown soldiers and radical civilians, at odds with the world and with each other, plunged Syria into factional strife in the name of revolution, leaving behind the party's earlier commitments to pan-Arabism and electoral democracy.

What did all this mean? Did the successive party congresses, with their lengthy discussions and declarations, really mean anything? Was a debate really going on about the means and ends of the party's programme, and if so, among whom, and to what end? Or had the Ba'th simply become the plaything of ambitious military officers, and was all the rhetoric just a smokescreen for factional power struggles?

The present book deals with these and similar problems. It concentrates especially on the years 1963–6, during which the Ba'th Party founded and consolidated its régime but concurrently underwent a profound metamorphosis, culminating in the internal *coup d'état* of 1966 which re-ordered the character of the party, the army, and the government in a new relationship. Thus, this book is an excellent and much-needed sequel to Patrick Seale's fine study, *The Struggle for Syria,* which charted the affairs of Syria from 1945 to 1958.

It is to the credit of the author, Itamar Rabinovich, that he has cut through the layers of fog in which Syria has been wrapped, and has managed to make sense out of what looked like nonsense. This is a considerable accomplishment, for it required not only the patience and thoroughness and mastery of the Arabic language with which he made his way through a mass of documentation (the Syrian, Lebanese, and Egyptian press, countless public manifestos and private circulars of the Ba'th Party, the published memoirs of numerous participants in recent Syrian events), but a keen analytical insight and scholarly detachment as well.

Where Patrick Seale, as a first-class journalist, relied mainly on the inside information he had gathered from interviews with several dozen retired Syrian politicians and soldiers, the author of the present book, as an Israeli citizen, has had no opportunity to interview his subjects. No one is more conscious of this limitation than the author himself. Yet his reliance on an exhaustive attention to written material, much of which has simply been ignored by scholars and much of which was not available until the aftermath of the 1967 war, gives his book a considerable strength all its own. He shows us that what happened in Syria in the 1960s was not really (as one of his sources puts it) "un combat de négres dans un tunnel", but a logical and comprehensible series of actions in which Syrian officers and politicians, like their counterparts elsewhere, played out their convictions, loyalties, and ambitions amidst the practical constraints and opportunities available to them.

Malcolm H. Kerr
University of California, Los Angeles

PREFACE

This study evolved from a broader interest in the contemporary history of Syria and in one of its major political parties, the Ba'th. It was mostly the availability of relatively rich documentation on the first phase of Ba'thi rule in Syria, from March 1963 to March 1966, which focused my interest on that period rather than on other, equally well-defined phases of Syria's recent history. The period opened with the *coup d'état* of March 8, 1963, which brought the Ba'th to power in Syria, and ended with another *coup* on February 23, 1966. Although the 1966 *coup* was an internal Ba'thi affair, it heralded the beginning of a new political order in Syria.

The annals of Syrian political history during these years present an interesting though often confusing picture and bring out several intriguing themes: the problems confronting an ideological party in power; the unique relationship between the military and civilian leaders of the Ba'th; the rapid transformation of that party; the rise of army officers and party militants from minority communities to political prominence; and other striking social changes. It is proposed here to establish the chronology of the period, to identify the issues and acting forces that shaped events, and, finally, to evaluate the significance of the changes and developments that took place in Syria between 1963 and 1966.

This study is defined as a "political history" in a rather narrow sense, since it focuses mainly on major aspects and issues of the political process. Social and economic questions are discussed only where they became political issues, and a continuous account of Syria's foreign policy during these years is not given. Syria's relations with other Arab states are discussed at some length as they constituted a cardinal issue of Syrian politics at that time.

Though concerned primarily with the Ba'th this is not a study of that party in its first years of power but of Syrian political history during a period in which the Ba'th Party played a crucial role. By mid-1965, Syrian politics had become practically coterminous with Ba'thi politics. Accordingly, the last three chapters of this book deal almost exclusively with intra-Ba'thi developments. The distinction between Ba'thi and broader Syrian politics is more marked in the earlier section.

THE SOURCES

None of the works previously published have covered the whole period or surveyed the subject fully. Those by Ben Tsur, Colombe, De Buck, Kerr, Rondot, Seymour, Torrey, and others, all cited in the bibliography, treat certain phases and aspects of the period and have been used to varying degrees as indicated in the footnotes to the text. K.S. Abu Jaber has written a history of the Ba'th Party in his *The Arab Ba'th Socialist Party: History, Ideology and Organization* (Syracuse, N.Y., 1966), but his discussion of the party's regime in Syria is cursory and at several points seems inadequate. Moreover, he often appears to express the views of, and to attribute too much importance to, Michel 'Aflaq's wing of the party, the emasculation of whose power was then a central issue.

A more recent history of the Ba'th Party is Ibrāhīm Salāmeh's *Al-Ba'th min al-madāris ilā ath-thakanāt* ("The Ba'th from the Schools to the Barracks"), Beirut, 1969. It is a short survey that is most informative on some issues and disappointing on others.

From the relatively rich documentation available, three principal categories of primary sources are used: Ba'thi documents, memoirs and books of polemics, and the Arabic press and radio broadcasts.

Ba'thi Documents

Most of the Ba'thi documents used in this study are yet unpublished records of the Syrian party, that were made available to the author through the archives of the Shiloah Center for Middle Eastern and African Studies at Tel Aviv University. Though originating in local centres, they are of a national rather than provincial interest. The Ba'th is a highly centralized party, and furthermore has upheld the

principle that one of the privileges of its member was to be better informed than the "uninitiated" general population. This accounts for the fact that the documents illuminate several unknown aspects of the internal workings of the Ba'thi political system. The documents consist of brochures distributed among party members, of bulletins (*nasharāt*) and circulars (*ta'mīmāt*) issued by the party's National and Regional Commands. The nature of each document cited in the text is explained in the footnotes, and each document should naturally be evaluated on its own merits. While in many respects this is a unique and most valuable source it also has two important limitations:
a. The documents represent a partial, often occasional, sample. Thus, while there is ample documentation on such episodes as the negotiations between the National Command of the Ba'th and the Syrian faction of the *Quṭriyyūn* in 1962, there are no details as to who these *Quṭriyyūn* were.
b. Research based on written documents of a general nature risks the danger of portraying the situation ideally, as it should have been according to the documents. This is all the more true when, as in this case, only a partial sample is accessible. Fortunately, however, the availability of other sources often provides a broader perspective.

Other Ba'thi documents have been published under the sponsorship of the party itself in the series *Niḍāl al-Ba'th* ("The Struggle of the Ba'th") issued in seven volumes by Dār aṭ-Ṭalī'a in Beirut. Volumes IV and VI, covering the activity of the National Command of the Ba'th in the years 1955–63, contain some particularly important documents on the UAR period and on the Fourth, Fifth, and Sixth National Congresses of the party. Earlier volumes in the series consist mostly of manifestos, declarations, and newspaper editorials. However, probably because the party's history from 1958 had already become the subject of open controversies, the Ba'th decided to publish, almost intact,[1] several documents that had previously been considered internal and even secret.

[1] A comparison of the resolutions of the Sixth National Congress as published in Volume VI of *Niḍāl al-Ba'th* with the brochure distributed to party members shows that a brief section including a strong criticism of 'Aflaq and his associate Salah al-Bitar was omitted by the former source.

Memoirs and Books of Polemics

The most important single source for the history of the period is *al-Tajriba al-murra* ("The Bitter Experience", Beirut, 1967), the memoirs written by Munif ar-Razzaz, secretary-general of the Ba'th Party from April 1965 to February 1966. The more significant parts of the book are the short survey of the party's history up to April 1965 and the detailed personal account of the struggle within the Ba'th regime which led to the *coup d'état* of February 23, 1966, and to Razzaz's own deposition. Razzaz has more than one axe to grind, and in his book he tried to settle accounts with both foes and apparent allies and to vindicate his own positions. But he was remarkably candid, and his account offers a detailed and vivid portrait of Ba'thi politics during those months.

Less helpful is the account titled *al-Ba'th* (Beirut, 1969) written by Sami al-Jundi, a veteran Ismā'īlī member of the party who had served in several Syrian cabinets in 1963 and 1964 and was then sent as ambassador to Paris. Jundi's description of the early years of the Ba'th is detailed and most illuminating, but the section dealing with developments from 1958 is somewhat disappointing. It does contain interesting new details and renders a vivid description of several events and institutions, but the narrative is often haphazard and sometimes seems unreliable. Not only does Jundi try to defend his conduct during the period but he is clearly hostile to such persons as Salah J'did, whom he probably holds responsible for the tragedies of the Jundi family from 1968. As a source Jundi is still indispensable but ought to be used very carefully.

Apparently it was also in response to the account given by Razzaz that Muhammad 'Umran, minister of defence in the Syrian cabinet ousted in February 1966, published a short version of the same events. He did so in the introduction to the first (and—due to his recent assassination—the only) volume of *Tajribatī fi ath-thaura* ("My Experience in the Revolution", n.p., 1970). 'Umran's account is disappointing—most controversial points are glossed over and his version of others often seems unacceptable.

The supreme commander of the Syrian army from September 1961 to March 1963, General 'Abd al-Karim Zahr ad-Din, has published his account of Syrian politics during that period under the title *Mudhakkirātī 'an fatrat al-infiṣāl fī sūriyya* ("My Memoirs of the Separatist Period in Syria"). It naturally focuses on the history of the Separatist Regime and does so from a very personal point of view; still, besides illuminating the context in which the Ba'th came to power in Syria, it contains important information on the making of the *coup* which brought the Ba'th to power and on the nature of military politics in Syria in the early 1960s. On the borderline between memoirs and polemics stands *Ḥizb al-ba'th, ma'sāt al-bidāya wa-ma'sāt an-nihāya* ("The Ba'th Party, the Misfortunes of Its Beginning and of Its End", Beirut, 1965) written by Mutā' aṣ-Ṣafadī, the Syrian novelist and publicist. A former Ba'thi disenchanted with the Ba'th and its leaders, Ṣafadī became an active supporter of Egyptian president Gamal Abdel Nasser and was jailed in 1963. Following his release he wrote anti-Ba'thi articles in Beirut newspapers, and his book is a more sophisticated attempt in the same direction. The author has an intimate knowledge of Ba'thi affairs, and despite its obvious bias his account not only represents a point of view shared by several other disillusioned Ba'this but also offers significant information.

Yasin al-Hafiz represents another dissident Ba'thi group, the Marxist faction which played a notable role in Syrian and Ba'thi politics late in 1963 and early in 1964 until its expulsion from the party. His critique of Ba'thi ideology in *Fī al-fikr as-siyāsī* ("On Political Thought", Damascus, 1963), which he coedited, and in the collection of his essays *Ḥaula ba'ḍ qaḍāyā al-ḥaraka al-qaumiyya al-'arabiyya* ("On Some Problems of the Arab Nationalist Movement", Beirut, 1965) tends to be of a general nature, but it sheds light on some of the central ideological and political issues of the period.

Several anti-Ba'thi books were published in Egypt during 1963 but even the more serious ones like those by Mahmud 'Abd ar-Rahim cited in the bibliography have little value as sources for Syrian and Ba'thi history. An apologetic rejoinder by Taufiq 'Indani, *al-Ba'th fī durūb an-niḍāl* ("The Ba'th on the Roads of Struggle", Damascus, 1965) is almost equally disappointing.

The Arabic Press and Radio Broadcasts

The Syrian press and radio broadcasts of the years 1963–66 are a basic and indispensable source for the chronology and some aspects of the political history of the period. The *coup d'état* of March 8, 1963, resulted in the gradual suspension of almost all the newspapers which had enjoyed a measure of relative freedom under the preceding regime. *Al-Muḍḥik al-Mubkī* ("The Sad Clown"), a humour weekly, sometimes containing esoteric political references, was the only significant non-Ba'thi publication tolerated during the first phase of Ba'thi rule in Syria.[2]

Consequently, the closely controlled press and radio[3] rarely offer political information beyond the daily chronicle, party and government bulletins, texts of public speeches, commentaries, and editorials. These are all important but reveal little about the internal workings of the Syrian-Ba'thi political system. The Syrian press and radio became more informative only in times of crisis. Thus, when the non-Nasserite elements in the Syrian government felt in May 1963 that they had to bring their case against the Nasserites to the public they did so in detail over the radio and in the press, and offered their version of the history of the March 8 *coup*. Later intra-Ba'thi rivalries were echoed in differences between *al-Ba'th* and *ath-Thaura*.

With the notable exception of the Lebanese press, reports on and analyses of Syrian affairs in the newspapers and radio broadcasts of other Arab states are generally more important as indicators of their relations with Syria than as a source of information on Syrian and Ba'thi politics. Of a different nature was the publication in Cairo of (the Egyptian version of) the protocols of the Tripartite Unity Talks held between Egypt, Syria and Iraq in March and April 1963. This unique document is of prime importance for understanding contemporary Arab politics; among other things it demonstrates the complex relationship between the Ba'th Party and President Nasser in the years 1958–63 and sheds some light on such questions as the antecedents of the March 8 *coup* and relations within the coalition government established in Syria following that *coup*.

The term Lebanese press is somewhat misleading when used to

[2] The newspaper published by the Kahhaleh family was suspended immediately after the *coup* of February 23, 1966—a symptom of the change of atmosphere brought about by that *coup*.

[3] The memoirs of Sami al-Jundi, several times minister of information under the Ba'th, clearly illustrate that control.

designate a single source, for it ignores important differences in quality and orientation. Most Beirut newspapers mirror in a more subtle fashion the propaganda warfare between rival Arab regimes. Thus, when writing or reporting on Syrian affairs in the years 1963–66, *al-Anwār, al-Muḥarrir, Kull Shay',* and a few other newspapers reflected Egyptian or Nasserite positions, *al-Ḥayāt* pursued a conservative anti-Ba'thi line (but was often informative), while *al-Kifāḥ* and sometimes *an-Nahār* tended to publish news that suited the Ba'th. *Al-Aḥrār,* the organ of the National Command of the Ba'th in Beirut, supported its cause against intra- and extra-party rivals. *Al-Jarīda,* and during most of the period *an-Nahār,* approached standards of objective reporting on Syrian affairs.

The latter two, and less frequently the partisan Beirut newspapers, provided useful and correct information on several episodes of Syrian political history during these years. In some instances revealing reports and documents published in these newspapers were leaked by interested Ba'thi sources.[4] The minutes of the Regional Congress of February 1964 (published by *al-Muḥarrir*) and 'Aflaq's addresses of December 19, 1965, and February 18, 1966 (published respectively by *al-Jarīda* and *al-Ḥayāt*) are notable examples of instructive documents published in the Lebanese press. The February 18 address is a most important document presenting 'Aflaq's interpretation of the regime's history and his position during the crisis which led to the *coup* of February 23, 1966.

The Arabic press and radio broadcasts have become more easily accessible through such publications as *Chronology of Arab Politics, Arab Political Documents, Middle East Record,* and *Cahiers de L'Orient Contemporain. Middle East Record* was not published during the years 1963–66, and *Arab Political Documents* and *Chronology of Arab Politics* (in both English and Arabic versions) together with the publications of 'Itim Mizraḥ, the Israeli monitoring service, proved the most useful research aids during the preparation of the present study.

[4] The *Organizational Report* submitted to the Syrian Regional Congress in February 1965 complained (p. 18) that reports submitted to previous congresses were quoted "literally" in the Lebanese press. For an earlier period, Zahr ad-Din (p. 345) complained that details from the most secret meetings were leaked to the local and Beirut newspapers.

All these sources make the history of the Ba'th regime in Syria from March 1963 to March 1966 relatively well documented, given the esoteric political system. Several aspects and episodes of the period are still obscured by insufficient information, and too little is known about the personalities and social backgrounds of its principal political figures, but this holds true for numerous aspects of Syria's modern history.

Transliteration and Appendices

Arabic names appearing in the text are rendered phonetically, only the 'ayn and hamza have been specifically designated. The spelling of names familiar to English readers from the daily press is given in the form commonly accepted by English publications. Arabic names are reproduced fully transliterated in Appendix E, which also includes an index of names and short characterizations. Appendix A consists of a list of all Syrian cabinets and their composition, from March 1963 to March 1966; Appendix B offers the composition of National and Syrian Regional Commands of the Ba'th during the same period; Appendix C lists all National Congresses from 1963 to 1966 with short explanations on each; Appendix D is a schematic description of the Ba'th Party's organization. Appendix F is a translation of the second section of *Ba'ḍ al-Munṭalāqāt an-Naẓariyya*, the important ideological text approved by the Sixth National Congress of the Ba'th that is discussed and analyzed in Chapter 4.

The translation of the Arabic term *ṭā'īfiyya* into English presents a problem. It has sometimes been rendered or referred to in the text as "communalism" or "sectarianism", but in certain cases it was found necessary to resort to the term "confessionalism", taken from the Lebanese context.

Finally, it gives me special pleasure to thank all those who have assisted me in preparing and publishing this study. My research was encouraged and supported by the Near Eastern Center at the University of California, Los Angeles, and the Faculty of Humanities and Department of Middle Eastern and African History of Tel Aviv University. The Shiloah Center of the same university and its staff, most notably Dr. Haim Shaked, were more than helpful in offering their aid and research facilities.

The manuscript in its original form as a Ph. D. dissertation owed much to the guidance of the late Professor G. E. von Grunebaum, to whose memory this work is dedicated. His recent untimely death was a great loss to Islamic and Oriental studies but for me it was primarily a personal loss.

My deepest gratitude goes also to Professor Malcolm Kerr of UCLA, who supervised the preparation of the dissertation, for his thoughtful advice and comment.

The manuscript has also been read by Professor Elie Kedourie of the London School of Economics and by my colleagues at Tel Aviv University, Professors Shimon Shamir and Uriel Dann. Credit is due to Dr. Joel Kraemer for his labours in improving the translation of Appendix F. Their advice was most helpful but the faults and shortcomings of the revised manuscript remain, of course, exclusively mine. I am especially indebted to my colleagues and former teachers for their encouragement and cooperation.

The manuscript was originally typed and corrected by Mrs. Teresa Joseph of Los Angeles. My sincere thanks go to the staff of Israel Universities Press and particularly to Mr. Robert Amoils who helped improve the English style.

Last but certainly not least, my affectionate gratitude to my wife Efrat, my daughter Iris, my parents and Esther and Abraham Silver who all have a share in the book.

ITAMAR RABINOVICH

1 SYRIAN POLITICS AND THE BA'TH, 1945–61

Syria's personality is the Arab unionist personality; its entity is moral, neither material nor political. It is an idea and a struggle and it is an anticipation and a preparation and materialization of the unified Arab entity. . . . (Resolutions of the Fifth National Congress of the Ba'th Party, June 1962).

THE SYRIAN POLITICAL SCENE, 1945–54

The Syrian state within its present boundaries is a novel entity to which relatively few of its citizens have owed the "terminal allegiance" that a political community expects from its members.[1] The notion of Syrian entity and nationhood was first formulated in the latter half of the nineteenth century by educated Syrian and Lebanese Christians. It seems that they were seeking a solution to their problems as members of closed minority groups through the creation of a new nation on a secular territorial basis.[2] But this notion was not entirely distinct from the feeling of an Arab identity; it referred to a wider territory than present-day Syria and has long been submerged by the idea of pan-Arab nationalism. This, too, was originally formulated by Christians moved by similar needs but was gradually taken over by Muslim Arabs and assumed an implicit Islamic content.[3]

The unification and independence of the area which constitutes present-day Syria was a major goal of the nationalist struggle against

[1] The terminology here follows L. Binder, *The Ideological Revolution in the Middle East* (New York, 1964), p. 116.

[2] For the most comprehensive analysis of the emergence of the ideas of Arab and Syrian nationalism in the nineteenth century see A. Hourani, *Arabic Thought in the Liberal Age, 1789–1939* (London, 1962) and especially pp. 273–280. Greater importance is attributed to the role of Muslims in the genesis of such ideas in a recent article, F. Steppat, "Eine Bewegung unter den Notabeln Syriens 1877–78", *Zeitschrift der Deutschen Morgenländischen Gesellschaft,* Supplementa I, Teil 2, 1969, pp. 631–649. A much heavier emphasis and from a Muslim partisan point of view is given to the Muslim role in A.L. Tibawi, *A Modern History of Syria* (London, 1969).

[3] For the implicit, sometimes even explicit, Islamic content of Arab nationalism see G.E. von Grunebaum, *Modern Islam* (New York, 1964), especially pp. 276–334;

the French, part of whose mandatory territory in the Levant it had become in 1920; however, achievement of this aim was regarded as a phase in the struggle for Arab independence and unity. The idea of a Syrian entity was revived in the 1930s by Antun Sa'adeh's Parti Populaire Syrien (PPS), but again it referred to a wider area and in Syria proper could not compete with the more prevalent ideology of pan-Arab nationalism.[4] By 1945 the newly born Syrian state had acquired a certain vitality through the nationalist struggle against the French and through the vested interests created by the very existence of a political unit. But in terms of the dominant ideology there was (and has remained) an aura of illegitimacy about it.[5]

While ideological allegiance was thus given, or at least professed, to a wider entity, effective political allegiance was often still vested in traditional social or regional units: the family, the religious community, the tribe, the locality. This is vividly suggested in the reply given by a somewhat marginal member of Syrian society to an American interviewer in the early 1950s: "Though I have a Syrian passport, still I don't feel I am so. We Bedouins are used to a different life and we are primarily loyal to our Amir. . . ."[6]

While such deep lines of division are familiar elsewhere in the Arab world, in Syria they seem to have assumed a particular significance because of the diversity and fragmentation of the society and the weakness of the political centre. This fragmentation is evident in a deep chasm between city and countryside, in regional rivalries and animosities, and, most prominently, in the population's communal structure. "The antagonism between the urban and rural populations reaches there such a degree", it has been observed, "that one can

Sylvia Haim, *Arab Nationalism: An Anthology* (Berkeley and Los Angeles, 1964), especially pp. 53–61; and C.E. Dawn, "From Ottomanism to Arabism: The Origin of an Ideology", *The Review of Politics,* XXIII (1961), pp. 378–400; and "The Question of Nationalism in Syria and Lebanon", in W. Sands (ed.), *Tensions in the Middle East* (Washington, D.C., 1956), pp. 11–17.

4 L.Z. Yamak, *The Syrian Social Nationalist Party* (Cambridge, Mass., 1966); Dawn, *op. cit.*, p. 17; and Hourani, *op. cit.*, pp. 317–318.

5 For a recent attack on the resurgence of Syrian particularism by a leading ideologist of Arab nationalism, see Sāṭi' al-Ḥuṣrī, *al-iqlīmiyya judhūruhā wa budhūruhā* ("Provincial Particularism, Its Roots and Seeds") (Beirut, 1964), pp. 141–142.

6 D. Lerner, *The Passing of Traditional Society* (New York, 1964), p. 272.

almost speak of two separate populations, that coexist in the same political framework".[7]

There are several ways of assessing the numerical strength and distribution of the various communities in Syria, but a distinction can be clearly made between the Sunni Muslim Arabs, the paramount element, who in the late 1950s constituted about 60 percent of the population (then estimated at about four million), and all other categories.[8] These included religious sects and minorities (approximately: Christians, 15 percent; 'Alawis, 11 percent; Druses, 3 percent; and Isma'ilis, 1 percent) and ethnic ones (approximately: Kurds, 8 percent; Armenians [being also a religious minority], 4 percent; Turkomans, 3 percent; and Circassians).

These figures by themselves do not convey the full significance of the problem. Historically, most of these communities had been largely autonomous groups, suspicious of and often hostile to one another. Their relations had been governed by what Weulersse calls the minority complex—". . . a collective and pathological susceptibility, which makes every gesture of the neighbouring community appear as a menace or a challenge to one's own community".[9] The French had fostered and exploited the differences and tensions among the minority communities, especially the "compact" Druse and 'Alawi minorities, and the Sunnis down to the eve of independence. Only then were autonomous Druse (around Sweida in southern Syria) and 'Alawi (around Ladhiqiyya on the coast) regions integrated into the Syrian state. The geographic concentration of these two communities (and to a lesser extent of others) served to enhance their solidarity and collective power. Communal differences were often hardly distinguishable from other lines of social division. The city of Ḥamā, where Sunni urban landlords dominated a countryside

[7] J. Weulersse, *Paysans de Syrie et du Proche Orient* (Paris, 1946), see especially pp. 85–88. The term "communal" is used here for the Arabic *ṭā'ifī* in its descriptive valueless quality.

[8] The figures follow the data given by G. Baer, *Population and Society in the Arab World* (New York, 1964), pp. 108–114.

[9] Weulersse, *op. cit.*, p. 77. Weleursse seems to reflect to a certain extent the French official outlook on the problem; for a more moderate view see A.H. Hourani, *Syria and Lebanon* (London, 1946), pp. 137–145, and the essay "Race, Religion and Nation State in the Middle East", in A.H. Hourani, *A Vision of History* (Beirut, 1961).

populated largely by a heterodox peasantry, provided a particularly striking example of the urban Sunni hegemony in Syrian society. Here, however, there was a significant difference between the Druses who were dominated mainly by their own leaders and the 'Alawis who were subjected to a greater measure of outside control.[10]

Within the communities themselves opposition to the traditional leadership had been developing, which often took the form of identification with a nationalist ideology, in Syria mostly that of Arab nationalism.[11] This met the expectation of the Arab Sunni majority that the minorities should assimilate into the dominant current of Arab nationalism but it did not alter the Sunni bias of that nationalism, which continued to regard Christians and heterodox Muslims as "imperfect Arabs".[12] Such an outlook has continued to disturb many members of minority communities—ethnic, Christian, and heterodox Muslim.

Upon achieving independence in 1945, then, Syria had yet to define the nature of its political community and to integrate within it a variety of minorities. These tasks were made all the more difficult by the ambitions of other Arab states and foreign powers in Syria. The doctrine of pan-Arab nationalism, the frail structure of the new state, and the traditional orientation of certain regions and groups towards neighbouring states (the Aleppo region towards Iraq, the Druses towards Jordan and Lebanon) facilitated outside interference in Syrian politics. These factors were long to remain below the surface of Syrian politics, though the actual political scene was often dominated or coloured by other, mostly related, issues.[13]

The important development in the first period of Syrian independence was the continuing gradual weakening of the political and, to a lesser degree, social power of the old ruling class challenged

[10] The most authoritative available description of social conditions in the 'Alawi region is still J. Weulersse, *Le Pays des Alaouites* (Tours, 1940), especially pp. 319–322 and 327–343. There is no comparable study of Jabal ad-Durūz, the Druse region.

[11] Hourani, *Syria and Lebanon,* p. 93. At that time quite a few members of minority communities in Syria sought to identify with the secular territorial Great Syrian nationalism propagated by the PPS. See also Yamak, *op. cit.,* p. 143.

[12] Hourani, *op. cit.,* pp. 127–128.

[13] The following discussion of post-1945 Syrian politics is generally based on P. Seale, *The Struggle for Syria* (London, 1965), and G.H. Torrey, *Syrian Politics and the Military, 1945–1958* (Columbus, Ohio, 1964).

by younger, more radical groups representing, to some extent, social strata that until then had little political power. The weakening of the older political groups had already begun in the late 1930s, and proceeded rapidly with their glaring failure to meet the tasks and counter the difficulties posed by independence.

The change was catalysed by the three *coups d'état* that took place in 1949. They brought the military to an active intervention and participation in politics, which has since remained a major aspect of Syrian political history. Though not necessarily conscious of it, the officers who initiated this process in 1949 served to break the political backbone of the traditional ruling class and to transfer a growing share of power to new groups and parties.[14]

These trends were more clearly evident in and accelerated by the period in which Adib Shishakli held power (December 1949 to February 1954), following the transitory regimes of Husni Za'im and Sami Hinawi (March to December 1949). Among other things, Shishakli introduced a more direct military dictatorship, a policy of centralization and assimilation, a state-organized single party, and a parliament, in which for the first time younger, urban, lower-middle-class elements were highly represented at the expense of the traditional landowning deputies.[15] A one-time PPS member, Shishakli was closely associated with Akram al-Haurani who had played a role in all three *coups* of 1949. The two quarrelled and Haurani joined forces with the radical ideological Ba'th Party to take part in toppling Shishakli in 1954.

[14] There is insufficient information about the social background of the Syrian officer corps in 1949 (and for that matter in later periods). The little that is known, however, suggests, that while there were officers in the Syrian army from prominent families, most officers at that time came from minority communities, a legacy of the French policy of recruitment to their "special forces", from which the Syrian army originated. See E. Beeri, *Army Officers in Arab Society and Politics* (New York, 1970), pp. 333–342, and M. Halpern, *The Politics of Social Change in the Middle East and North Africa* (Princeton, N.J., 1963), pp. 266–268 (based on an unpublished paper by R.B. Winder).

[15] R.B. Winder, "Syrian Deputies and Cabinet Ministers 1919–1959", Part II, *Middle East Journal,* XVII (1963), p. 44.

HISTORY AND IDEOLOGY OF THE BA'TH PARTY, 1941–54[16]

The Arab Socialist Renaissance (or Resurrection) Party (*Ḥizb al-ba'th al-'arabī al-ishtirākī*), as it came to be known in the 1950s, was formed in 1953 by the merger of the Party of the Arab Renaissance, led by Michel 'Aflaq and Salah al-Bitar, with Akram al-Haurani's Arab Socialist Party.

The movement led by 'Aflaq and Bitar was constituted in 1947 as a full-fledged political party with branches outside Syria but had existed as a political-intellectual circle since 1941. 'Aflaq and Bitar were high school teachers who had studied in France in the late 1920s and early 1930s, where they had been exposed to both Marxist and ultra-nationalist influences. Their circle included several young fellow intellectuals from urban lower-middle-class families and younger university and high school students; the atmosphere was intimate, even close, and less sympathetic observers tend to liken the original Ba'thi groups to a Sufi teacher and his disciples (*murīdūn*).[17] The rise of the party and the development of its ideology should be seen against the background of the national humiliation, social agitation and intellectual ferment of the period.[18] The Ba'th, in fact, filled a vacuum created by the disintegration of the "League of Nationalist Action" (*'Uṣbat al-'amal al-qaumī*), a radical nationalist group, that

[16] The major sources for this account of the history of the early years of the Ba'th were: Sami al-Jundi, *al-Ba'th* (Beirut, 1969); Mutā' aṣ-Ṣafadī, *Ḥizb al-ba'th ma'sāt al-bidāya wa ma'sāt an-nihāya* ("The Ba'th Party, the Misfortunes of Its Beginning and End") (Beirut, 1964); Nājī 'Allūsh, *ath-Thaura wa-al-jamāhir* ("The Revolution and the Masses") (Beirut, 1962); Muḥammad 'Umrān, *Tajribatī fi-ath-thaura* ("My Experience in the Revolution") (Beirut, 1970); Y. Oron, "The Arab Socialist Renaissance Party, Its History, and Ideas" (in Hebrew), *Hamizrah Hehadash,* IX (1959), pp. 241–263; and K.S. Abu Jaber, *The Arab Ba'th Socialist Party: History, Ideology, Organization* (Syracuse, N.Y., 1966).

[17] See, for example, Safadi, *op. cit.*, p. 83. The same expression is often used by Jundi when describing the intimate relationship between Arsuzi and his own circle (see, e.g., p. 27).

[18] For a literary portrayal of the mood and outlook of the Ba'th's young adherents see Mutā' aṣ-Ṣafadī's *Jil al-qadar* ("The Generation of Fate") (Damascus, 1960). This novel was written prior to Ṣafadi's disenchantment with the party, which is clearly evident in the account he renders in the history mentioned above.

in the late 1930s had attracted members of the younger generation disillusioned with the traditional political leadership as represented by the "National Bloc".[19] Two events loom most prominently in this background: the loss of Alexandretta to Turkey (1939) and the campaign to aid the Rashid 'Ali movement in Iraq (1941), in which the Ba'th and other nationalist groups in Syria took part.

Among those who emigrated from Alexandretta to Syria was Zaki al-Arsuzi, an 'Alawi member of the League of Nationalist Action who had studied in France, organized resistance to the Turks in Alexandretta, and then left for Damascus with a group of followers. There he held a circle of his own and having seceded from the "League", founded in November 1940 a movement called *al-Ba'th al-'arabī*. It was small and short-lived and by 1944 most of its members had left and joined the kindred group organized at about the same time by 'Aflaq and Bitar and called interchangeably *al-Ba'th al-'arabī* or *āl-iḥyā' al-'arabī*.[20] Arsuzi's true role in the genesis of the Ba'th is a matter of controversy but it seems to have been consequential not only in bringing a sizable group of 'Alawis into the party but also in accentuating the nationalistic and mystical elements in its thought.[21]

19 On the "League of Nationalist Action" see Hourani, *Syria and Lebanon*, pp. 197–198. Jundi, *op. cit.*, p. 20, points to the fact that many of the original members of the Ba'th had previously adhered to the "League". Some of the ideas preached by 'Aflaq in the 1940s had already been adumbrated in the teachings of the "League".

20 The short history of Arsuzi's movement is described in detail by Jundi in the most interesting and convincing section of his book (*op. cit.*, pp. 19–35).

21 Ṣafadi, hostile to 'Aflaq, stressed in his account Arsuzi's role in the genesis of the Ba'th, as did E. Rouleau in the interesting article "The Syrian Enigma: What is the Ba'th", *New Left Review*, No. 45 (September-October 1967), pp. 53–65, of interest because the French correspondent seems to reflect a version of the party's past convenient to 'Aflaq's intra-Ba'thi rivals, Syria's rulers at that time. Abu Jaber, whose views often coincide with those of 'Aflaq's wing, does not mention Arsuzi in his account. Jundi (*op. cit.*, p. 19) regrets the fact that the old Arsuzi placed himself at the disposal of 'Aflaq's rivals, but he himself is often quite vague when describing the relationship between the two leaders and their groups in the early 1940s. According to Rouleau, Salah J'did, and Hafiz al-Asad, two 'Alawi officers who were to play a crucial role in the party's later history, joined it through Arsuzi. More probably, they did so through Wahib al-Ghanim, an 'Alawi who came with Arsuzi from Alexandretta and settled in Ladhiqiyya. A recognition of Arsuzi's role in the formulation of the Ba'th's nationalist ideology presents an interesting analogy of the part exiles took in the genesis of other nationalist ideologies (e.g., Akchuraoghlu

During the 1940s the Ba'th expanded its activity among young educated elements of the urban middle classes and spread to several Syrian cities and towns. 'Aflaq and Bitar resigned their teaching positions and began to issue the party's organ *al-Ba'th.* In keeping with its pan-Arab ideology, in the later 1940s the party recruited members from other Arab countries who came to study in Beirut and Damascus. In 1947 the first formal party congress took place, and a constitution (*dustūr*) and an Internal Regulation (*niẓām dākhilī*) were issued.

The party agitated against French rule and was unsuccessfully active in Syrian politics of the late 1940s. 'Aflaq and his circle had made a considerable impact on educated youth in Syria, but their ability to attain effective political power was very limited under the traditional political system. Their party had less than 500 members and could mobilize little support in an election campaign. The change came with the *coups d'état* of 1949, not because the Ba'th fared well under the military rulers, but rather since the latter undermined the old system while 'Aflaq and Bitar united their forces with those of Haurani's kindred movement.

Haurani was a different representative of the same generation, moved by social ferment and nationalist agitation. An ambitious lawyer-politician, he came from an impoverished landowning family of Ḥamā in north-central Syria and realized that he had little chance of competing in the traditional channels of Syrian politics against members of the "feudal" families of his constituency. He became leader of the "Youth Movement" (*ḥarakat ash-shabāb*), which was first affiliated with the PPS and then became independent and developed into the "Arab Socialist Party" (*al-ḥizb al-'arabī al-ishtirākī*).

The movement possessed two advantages which made it exceptional in Syria of the 1940s. Haurani was able to organize peasants in the Ḥamā area against their landlords, for having come from within the landowning class himself, he was an effective rival, and he built up a lasting clientele around Ḥamā and in the neighbouring areas. Haurani's other asset was his contacts in the army, which he had

Yusuf and Turkish nationalism in the nineteenth century) and justifies the discussion of irridentist elements in Ba'thi ideology in M. Khadduri, *Political Trends in the Arab World* (London, 1970), pp. 206–207.

established during the campaign to aid Rashid Ali and developed in the later 1940s when he took part in al-Kaukji's campaigns in Palestine. Additionally, he had a special relationship with a group of younger officers, natives of Ḥamā and graduates of the officers' academy in that city.[22] His close contacts with several politically minded officers enabled Haurani to play an important role in the 1949 *coups*. Later, having quarrelled with his former associate, Shishakli, he came to cooperate with the Ba'th in opposing him. The two parties had reportedly considered a merger in 1946 and the common opposition to Shishakli brought it about. The merger was a crucial turning point in the party's history. Haurani's ambition and cunning, and the following he had in the army and among the peasantry were indispensable in forging the Ba'th into the political force it was to become. The combination of a well-developed popular ideology and a strong political basis was exceptional for a secular Arab party. However, the fusion never became complete. The union of the practically minded, often opportunistic, Haurani with the idealist (in both senses of the term) 'Aflaq and his group was somewhat incongruous. This duality is a key factor in understanding the party's later history.

The ideology of the Ba'th Party in the mid-1950s as expounded in its constitution and in the writings of its principal thinkers[23] is essentially a nationalist doctrine that views the Arabs as a "single,

[22] This account of Haurani's early career is based on Jundi, *op. cit., passim,* Seale, *op. cit.*, pp. 38–41, Oron, *op. cit.*, Ṣafadi, *Ḥizb al-Ba'th,* pp. 342 ff., and B. Vernier, *Armée et Politique en Moyen Orient* (Paris, 1966), *passim.* According to Jundi, there was a tradition of "anti-feudalism" in Hama dating back to the early years of the present century: *Ḥizb ash-shabāb,* writes Jundi, had been founded in 1938 by one 'Uthman al-Haurani and its leadership was later taken over by Akram al-Haurani (presumably his relative). Jundi's version also serves to correct the impression that Haurani alone had contacts with army officers. According to him (*op. cit.*, pp. 50, 51, 54), 'Aflaq's party too had sympathizers in the army (most notably Colonel Ibrahim al-Husaini) and in 1949 it even began to prepare for a *coup d'état*. This, however, has yet to be corroborated by another source.

[23] The following analysis is based on the Ba'th's constitution and on 'Aflaq's two books *Ma'rakat al-maṣīr al-wāḥid* ("The Battle of the One Destiny") (Beirut, 1958) and *Fi sabīl al-ba'th* ("For the Ba'th" or, possibly, "On the Road to the Renaissance") (Beirut, 1959). Other aspects of Ba'thi doctrine and its further development are discussed below, particularly in the second and third chapters.

eternal nation". The Arabs have always formed one nation in this conception, and their reunification in one state is the party's main goal. The goal of unity, however, is not ultimate, but should serve only to resuscitate the Arab nation so that it can play its proper role in contributing to world civilization. But ends and means are sometimes difficult to distinguish and unity can only be achieved following a social and spiritual revolution. This revolution will liquidate the force of (internal) feudalism and (external) imperialism and prepare the popular forces for their role in the future Arab state. The party is therefore revolutionary (*inqilābī* in the terminology of the early 1950s) and popular.

The future state will have a democratic parliamentary regime, which will guarantee freedom (*ḥurriyya*) and carry out the policy of social justice and economic reform called Arab Socialism. This socialism is moderate (the rights of inheritance and of limited nonexploitative ownership are recognized) and "spiritual", as opposed to "materialist" Western socialism. Thus the masses will be given the leading role in the future Arab society not just because they are the majority but because they have suffered. In the original Ba'thi teaching, socialism was clearly of secondary importance compared with the theme of Arab unity, and this preference became all the more pronounced through the party's anti-Communist polemics.

Arab nationalism is defined by the Ba'th on a secular basis, but the special role of Islam in Arab history is recognized. Islam is acknowledged as the basis of the most glorious phase of Arab history, but then this is a past that has by now become part of the heritage of Christian (and other non-Sunni) Arabs as well. This formulation could in theory help to integrate non-Sunni Arabs like the Greek Orthodox 'Aflaq on an equal footing into the secularly defined Arab nation, while still gratifying the Sunnis. Relevant in this context is the fact that the Ba'th's constitution implies secularist tendencies (i.e., it advocated state control of marriage and education) and that 'Aflaq's writings reflect what may have been the impact of Christian mystical motifs (Suffering, Love, Pain).

Even this short sketch indicates some of the internal contradictions and incongruities of the doctrine. Humanitarian universalist elements of nineteenth-century liberal nationalism are grafted onto ultranationalist elements of the late nineteenth and early twentieth centuries. A violent feeling of struggle and rapid, deep change coexists uneasily with a belief in parliamentary democracy. Individual liberty is cherished but then is subjected to collective criteria. The forced treatment of the place of Islam in Arab nationalism, together with the implicit secularist tendencies, has been suspiciously regarded by devout Sunni Muslims. The Ba'th has never been a party of minorities like the PPS, but it has still attracted a large proportion of its membership from the ranks of the minority communities. The Ba'th's doctrine as a whole is idealistic and remains vague about most practical questions, especially with regard to politics and political action.[24]

The full significance of these contradictions and weaknesses, together with the inherent structural frailty of the unified party, became clear only when it later achieved real political power; in the early and mid-1950s they were hardly apparent. The party's doctrine then satisfied the needs of its adherents. The combination of nationalist and socialist ideas attracted younger radical elements[25] and the forceful simplicity of its slogans ("Unity, Freedom, Socialism" or "One Arab nation with an eternal mission") appealed to humbler adherents. Armed with this doctrine and with the political muscle of Haurani, the party seemed ready to play a crucial role in the later 1950s.

THE ROAD TO UNION, 1954–58

The unified Ba'th Party took an important part in the heterogeneous coalition which led the opposition to Shishakli's regime and then toppled it in a military *coup* in February 1954. Active in this coalition were also the Druse community and some traditional political circles, most notably the Atasi family, based in the central Syrian city of Ḥomṣ and affiliated with the People's Party. As in 1949, the *coup*

[24] See the interesting discussion in J.P. Viennot, "Le role du Ba'th dans la genèse du nationalisme arabe", *Orient*, IX (1965), pp. 65–80.

[25] 'Umran (*op. cit.*, pp. 8–9 and 139 ff.) describes what it was that appealed to young adherents like himself in the party's doctrine. Similarly, Jurj Ṭarābīshī in *Sartre wa-al-marxiyya* ("Sartre and Marxism") (Beirut, 1964), pp. 8–9, explains how the party's doctrine attracted him as a young man in the early 1950s.

could not be divorced from the broader context of inter-Arab rivalries; Iraq played an almost overt role in the preparations for Shishakli's overthrow.

An interesting aspect of the February 1954 *coup* was that the division within the army, largely on a regional basis, ended in a compromise following a conference in Ḥomṣ. This was to become a recurrent theme in Syrian military politics: on the verge of crisis a fragmented, divided officer corps, reflecting the country's social and political diversity, often closed its ranks and demonstrated not only a measure of prudence but also a sense of corporate and professional solidarity.

Following the February *coup* the Ba'th disappointed some of its impatient military supporters by refusing to use their help in order to take power directly into its own hands.[26] Instead the party cooperated with the traditional Syrian parties in restoring constitutional rule. In the much recalled, relatively free elections of 1954 the Ba'th, which then had about 2,500 members, won 22 seats out of 142. (The People's Party won 32 seats, the Nationalist Party, 25, and the largest bloc, composed of independents, 55.) This was an unprecedented achievement for a modern radical party in the Arab world, and with the election of the Communist leader Khalid Bakdash it marked the beginning of a four-year period of parliamentary government characterized by the rising power of the left.

In the Syrian context the leftward trend was manifested primarily in the domain of foreign relations and in the gradual waning of the country's traditional and right-wing parties. The combination of left-wing parties (the Ba'th and the Communists whose rivalry was eclipsed by a period of cooperation) and the opportunism and anti-Western sentiment of several independent and even right-wing deputies brought Syria close enough to the Soviet Union to make it the centre of a minor international crisis in 1957. In the Arab context this was matched to a degree by the growing influence in Damascus of the Nasser regime, which since 1956 had become more identified with a

[26] 'Umran, *op. cit.*, p. 11. The Sixth National Congress of the Ba'th in October 1963, in which some of those officers frustrated in 1954 would figure prominently, was to consider a resolution denouncing those leaders who among other things were accused of being "responsible for the failure to take power before 1958".

neutralist anti-Western line and had begun to pursue a more active Arab policy.

The Egyptian position in Syria was based on the appeal of Nasser's leadership (*zi'āma*) and the close relationship established with a group of officers and with the Ba'th Party. The emergence of Nasserite Egypt as a geographically close "progressive" Arab power gave the Ba'th for the first time a suitable partner for Arab union, and beginning early in 1956 the Ba'th made a point of calling for some form of a union with Egypt.[27] While the call was not then shared by other political forces in Syria, it seems to have familiarized the idea on the Syrian political scene.

In Syria an uneasy alliance (or front) of the Ba'th with the Communists and with a group of "progressive" independent deputies headed by Khalid al-'Azm was sufficiently strong to sap the power of several traditional and right-wing groups and to control the cabinet (in which the Ba'th participated from 1956 with Bitar as minister of foreign affairs). In reality, however, the power of this alliance was derived largely from the support of the army, which after February 1954 chose to exercise its influence from behind the scenes. The army's support was vital for the left, since in the absence of deep changes and sweeping reforms in the country's socioeconomic structure, much social and political power still remained in traditional hands. The Ba'th could not, for instance, hope to win elections decisively so long as landlords and notables dominated the countryside and many urban areas. The process of social change was discernible[28] but most Ba'this were too impatient to wait for its results.

While the Ba'th and its allies relied on the army's backing, this support was quite a tenuous one. The politically involved section of the Syrian officer corps was fragmented and divided into numerous rival factions. Moreover, even after the purges that followed the assassination of the Ba'thi military leader 'Adnan al-Maliki in 1955,

[27] Documented in 'Allush, *op. cit.*, pp. 94–97.

[28] Thus an important change became evident in the later 1950s as Trade Unions, which in the early 1950s had largely been controlled by right-wing parties, came under growing Ba'thi and Communist influence. See H.M.S. Nabulsi, "Labor Organization and Development in Syria: 1946–1958" (unpublished Ph.D. dissertation, Georgetown University, 1960), pp. 325–335, and F. Chevallier, "Forces en présence dans la Syrie d'aujourd'hui", *Orient*, I (1957), pp. 181.

by a member of the PPS, there remained a sizable conservative element among the military. The Ba'thi faction, headed by such officers as 'Abd al-Ghani Qannut and Mustafa Hamdun, allied with such sympathizers as the director of military intelligence, 'Abd al-Hamid Sarraj, was perhaps the strongest but still only one of several military factions. Its power was to be severely tested in the spring and summer of 1957 when attempts were made to transfer Sarraj and other leftist officers from their positions.[29]

The Ba'thi officers were only loosely tied to the party, and their contact with it was generally maintained through Haurani. The party's relationship with the military was an important aspect of a persistent conflict between the 'Aflaq and Haurani wings, which focused on the party's approach to power and politics. 'Aflaq and, seemingly to a lesser extent, Bitar resented what they regarded as Haurani's unprincipled meddling in politics and his bidding for more power through the army, but their own attitude to these issues was at best ambivalent.[30] While they still preached a doctrine of long-term revolutionary preparation and conversion as a precondition to the assumption of power, they seem actually to have become ready to do so by a short cut.

All this goes far to explain how the grave political crisis of 1957 led the Ba'th and its military allies to push Syria into a union with Egypt in February 1958.[31] At the heart of the crisis was the combined threat of a more ambitious and assertive policy adopted by the Ba'th's Communist allies[32] and of the counterpressure applied by the West,

[29] See 'Umran, *op. cit.*, p. 13, Seale, *op. cit.*, pp. 293–294, and Torrey, *op. cit., passim.* The incident is known in Ba'thi literature as *'uṣyān qaṭana* (the Qaṭana Insurrection). According to Jundi, *op. cit.*, p. 85 (whose version seems to be supported by that of 'Umran), the incident also contributed to widening the rift between the officers belonging to 'Aflaq's Ba'th and Haurani's supporters.

[30] Munif ar-Razzaz, *at-Tajrriba al-murra* ("The Bitter Experience") (Beirut, 1967), pp. 31–36, 'Allush, *op. cit.*, pp. 49–50, and 'Umran, *op. cit.*, pp. 11–15.

[31] The following analysis is based on Seale, *op. cit.*, Torrey, *op. cit.*, M. Kerr, *The Arab Cold War* (2nd ed.; London, 1967), pp. 10–14, Muḥammad Ḥasanain Haikal, *Ma alladhī jarā fī surya?* ("What Happened in Syria?") (Cairo, 1962), and the protocols of the March-April 1963 Unity Talks as published by Haikal in *Maḥāḍir muḥādathāt al-waḥda* ("Protocols of the Unity Talks") (Cairo, 1963).

[32] An interesting criticism from "within" of this policy by an ex-Communist, who calls it the policy of "leaping to power" (*al-wuthūb ila-al-ḥukm*) can be found in Eliās

by pro-Western Turkey and Iraq, and by conservative elements at home, all alarmed by the growing power of the left. The increasing tensions were mirrored in the army where rival factions were on the verge of clashing. The Ba'th and the large group of senior officers who were allied with it or shared its outlook felt that they could not cope with this combined pressure. It seemed to them that the only way to get out of the crisis and to stop Syria's disintegration as a political unit was through a federal union with Egypt.

The military, apparently, looked to the authority of President Nasser and Field-Marshal 'Abd al-Hakim 'Amer as a remedy for their suicidal factionalism. They could also presume that under a union with an essentially military regime, their own paramount position would be preserved. For the Ba'th, too, the union with Egypt was not merely an escape from an odious situation. Such a union would be an implementation of the call for unity which the Ba'th had been preaching for almost 20 years. The Ba'th, furthermore, could hope not only to consolidate its shaky position in Syria but also to radiate its influence beyond it through the union. Possibly, Haurani and 'Aflaq each calculated that with Nasser's help they could neutralize the other.[33]

Additional political forces provided a more passive support for the establishment of the union, which they regarded as a lesser evil than the 1957 crisis and the even graver ones that seemed to be in store. Those who opposed the union preferred to jump on the wagon once the issue had been finalized, so that Syria's decision to forsake its independent political existence appeared to be unanimous.

During the negotiations which preceded the formation of the United Arab Republic (UAR) an important change occurred. When the Ba'th and the military approached Nasser it was a federal union that they had in mind. But so anxious were they to achieve the union that they agreed to unite on Nasser's terms: a unification of the political patterns in both parts of the united state, the dissolution of all political parties, and termination of the army's political role. That Ba'thi leaders and officers agreed to these conditions (which were

Murquṣ, *Ta'rikh al-aḥzāb ash-shuyū'iyya fi-al-waṭan al'arabi* ("History of the Communist Parties in the Arab Homeland") (Beirut, 1964), pp. 91–92.

33 At least one passage in the 1963 Protocols suggests that this may have been the case (see, e.g., p. 56).

indeed accompanied by some assurances) evidences not only naïveté and misunderstanding of the Nasserite regime but also the depth of the 1957 political crisis in Syria. Furthermore, it seems that the agents of the union in Syria could not have arrived at such a solution and have carried their country with them in such a manner but for the strength of Arab sentiment there and the frail structure of the Syrian state.

THE FAILURE OF THE UAR AND ITS IMPACT[34]

The depth of the 1957–58 crisis, Syrian yearning for Arab union, and the charisma of Nasser's personality won the Union's regime initial wide support in Syria in addition to the commitment of the Ba'th and officers who had cooperated with the Egyptians in establishing it. But the centralized regime that the Egyptians established in February-March 1958 and their conception of the Union as a gradual incorporation of Syria disregarded the important differences between social and political conditions in the two regions, offended Syrian sensibilities, and resulted in a progressive erosion of the public's support of the regime. The dissatisfaction of a large section of the Syrian populace with the Union contributed to its eventual fall by creating an atmosphere suitable for the preparation and execution of the *coup d'état* of September 28, 1961, which led to Syria's secession from the UAR. The estrangement of the Ba'th and of a considerable body of army officers, and Nasser's failure to find effective political partners in Syria, had a more direct bearing on the course of the Union's history and on its failure.

To understand the deterioration of Nasser's relations with the the Ba'th during 1958 and 1959 one has to go back to the misconceptions and ambiguities which characterized Ba'thi considerations on the eve of the establishment of the UAR. Not only did the Ba'this fail to perceive the nature of Nasser's regime, in whose scheme there was no

[34] This analysis of the failure of the UAR and of Nasser's partnership with the Ba'th is based on Kerr, *op. cit.*, pp. 14–34, C.R. Frost, "UAR: A Study in Arab Nationalism and Unity" (unpublished Ph.D. dissertation, University of Denver, 1966), M. Palmer, "The U.A.R.: An Assessment of Its Failure", *Middle East Journal,* XX (1966), pp. 50–67, 'Allush, *op. cit.*, pp. 128–144, Y. Oron (ed.), *Middle East Record: Vol. II, 1961* (Jerusalem, 1966), pp. 605–623, and *Maḥaḍir, passim.*

place for other distinct political entities, but they also concluded naïvely that after relieving them from their plight in Syria, Nasser would entrust them with the major political and ideological role in Syria and beyond it. The Ba'thi leaders agreed to the party's dissolution in Syria but expected to resume its activity under a new guise within the projected National Union in which, they believed, Ba'thi cadres were destined to play the principal role. The party's organization outside Syria was not dissolved, thus leaving 'Aflaq at the head of a distinct political party.

During the Union's first months it became apparent that this was not how Nasser viewed his relationship with the Ba'th or the future of the UAR's government. Ba'thi leaders were appointed to the UAR's central government and were offered power and positions in Syria, but Nasser did not give them a free hand in running Syria nor would he let them organize the National Union as an extension of their party. The relationship further worsened as the messianic fervour which had accompanied the formation of the Union cooled off (particularly after the emergence of Qassem in Iraq and Nasser's adoption of a more moderate Arab policy) and public disenchantment with it became apparent. As preparations for the elections to the National Union proceeded in 1958 and 1959, it gradually surfaced that: (*a*) the Syrian public's disaffection with the Union was directed largely at the Ba'th; and (*b*) partly as a result of this, Nasser and the UAR authorities refused to support the Ba'th in the elections (the Ba'this would even say they were opposed by the Egyptians and by Sarraj) so that it was about to lose them to independent, mostly conservative, candidates. In July 1959, after partially boycotting the elections, the Ba'th suffered a humiliating defeat and won only about 250 out of 9,445 seats.

The deterioration of the Ba'th's relations with Nasser proceeded rapidly and culminated in the collective resignations of the Ba'thi ministers in December 1959. To make things worse, the Ba'this tried to persuade some Egyptians to follow suit. Certain Ba'this continued to cooperate with Nasser but the party as such drifted to a passive opposition to the UAR government. These developments were made all the more significant by Nasser's failure to find other political allies in Syria who would provide a meaningful framework for Syrian self-expression within the UAR. The National Union never developed into a viable political organ nor could the 200 Syrian delegates to the

National Assembly nominated in July 1960 fill that function. Nasser came to rely on a more direct Egyptian control personified by Field-Marshal 'Amer, who in October 1959 was dispatched to Syria, and on a group of Syrian army officers and bureaucrats headed by 'Abd al-Hamid Sarraj. This was an inadequate basis of support in territorially separated Syria. From October 1959 to September 1960 'Amer presided over Syrian affairs while trying to reconcile the urban middle classes and to attract a group of veteran politicians into actively supporting the government. As this approach failed and opposition to the Union continued, Nasser decided late in 1960 to pursue a policy of further integrating Syria into Egypt.

During 1961 the inherent weaknesses of the Egyptian policy in Syria were brought to a sharp focus. When a controversy arose between the Egyptian 'Amer and the Syrian Sarraj, Nasser's most loyal and important local supporter, the Egyptian president was bound to back the former and by alienating the latter he lost a crucial prop. The policy of integration and the tighter economic controls it involved alienated the Syrian bourgeoisie whose antagonism was later brought to a head by the nationalization decrees of July 1961. In Egypt these decrees hit a politically powerless bourgeoisie composed largely of foreigners and minoritarians, but in Syria their effect was different, as they hurt a class that was politically significant and still represented in the army. The effectiveness of their representation was enhanced by the widespread resentment among Syrian officers of highhanded treatment by the Egyptians and by the transfer of no longer reliable Ba'thi officers from sensitive command posts, mostly by sending them to Egypt.

The conspiring group of officers which plotted the *coup* against the Egyptians was composed of at least two distinct elements. On the one hand were rightist officers like Haidar al-Kuzbari and Faisal Sirri al-Husaini, who seem to have been linked to the Syrian bourgeoisie and possibly also to conservative Arab regimes. The other group headed by 'Abd al-Karim Nahlawi, the director of officers' affairs in the First (Syrian) Army and the director of 'Amer's (Syrian) office, seems to have had no strings attached but rather to have been moved by personal ambitions and by the grievances of the Syrian officer corps. The latter group, moreover, apparently included officers (like Faiz ar-Rifa'i and Muhib al-Hindi) who did not really

View of Damascus

A pro-Nasser demonstration in Damascus

want to break away from the Union but sought to try to reform it by imposing certain conditions on the Egyptians.[35] President Nasser, however, would not negotiate with rebels against his authority and the revolting officers declared Syria's secession from the UAR and reconstituted it as an independent state.

Perhaps the most profound and certainly the most immediate effect the Union and its failure had on Syrian politics was to reopen the issue of Syria's national identity as a cardinal political question. The experience of union with a much larger, stronger and rather self-assertive nation-state strengthened the feeling of Syrian distinctiveness and the notion of a Syrian entity, which in early 1958 had been very weak. But this change found no overt ideological expression as no one dared challenge the doctrine of pan-Arab nationalism and unity. The proponents of Syria's renewed independence and sovereignty found themselves in the awkward situation of having to defend their position while professing allegiance to a doctrine that denounced it.

Their dilemma was further increased by Nasser's refusal to acknowledge the legitimacy of the Syrian independent regime[36] and by the existence of a body of politicians, army officers, and bureaucrats whose political and personal future depended on Syria's relationship with Egypt. Several of those who had cooperated with Egypt managed to detach themselves at the right moment, while others were too deeply involved or identified with Egyptian rule to dissociate themselves. Whether in Syria or in Egypt, they remained a strong pressure group for a reunion with Egypt or at least for a return to a close relationship with it on Nasser's terms (which would include the accomodation of his supporters). Thus, while the UAR period served on the one hand to intensify the feeling of Syrian unity and solidarity, it also created another line of deep division in the already fragmented Syrian polity.

[35] The existence of a more moderate group within the rebellious faction could be learned from the communiqués issued on the day of the *coup* (in particular communiqué number nine) and from later information released by the Egyptians in 1962. This is all corroborated by the illuminating discussion of Nahlawi and his faction by Luayy al-Atasi and President Nasser during the 1963 Unity Talks as recorded in *Maḥāḍir*, p. 126.

[36] Only in November 1966 would Nasser agree under pressure to exchange ambassadors with Syria.

Of long-lasting effect were the practical socialist measures passed by the Union government—the Agrarian Reform Law of September 1958 and the nationalization decrees of July 1961. The Agrarian Reform Law was only partially carried out[37] and the nationalization decrees were passed only a short while before Syria's secession (to which they contributed). However, they sufficed to establish new standards from which no future government could deviate too sharply if it wished to retain a progressive image. This applied not only to intellectuals but also to workers and peasants who had materially benefited from these measures.[38] The effect of these developments was not tangible in September 1961; at that stage only the reaction to them was manifested, but it would be felt later on.

The Syrian army underwent profound changes during the 1958–61 period. The Egyptians eliminated two major factions that had been active in Syrian military politics from 1954 to 1958—the Ba'thi faction and the group centred around Amin an-Nafuri and Ahmad 'Abd al-Karim, two independent officers who had risen to prominence under Shishakli, shifted loyalties after his fall, and were generally considered close to Khalid al-'Azm and jealous of Sarraj. On the other hand, the Egyptians promoted the factions headed by Sarraj, Tu'meh al-'Audatallah and Ahmad al-Hunaidi (the latter two had vacillated between Nafuri and the Ba'th) and the "Damascus Group" headed by Akram ad-Dairi as well as several individual officers.[39] The military leaders who had prospered under the Egyptians (as army officers or cabinet ministers) were mostly ousted after September 28, 1961. The result was a transformation of the upper echelons of the Syrian army, but its notorious factionalism and penchant for intervention in politics were only heightened. Thus, by carying out the *coup* of September 28 the army again became the source of power in Syria, which it then chose partially to deposit with the politicians.

The tension and conflict with President Nasser and its later

[37] See E. Garzouzi, "Land Reform in Syria", *Middle East Journal,* XVII (1963), pp. 85–86, and S.M. Dabbagh, "Agrarian Reform in Syria", *Middle East Economic Papers,* 1962, pp. 6–15.

[38] According to Dabbagh (*op. cit.*, p. 13), the income of land recipients was estimated to have trebled by 1962.

[39] The composition of the major military factions in the Syrian army on the eve of the Union is described in some detail by Seale, *op. cit.*, pp. 244–246.

eviction from actual participation in UAR government and politics seemed to have eclipsed the Ba'th Party. Faced with a situation in which it could neither operate as a party within the Union nor openly oppose it, the Ba'th under 'Aflaq and Bitar drifted into actual but unadmitted opposition to Nasser's policies under the slogan "correction within the Union for the Union's protection".

This compromise solution satisfied but few. By placing itself in virtual opposition to the UAR government, the Ba'th estranged those party members who identified themselves with the regime. Some of them, headed by 'Abdallah ar-Rimawi of Jordan and Fu'ad ar-Rikabi of Iraq, dissented (and were expelled) from the party (dissolved only in Syria) following the Third National Congress held in Lebanon late in 1959, and organized a pro-Nasserite party of the same name.[40] Other Ba'thi supporters of the Union, who refused to follow Rimawi, declined also to rally behind 'Aflaq's line. At the other end of the spectrum Haurani and his group advocated a more resolute opposition to the UAR's government, and the two wings of the party were drawn further apart.

Less visible at the time but of great import for the future was the impact of the Union and its failure on the Ba'thi rank and file, called in the party's jargon "the bases" (*al-qawā'id*) or "the second rank" (*aṣ-ṣaff ath-thāni*). Confused by the rapid change in the party's fortunes and often harrassed by the UAR authorities, many of them nurtured a grudge against the Union and the veteran Ba'thi leaders, whom they held responsible for plunging into the Union and for dissolving the party without consulting the membership.[41] Resentment against the veteran leaders was in many cases grafted on a pre-existing feeling of inferiority and deprivation felt by those "second rank" members

[40] The Ba'th's first major and formal congress in 1947 is considered the First National Congress and the one held in 1954 is counted as the second. For details on the Third National Congress see 'Allush, *op. cit.*, pp. 131–134, and Bashīr Da'ūq (ed.), *Niḍāl al-ba'th, wathā'iq ḥizb al-ba'th al-'arabī al-ishtirākī* ("The Struggle of the Ba'th, Documents of the Arab Ba'th Socialist Party"), Vol. IV (Beirut, 1964), pp. 92–112. For Rimawi's point of view see his *al-Manṭiq ath-thauri li-al-ḥaraka al-qaumiyya al-'arabiyya al-ḥadītha* ("The Revolutionary Logic of the Modern Arab Nationalist Movement") (Cairo, 1961), pp. 129–132, 154.

[41] 'Allush, *op. cit.*, pp. 128–131, and the interesting account called "The View of the Command of the Yemenite Region's Party Branch Concerning the Latest Crisis" published in the party's internal organ *al-Munāḍil* ("The Militant") in June 1966.

(especially in the more remote provinces) who during the fifties had not been fully integrated into the original and rather intimate circle of the Ba'th.[42]

Such feelings were matched, particularly among educated members of the same stratum, by disenchantment with the party's original ideology and adoption of a more leftist stance. The process had begun earlier but was catalyzed by the failure of the UAR, which undermined the party's unionist ideology, and apparently also by a broader leftward trend in the Arab world that was particularly noticeable in Egypt.[43] These developments were descriped in January 1963 by a young Ba'thi who by then had been converted to a more radical, heavily Marxist, conception of socialism:

> But the union between Syria and Egypt and then its breakdown and the crises through which the Arab left and especially the Ba'th lived during the Union and the Secession were bound to tear the veil from our eyes, that is if we still wanted to be leftists and socialists. We then understood the glaring truth—we had to review everything in our views, thoughts, sympathies, expectations. We felt that the period of political adolescence was over, that we should move from revolt to revolution.[44]

These changes, as well as the erosion of 'Aflaq and Bitar's hold on the Ba'th, surfaced at the Fourth National Congress held in Lebanon in August 1960. Owing to the circumstances (the party was, after all, formally dissolved in Syria), the congress was mainly attended by delegates representing the Lebanese Ba'th, among whom currents similar to those just described had also developed.[45] They gave the

Whether written by Yemenites or not, this is a detailed and most illuminating survey of the internal struggle in the Ba'th; it stresses the significance of the party's dissolution as a turning point in this struggle.

[42] On the party's organizational problems in the later 1950s see 'Allush, *op. cit.*, pp. 102–106, and Jundi, *op. cit.*, *passim* and especially p. 71.

[43] *Cf.* M. Kerr, "The Emergence of a Socialist Ideology in Egypt", *Middle East Journal,* XVI (1962), pp. 127–144.

[44] Tarabishi, *op. cit.*, pp. 12–13. The quotation is from the introduction written in January 1963.

[45] Later the party's National Command decided to disband the Lebanese Regional Command, but in August 1960 it could not afford to quarrel with the only party branch that was practically free to operate.

resolutions of the congress a more pronounced anti-Nasserite tone and then turned their criticism against 'Aflaq and Bitar's past record and ideological preferences. The resolutions denounced the leaders' conduct in having relied on the armed forces and in hastily entering the Union and dissolving the party. The resolutions also deplored the emphasis that the party's doctrine had in the past placed on (Arab) unity rather than on socialism and democracy. At the present phase, it was stated, there was no more need to stress the nationalist cause; rather, the tools for a scientific analysis of the context in which the party operated should be borrowed from Marxism. Also, the party should strengthen its position among the popular classes—workers, peasants, artisans, and shopkeepers.[46]

The experience of the Union period had a somewhat different but certainly very consequential impact on the Ba'thi military, particularly those who were stationed in Egypt in what was virtual political exile. The miserable feeling of these officers would be later expressed during the 1963 Unity Talks by a non-Ba'thi officer, Ziyad al-Hariri from Hama, who had led the *coup d'état* of March 8, 1963: "We felt as if we were lost . . . we were here in an inferior position and we did not know why. . . ."[47]

Apparently, an experience of this kind led a group of Ba'thi officers in Egypt, several of them 'Alawis,[48] to form a secret cabal made up of 13 members and called "The Military Committee" (*al-lajna al-'askariyya*). There is no trustworthy information as to the group's original aims and designs. It seems, however, that the formation of the group represented an attempt to revive the informal "military organization" of the Ba'th, which had existed in the 1950s, under a new guise and according to a new concept. The leaders of the Committee saw themselves as the inner core of such a revived organization. They were opposed both to the authorities of the UAR and to their party's veteran leaders whom they held responsible for their plight. The new organization, it seems, was also fed by a current of opposition to the traditional leaders of the Ba'thi military, mostly high-ranking officers associated with Haurani.[49]

[46] *Niḍāl al-Ba'th*, IV, pp. 200–204, 208–212.

[47] *Maḥāḍir*, p. 16.

[48] Razzaz, *op. cit.*, pp. 87–88, and 'Umran, *op. cit.*, pp. 18–19.

[49] *Ibid.*; Jundi, *op. cit.*, p. 85, and see n. 29 above.

The Military Committee was founded and led by three 'Alawi officers: Muhammad 'Umran, Salah J'did, and Hafiz al-Asad. (Salah J'did's brother, Ghassan, it should be noted, was murdered by Syrian Intelligence for his share in the assassination of the Ba'thi military leader 'Adnan al-Maliki, and another brother, Fuad, was imprisoned in Syria.) Two factors combined to give 'Alawi (and other minoritarian) officers dominance in the new cabal. There were, to begin with, several minoritarian Ba'thi officers in Egypt, since the minorities had traditionally been heavily represented in the Syrian officer corps,[50] and many of them had been attracted to the Ba'th by its secularist ideology and for a variety of other reasons.[51] Second, while in Egypt these officers must have felt even more downtrodden than the Sunni Hariri, and one can imagine how under the pressure they were drawn together.

The Military Committee did not play any political role during the Union period, and its existence seems to have remained unknown to the party's leaders for quite some time. However, under the conditions that would result from the break-up of the UAR, it was to achieve a prominence that was perhaps not expected even by its own members.

[50] See Beeri, *op. cit.*, pp. 334–342, for a discussion of this question.

[51] See above pp. 10, 11. The role played by Arsuzi and Wahib al-Ghanim in the early years of the Ba'th seems to have been another factor in attracting 'Alawis to the party. 'Alawis from poor families (as 'Umran is said to have been) may have been drawn by the party's socialist ideology, but this could hardly apply to earlier years when this aspect of the party's doctrine had been rather opaque. That Salah J'did joined the Ba'th while his brothers Ghassan and Fuad had been affiliated with the PPS is not as surprising as it may seem at first. Both parties, after all, offered solutions to the problem of Syria's political community to which members of minority communities were attracted.

2 THE MARCH 8 COUP D'ÉTAT IN THE MAKING, SEPTEMBER 1961 TO MARCH 1963

. . . I read the articles by Salah al-Bitar and the articles of Jamal al-Atasi and those by ('Abd al-Karim) Zuhur . . . in *al-Ba'th* . . . they contained both poison and sweetness, namely the poison was directed at the UAR regime and at Abdel Nasser and the sweetness was in speaking of Arab unity and in endorsing the secession in the full sense of the term (Gamal Abdel Nasser to the Ba'thi delegates in the 1963 Unity Talks).

The 18 months known as the Separatist (or Secessionist) Period provide several interesting insights into the nature of Syrian politics, as the relatively liberal political climate again brought into the open the variety of the Syrian political scene. In the present context, however, they will rather be analyzed as the period that provided the immediate setting for the *coup* of March 8, 1963, which brought the Ba'th to power in Syria. The problems which plagued the Separatist Regime prepared the way for the Ba'th's assumption of power, but the Ba'th would also inherit some of them to contend with. During this period the Ba'th itself underwent changes profound enough to invite the question: What Ba'th was it that came to power in Syria in 1963? Finally, the events of the period shaped the group of military conspirators who were the real power behind the *coup* of March 8.

THE POLITICS OF THE SEPARATIST REGIME

The regime which emerged in Syria following the secession from the UAR was based on an alliance between the new leadership of the Syrian army and a loose, heterogeneous coalition of civilian politicians. Its failure to establish a normal relationship with Egypt, the conservative outlook and image of several of its leaders, and the sharp divisions between military and civilian and within each sector had from the outset hampered the new regime and facilitated its downfall.

By refusing to acknowledge its legitimacy and by actively trying to undermine it, President Nasser kept the new regime under permanent pressure. The attempts by its leaders to outbid Nasser with comprehensive schemes of Arab union, to balance his enmity by drawing closer to the conservative Arab regimes and to Qassem's Iraq, and to contest Nasser's right to speak in the name of Arab nationalism[1] were all abortive.

Nor could the domestic policies of the new regime compensate for the disappointment felt by Arab nationalists in Syria.[2] The first new Syrian cabinet was dominated by a group of traditional politicians of the pre-UAR period who enjoyed two assets important at that stage: the backing of the conservative element among the *coup* makers of September 1961; and their own unequivocal support of renewed Syrian independence. The elections of December 1961 produced a parliament strikingly similar to that of 1954[3] and strengthened the standing of the traditional politicans, particularly those of the old People's Party (*ḥizb ash-sha'ab*). Nazim al-Qudsi and Ma'ruf ad-Dawalibi of that party were elected president and premier, and Dr. Mamun al-Kuzbari, a past leader of Shishakli's Liberation Rally, was elected speaker.

But the elections did not reflect what seems to have been the true mood of the country. Their outcome was largely determined by the electoral system and by the unique circumstances in which the elections were held. The significance of this, however, was ignored by the victorious politicians, who seemed "to have learned and to have forgotten nothing". Thus they (practically) abolished the nationalization measures and curtailed the Agrarian Reform, ignoring the fact that in 1962 socialism (vaguely defined) had become a constituent element of "progressive" Arab nationalism.[4] The Syrian govern-

[1] This was done in a series of revelations and accusations in the Syrian press and broadcasts, most prominently by Haurani. They are also documented in a number of books published in 1962 in Syria, best known of which is Nihād al-Ghādiri's "Black Book" (*al-Kitāb al-aswad fī ḥaqiqat 'Abd an-Nāṣir* [Damascus, 1962]).

[2] The feeling that the break of the first Arab Union should at least have been compensated by achievements of the successor regime within Syria is well illustrated in a commentary by the level-headed Lebanese columnist Michel Abu Jauda written in *an-Nahār* (Beirut) on March 5, 1963, under the title "The Syria of September 28 Had Not Yet Justified Its Existence" (quoted by Zahr ad-Din, *op. cit.*, p. 412).

[3] For this comparison and on the December 1961 elections in general see Y. Oron (ed.), *Middle East Record: 1961*, pp. 499–505.

[4] For the details of the new laws see 'Adlī Hashshād and 'Abd al-Jawād 'Atiya, *Suqūṭ al-infiṣāl* ("The Fall of Secessionism") (Cairo, 1963), pp. 115–119. See also A. Hottinger, "How the Arab Bourgeoisie Lost Power", *Journal of Contemporary History*, III (1968), pp. 122–123.

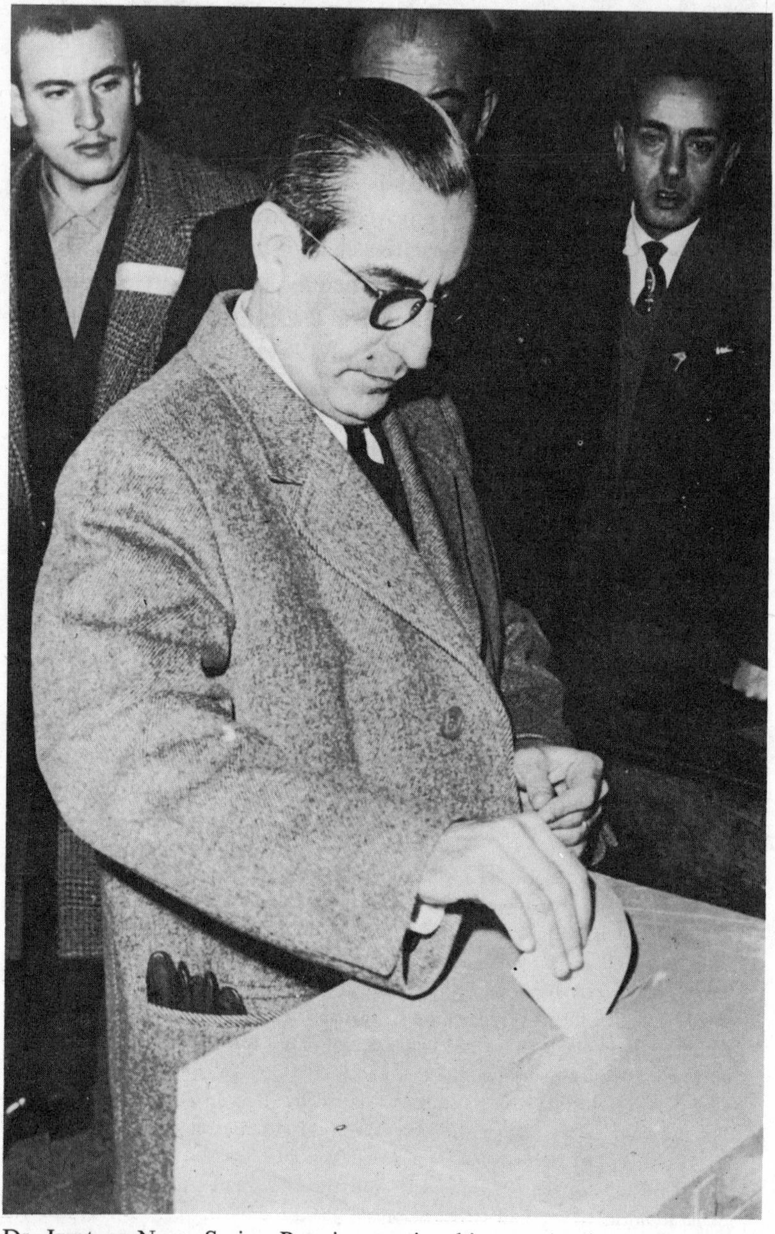

Dr. Izzat an-Nuss, Syrian Premier, casting his vote in the parliamentary elections of December 1961

ment's action antagonized not only the beneficiaries of these laws but also politically minded nationalists, who regarded the new regime as "reactionary".

Such ideological differences were a source of friction between the conservative politicians and those elements, especially Haurani, who shared their anti-Nasser sentiment, but could hardly reconcile themselves to their social and economic policies.[5] More significantly still, these policies as well as the government's failure to normalize relations with Egypt antagonized the political leadership of the Syrian army. The conservative partners to the *coup* of September 28, 1961, were ousted from the army later in the year, and the remaining senior officers seem to have been more susceptible than the civilian government leaders to ideological pressures for Arab unity and socialism, and they felt that ignoring such pressures endangered the stability of the regime.[6]

When they deposited constitutional and political powers with the civilian government in the autumn of 1961, the leaders of the Syrian army still saw themselves as the final arbiters of the country's destiny and they accordingly sought to intervene in every major policy decision. The officers made several attempts to institutionalize their participation in policy making, which culminated in the formation of a "National Security Council" (*majlis al-amn al-qaumī*), in which they had a guaranteed majority and whose function they defined as "formulation of the broad lines of the state's policy".[7]

Nevertheless, for a number of reasons the military's ability to force their views on the civilian politicians proved to be quite limited. For one thing, the military lacked effective leadership. The coalition of officers led by Nahlawi, which had carried out the *coup d'état* of September 28, soon disintegrated, and Nahlawi remained at the head

[5] The Communists, it seems, found it easier to reconcile themselves to the social and economic policies of the regime. See Murqus, *op. cit.*, pp. 124–125, and see also Yāsīn al-Ḥāfiẓ, *Haul ba'ḍ qaḍāya ath-thaura al-'arabiyya* ("Concerning Some of the Problems of the Arab Revolution") (Beirut, 1965), pp. 71–86, for a refutation written in 1962 of the Communist attempt to find a doctrinal justification for the role of the Syrian bourgeoisie.

[6] Zahr ad-Din, *op. cit.*, *passim*, and M. Colombe, "La république arabe syrienne à la lumière du coup d'état du 28 mars", *Orient*, VI (1962), pp. 11–17.

[7] Zahr ad-Din, *op. cit.*, p. 152. For several most interesting references to military intervention in politics see *ibid.*, pp. 66, 147, and again 152.

of a rather small faction of mostly Damascene officers. This faction lost its hold over the army and had to share military—and political—power with several other military groups. Their factiousness reduced the ability of the military to exert pressures and even enabled the civilian leaders to intervene in the politics of the army. The officers' desire to maintain a constitutional façade and their awareness of the regime's frailty made them averse to creating constitutional crises. Some of them, moreover, seem to have been impressed with the personal and social prestige that several veteran politicians like Khalid al-'Azm and Nazim al-Qudsi still carried.

THE ABORTIVE COUP OF MARCH 28, 1962

On March 28, 1962, Nahlawi and his group staged a "corrective" *coup* against the government which they presented as complementing the original *coup d'état* of September 28, 1961. It seems that they were primarily moved to do so by their inability to impose their outlook on the Qudsi-Dawalibi government and by the feeling that the policies it pursued endangered the regime. They apparently wanted to install a more obedient civilian government, to tighten their own hold on the army, and to try their hand at another attempt to reconcile President Nasser to their rule.[8] But Nahlawi's second *coup* surprised only a few of his fellow officers, many of whom expected him to act, some with designs of their own. This resulted in a confused, sometimes confusing,[9] chain of events which between March 28 and April 2, 1962, unfolded as a most illuminating and consequential episode of Syrian and Ba'thi military politics. These events were governed by the reaction of two broad groups of officers—a Ba'thi-unionist bloc and the faction centred on the army's supreme commander, General 'Abd al-Karim Zahr ad-Din—to Nahlawi's *coup* and by the division which later occurred within the former group.

That group was a rather loose alliance based on cooperation between the Military Committee, certain Ba'thi officers, a group of Nasserites headed by the cashiered Colonel Jasim 'Alwan, and several

[8] See Colombe, *op. cit.*, and Zahr ad-Din, *op. cit.*, pp. 209–219.

[9] Saab, *op. cit.*, p. 110, quotes the Lebanese editor G. Naccache, who characterized these events as "un combat de négres dans un tunnel".

other officers, unionists of various shades like Luayy al-Atasi and Fahd ash-Sha'ir.[10] The collaboration of the Military Committee, most of whose members had become anti-unionists at heart, with the hard-core Nasserites and with other non-Ba'this is to be explained by its weakness—several members of the Committee and other Ba'this affiliated with them constituted the majority of 63 officers that Nahlawi had cashiered in 1961 in his capacity as director of officers' affairs.[11] The Military Committee could hope to achieve its goals, the most immediate of which seems to have been the return of its members to the army, only if it worked together with other factions that were still represented in the army. When early in 1962 Sami al-Jundi, who served as a liaison between the Nasserites and the Ba'this, protested to one of the members of the Military Committee that he was aware of Salah J'did's relations with the anti-Nasserite Ba'thi *Quṭriyyūn,* he was told that "necessities make them maintain contacts with all movements, but contacts do not (necessarily) mean commitment".[12]

Much has yet to be uncovered about the aims and activities of the Ba'thi, Nasserite, and so-called unionist officers in early 1962 and about their mutual relations. It is definitely known that there were unionist cells in various units of the Syrian army, that these cells were linked to the Military Committee and to the cashiered Ba'thi and other unionist officers, and that the Nasserite officers who participated in the schemes of this loose group maintained contacts with Cairo.[13] It appears that the unionist cells in the army had been preparing for a *coup* and Nahlawi's decision to act may have been influenced by his anticipation of such a move.[14] As he and his as-

[10] Not much is known about this unionist grouping in the Syrian army in early 1962. Some details can be found in Jundi, *op. cit.,* pp. 88 ff., Zahr ad-Din, *op. cit.,* pp. 281 ff., *Maḥāḍir,* p. 67, and the communiqué issued by the Syrian National Council of Revolutionary Command on May 19, 1963, and published in the Syrian press of May 20, 1963.

[11] See Jundi, *op. cit.,* p. 88, and Zahr ad-Din, op. cit., pp. 174–175. Presumably Nahlawi suspected the Ba'thi officers of being unionists (which, in fact, most of them were not) and did not like their affiliation with a political party.

[12] Jundi, *op. cit.,* p. 90. On the *Quṭriyyūn* see below, p. 39.

[13] *Ibid.* and Zahr ad-Din, *op. cit.,* pp. 281 ff.

[14] A. Horton, "Syrian Stability and the Ba'th", *American Universities Field Staff Reports Service, Southwest Asia Series* (1965), No. 1, p. 3, and see the most interest-

sociates staged their *coup* on March 28 and arrested the president and other government leaders, they encountered resistance from unionist officers particularly in Ḥoms, where the army units commanded by Badr al-A'sar revolted against them. Nahlawi's ability to deal with this resistance was hampered by the uncooperative attitude of an important group of senior officers represented by General Zahr ad-Din.

Zahr ad-Din, a professional, colourless Druse officer, was picked in September 1961 to be the nominal head of the Syrian army since as a respectable but powerless senior officer he was considered a convenient and harmless choice. He proved, however, to be more ambitious and cunning than had been anticipated and was able to use the powers vested in his office, his apparent indispensability as a compromise candidate, and the rivalries of the strong contending factions to bolster his own position. He and several other senior officers had known in advance of Nahlawi's plans and may even have encouraged him to carry them out,[15] since they shared his dissatisfaction with the Qudsi-Dawalibi government. However, they had no desire to see Nahlawi succeed and become the strong man of the Syrian army (at their expense). Therefore, they did not lend him assistance against the unionist rebels and he was left to rely on his own (mostly Damascene) supporters to contend with them. This resulted in a stalemate which threatened to deteriorate into violent confrontation. In order to avert this danger it was decided to convene a Military Congress in Homs on April 1.

Composed of representatives from all military regions and major units (41 officers in all), the congress represented, as it were, the corporate identity and interests of the Syrian officer corps. Its meeting

ing version given by Luayy al-Atasi during the 1963 Unity Talks as reproduced in *Maḥāḍir*, p. 126. According to this version, Atasi and other unionist officers were involved in the preparations for the *coup* against the Qudsi-Dawalibi government together with several other factions (including that of Nahlawi) and withdrew from it when they became aware of its anti-unionist orientation (Atasi, it should be remembered, was addressing Nasser). It follows from this version that the various factions were aware of each other's plans.

[15] This is implied in Zahr ad-Din's account in his memoirs and explicitly charged by Ma'ruf ad-Dawalibi, the Syrian premier at that time, in a series of articles published in the Lebanese weekly *al-Jadīd* between May 24 and July 19, 1968, in which he took issue with Zahr ad-Din's memoirs.

in what was in effect a parliamentary capacity was an expression of the army's decision to close its ranks rather than let the rival factions clash. By deliberating the issues a course of action acceptable to the army as a whole could be found. The proceedings of the Homs Congress again indicated what influence the close contact with the Egyptian army had had on the pattern of Syrian military politics. The newly independent Syrian army inherited from the UAR period such forums as the Military Defence Council (*majlis ad-difāʿ al-ʿaskarī*), which included all senior officers in the army, and the Officers' Committee (*lajnat aḍ-ḍubbāṭ*), in which was vested authority for cashiering officers. In search of formal, institutionalized ways for regulating their affairs and settling their differences, the Syrian officers often found it convenient to activate this legacy of the Union period. Such was decidedly the case in March and April 1962.[16]

There were many interesting aspects to the Homs Congress and it adopted several important resolutions that can not be surveyed here. Four points, however, appear to merit special mention:

a. It was decided to exile Nahlawi and his close associates. All those exiled happened to be Damascenes and it seems that besides widespread resentment in the army against Nahlawi's personality and ambitions, the decision to exile him and his group reflected an element of provincial jealousy.[17]

b. The congress decided to restore the civilian government.

c. On the question of union the majority of votes was cast in favour of a resolution calling for a union "with the liberated Arab states", which meant a virtual rejection of the more specific demand for an immediate return to union with Egypt.

d. The congress made no decision with regard to the case of the (mostly Baʿthi and other unionist) officers who were retired after September

[16] See Zahr ad-Din, *op. cit.*, pp. 216–217, 146, 174, *Maḥāḍir*, pp. 220–222, and see Amin Nafuri,*ʿAbd an-Nāsir bada'a fi dimashq wa-intaha fi-shtūra* ("Nasser Began in Damascus and Ended in Shtura") (Damascus, 1962), p. 177, for the operation of the Officers' Committee under the Union.

[17] Zahr ad-Din, *op. cit.*, p. 216 n. 1. On p. 372 he tells how during a later struggle one of the military factions tried to encircle Damascus with units commanded by officers "who felt nothing but hatred and resentment towards Damascus and its inhabitants". On the Damascene faction of officers in the 1950s see Torrey, *op. cit.*, p. 355.

1961 and referred the matter to the Officers' Committee (to whose province the matter technically pertained).

The decisions of the Homs Congress disappointed several of the unionist officers. Some of them regarded Nahlawi's *coup* as an opportunity to carry out their own plan to overthrow the regime; certain retired officers saw in it their chance to return to service. They rejected the compromise achieved at Homs and wanted to take up arms against it. But these views were not shared by all partners to the loose unionist coalition. Some of them considered armed resistance useless and many Ba'this were disconcerted by the Nasserite's insistence on an immediate return to union with Egypt. Consequently, when unionist officers tried, on April 2, to stage a *coup* in Homs and Aleppo (under Jasim 'Alwan, Muhammad 'Umran, and Hamad 'Ubaid) and in Deir az-Zor (under Luayy al-Atasi), they were not joined by some of their Ba'thi and other colleagues who, according to the original scheme of the unionists, were to act in such places as Sweida and the Southwestern (Israeli) Front.[18]

Still more decisive was the fact that the bulk of the Syrian army stood by the decisions of the Homs Congress, and the revolt in the north was easily suppressed by forces from other parts of Syria. Even the units commanded by Badr al-A'sar, who had initiated the resistance to Nahlawi on March 28, took part in the pacification of Aleppo. This is most illuminating—once the army had taken a collective decision, a dissenting minority could hardly count even on those officers sympathetic to its cause.

The events of April 2 drove a deep wedge between the Ba'thi and Nasserite officers which goes a long way in explaining the development of their complex relationship in 1963. Apparently, much of the resentment felt by those officers who fought to the end until they were arrested (to be tried later) was directed against 'Alwan and 'Umran who managed to escape in time. The Ba'thi as well as other officers

[18] Jundi, *op. cit.*, pp. 91–95, Razzaz, *op. cit.*, p. 86, and Taufiq 'Indānī, *al-Ba'th fī durūb an-niḍāl* ("The Ba'th on the Roads of Struggle") (Damascus, 1965), pp. 154–155. 'Indani wrote a Ba'thi-inspired version of the party's and regime's history that seldom adds significant new details. According to Jundi, Salah J'did was in charge of the units that were to revolt in the Sweida region, but the plan was not carried out there and in other regions.

may have learned a more general lesson from the events that followed this episode—military control without a civilian basis of support created a vacuum and was politically meaningless. Thus the army, after protracted negotiations, was able to impose a more forward-looking premier, but it had to restore President Qudsi to his office, his position now strengthened after his indispensability had been demonstrated.

The new cabinet headed by a moderate unionist, Dr. Bashir al-'Azma, represented an attempt to stabilize the regime by giving it a more progressive image and by attempting to mend fences with Egypt. 'Azma, a physician from a noted Damascene family, was close to the Ba'th and his cabinet included one of Bitar's confidants and two of Haurani's associates ('Abd al-Halim Qaddur and Ahmad 'Abd al-Karim). It amended the Agrarian Reform Law, renationalized the Khumasiyya Company (a large industrial concern), and made a number of gestures towards Egypt.[19] 'Azma's efforts seem to have been the utmost to be expected of a cabinet operating within the framework of the Separatist Regime and were to no avail. Relations with Egypt deteriorated—the propaganda warfare was renewed (during these months Haurani came out with the sharpest denunciations of President Nasser and his policies), an Egyptian plot to topple the Syrian regime was exposed, and Nasserite terrorist groups operated in Syrian cities. On July 28 Syria took its case to the Arab League and filed a complaint against Egyptian meddling in its internal affairs and Egypt's violation of Syrian sovereignty. In its famed session in Shtura (August 22–30) the League's Council listened to acrimonious exchanges between the Syrian and Egyptian delegations (the latter composed of exiled Syrian Nasserites), but in view of an Egyptian threat to withdraw from the League it was finally decided to suspend the Syrian complaint. In Syria itself 'Azma ran into difficulties that in September 1962 led to his resignation. He was replaced by the veteran Khalid al-'Azm, who again headed a broad and incongruous coalition cabinet and like his predecessors was unable to cope with the regime's underlying problems.

[19] For details see *Cahiers de l'Orient Contemporain* (in short, *Cahiers*), No. 48 (1962), pp. 74–89, and *ibid.*, No. 49 (1962), pp. 235–240.

THE TRANSFORMATION OF THE BA'TH PARTY

Syria's secession from the UAR and the establishment of the Separatist Regime immediately exacerbated the difficulties that had confronted the Ba'th Party since the failure of its partnership with Nasser had become apparent. As long as it wished to remain a unionist party, the Ba'th could not afford to sanction the breach of the first Arab union by working within the regime created by this breach. On the other hand, the Ba'thi leaders, at odds with Nasser, neither wished for nor saw any political prospects in a return to union under him. The predicament resulting from this dilemma was illustrated by the conduct of Bitar, who endorsed the secession only to regret it later, and by the ambiguous public line that the party's National Command adopted in the first few months following the secession.[20]

The choice was simple for Ba'this at both ends of the spectrum. Rimawi, Rikabi, and their followers remained all-out Nasserites, and the more moderate supporters of President Nasser in Syria, later known as the Socialist Unionists (*al-Waḥdawiyyūn al-ishtirākiyyūn*), also placed themselves, though with more reservations, within the Nasserite pale. At the other end, Haurani and his group readily identified themselves with the Separatist Regime and sought to pursue their political careers within it.

It was only gradually, as the new conditions obtaining in Syria and the Arab world crystallized, that 'Aflaq and the National Command in Beirut formulated a better defined policy. The series of circulars (*ta'mīmāt*) and policy statements issued by the National Command in the latter part of 1961 and early in 1962 reflected its growing conviction that the party's future lay in opposing the Separatist Regime and in proposing a unionist-socialist alternative to it. The

[20] On October 2, 1961, Bitar and Haurani together with 14 other prominent politicians, most of them conservative, signed a manifesto supporting the secession. This would be used against Bitar by Nasser in the 1963 Unity Talks and by other political foes. Just as significant but of a lesser emotional impact (and therefore rarely mentioned) was Bitar's signature two months later of a National Charter for the Separatist Regime (see *Middle East Record, 1961,* pp. 493, 497). For the first communiqués published by the National Command of the Ba'th on October 5 and 14 see *Niḍāl al-Ba'th,* Vol. VI (Beirut, 1965), pp. 11–19. An explanation of these communiqués and an apology for their ambiguity can be found in a circular issued by the National Command early in December 1961 and reproduced *ibid.*, pp. 20–43.

new policy was for the first time fully presented in a statement issued by the National Command on February 21, 1962, on the eve of the fourth anniversary of the UAR's establishment.[21] In it 'Aflaq (who is known to be the author) criticized the mistakes of the UAR period (including some of his own) and proposed a return to a federal union. The advantages of the course 'Aflaq chose are evident: it enabled him to "finesse" for the time being the dilemma of the Ba'th's relationship with Nasser, while at the same time it still placed the party within the unionist orbit.

But this line was unacceptable to many of the party's rank and file and lesser functionaries, whose disenchantment with unionism and with 'Aflaq himself had already been evident in 1960, and became even more so when preliminary attempts were made to reorganize the party early in 1962.[22] It then became evident that if 'Aflaq wanted to control the party that was about to re-form in Syria, he had to build it on a new basis.

This 'Aflaq and his confidants set out to do at the Fifth National Congress, convened in mid-May 1962 in Homs. Only a few dependable delegates were invited from Syria, and the strong "leftist", anti-unionist, and anti-'Aflaq faction of the Lebanese Ba'th was neutralized by the Iraqi delegation that dominated the congress. The leadership of the reorganized Iraqi Ba'th, headed by 'Ali Salih as-Sa'di, was young and militant and at that time supported 'Aflaq and his policy.[23]

With Iraqi support the congress endorsed 'Aflaq's approach to Egypt and to the question of union and further elaborated the position enunciated on February 21. The congress in effect placed the Ba'th in a

[21] *Ibid.*, pp. 44–60.

[22] See *Nashra dākhiliyya 'an al-mu'tamar al-qaumī al-khāmis* ("Internal Bulletin on the Fifth National Congress") issued in June 1962 and reproduced in *ibid.*, pp. 80–93. The relevant passage is on pp. 88–89. 'Umran, p. 28, even mentions a congress held in February 1962 for that purpose.

[23] For details on the reorganization of the Iraqi Ba'th following the Rikabi split see U. Dann, *Iraq under Qassem* (New York and London, 1969), p. 327. On the role played by the Iraqi Ba'this in supporting 'Aflaq at the congress see Ṣafadī, *Ḥizb al-Ba'th*, pp. 287–290, and Naṣr Shimālī, "Ayyām ḥāsima fī ta'rīkh al-ḥizb" ("Crucial Days in the Party's History"), *ath-Thaura* (Damascus), November 18, 1968. Sa'di himself would mention this episode during his argument with 'Aflaq at the Extra-ordinary Syrian Regional Congress in February 1964 (see American University of Beirut, *Arab Political Documents* [1964], p. 33).

middle-of-the-road position, rejecting both secessionism and precipitate return to a union with Egypt. This position was yet to be practically tested, and the Ba'this themselves must have known that it was unacceptable to Egypt. However, it was precisely its nonbinding nature and dim prospects that made it acceptable to such anti-Nasserites as Sa'di.[24]

The most important resolution passed by the congress concerned the formal re-establishment of the party organization in Syria on new foundations and exclusion from it of all those militants who opposed the veteran leadership and its unionist orientation. This was quite plainly stated and explained in an Internal Bulletin (*nashra dākhiliyya*) issued by the National Command on the results of the congress:[25]

> The experience that had taken place in Syria underscored the need to restore the organization without taking into account past positions of responsibility as a sufficient criterion for party work in the present time. The excitement and individualism[26] that have dominated the minds of most functionaries have made them unsuitable for responsible, disciplined party work and certainly for reorganizing a Party in which the attitude of most members was distorted by the divisions and doubts that resulted from the dissolution. To this should be added the appearance of doctrinal and political deviations among certain Party members, most prominently their rejection of the Party's creed and its mode of political action and its spirit of discipline.

In line with these resolutions the new National Command appointed a four-man Temporary Regional Command for Syria and a supervisory committee, whose task was to guide the new organization on its behalf. The committee set to work immediately

[24] While Sa'di seems to have been opposed to concessions to Nasser, as were the Syrian and Lebanese anti-unionists, he apparently supported 'Aflaq's line because he desired the latter's cooperation and because in the struggle against Qassem he needed the collaboration of nationalist, non-Ba'thi, officers.

[25] *Niḍāl al-Ba'th,* VI, p. 89.

[26] The original term is *fardiyya,* a pejorative often used in Ba'thi parlance to deplore Nasser's political style and, in a more general way, any deviation from collective leadership and conduct.

and began to build a new and clandestine party organization in Damascus.[27]

All this drew a rapid response from Akram Haurani and from the intra-party opposition that had not been invited to the Homs Congress and by its decisions was to be excluded from the re-formed party. The opposition cooperated with Haurani whose anti-unionism and enmity to 'Aflaq it shared, but it had remained aloof from his faction and disputed his leadership as it repudiated that of 'Aflaq.[28] This opposition was itself divided into several groups, but it was generally called *Quṭriyyūn* (Regionalists) after the *tanẓīm quṭrī* (Regional Organization) that some of them established in Syria independently of the National Command following the secession from the UAR. Their origins can be traced in the Syrian provinces, most notably Deir az-Zor in the North East, Ladhiqiyya, and the Hauran, where sections of the party had never really dissolved themselves during the union with Egypt. Led by such party militants as Fa'iz al-Jāsim, Yusuf Z'ayyin, Munir al-'Abdallah and Ibrahim Makhus, the *Quṭriyyūn* did not represent a coherent organization or a definite point of view. Some of them were close to Haurani, some cooperated with the Separatist Regime, while others were affiliated with the Military Committee. Munir al-'Abdallah, for instance, an influential but little known 'Alawi lawyer from Ladhiqiyya, was close to Salah J'did and following the abortive *coup* in Aleppo he defended Hamad 'Ubaid in court.[29]

The *Quṭriyyūn's* reaction to the Fifth National Congress and to the formation of the first cells of the new party was to convene a

[27] *Niḍāl al-Ba'th,* VI, pp. 89–90, Razzaz, *op. cit.,* p. 109, "Internal Bulletin of the Organizational Bureau of the Syrian Ba'th, May 15, 1963", and Ibrahīm Salāmeh, *Al-Ba'th min al-madāris ilā ath-thakanāt* ("The Ba'th from the Schools to the Barracks"), Beirut 1969, p. 19. According to the sources, the supervisory committee seems to have been composed of Iraqi Ba'this and of two Syrian supporters of 'Aflaq, Shiblī al-'Aisami and Al-Walid Talib. The sources sometimes confuse this committee with the four-member Temporary Regional Command.

[28] Internal Bulletin issued by the National Command in July 1962. Similarly the leftist, anti-unionist wing of the Lebanese Ba'th, mistakenly called the Haurani Group, was actually opposed to him and his policies. See Abu Jaber, *op. cit.,* p. 195 n. 31, and *Maḥāḍir,* pp. 121–122.

[29] The most authoritative history of the *Qutriyyūn* can be found in N. Van Dam, "De Ba'thparty in Syrie (1958–1966)," *Internationale Spectator* XXV, (November 1971), pp. 1899–1933. Much of the author's information seems to have been gath-

Regional Congress in cooperation with Haurani some time in May or June 1962, and elect a Regional Command of their own. The National Command, apparently aware of their numerical strength, entered into negotiations with them that lasted throughout the month of June. However, these negotiations only served to bring out the mutual dislike and distrust of both sides, and in June 25 the *Quṭriyyūn* came out with a public statement in the name of the Ba'th Party, thus signifying the failure of the discussions and the *Quṭriyyūn*'s claim to speak for the true Ba'th. It is not known what relation the publication of this statement bore to the publication on June 18 of a statement by Haurani, announcing the re-establishment of the Ba'th Party and denouncing 'Aflaq and Bitar.[30]

In the summer of 1962, then, the Ba'th Party in Syria was divided into four distinct organized groups. Haurani's faction and the *Quṭriyyūn* supported the existing order and operated within it, while 'Aflaq's new party and the Socialist Unionists were counted among the unionist opposition. In addition, there were several ex-Ba'this who did not formally join any of these groups but were still considered close to the party. Thus, the intellectual circle around Dr. Jamal al-Atasi, 'Abd al-Karim Zuhur, Yasin al-Hafiz, and Elyas Murqus, though it published in *al-Ba'th*, the organ of 'Aflaq's party (that renewed publication in July 1962), was not formally linked to it.

ered in an interview with Munif ar-Razzaz. See also *al-Munāḍil*, appendix to June 1966 issue, Jundi, *op. cit.*, p. 80, and Shimali, *op. cit.* Shimali mentions another group active in 1962, close in outlook to the *Quṭriyyūn* but distinct from them, which he calls *al-lajna al-jāmi'iyya* (The University Committee). Abu Jaber, *op. cit.*, pp. 63–64, writes of a split in the Syrian Ba'th and of the "Syrian region" of the Ba'th welcoming the secession, and it is probably the *Quṭriyyūn* that he has in mind.

[30] The statement was published in *an-Naṣr* (Damascus), June 25, 1962, and its general tone was in line with Haurani's views. On Haurani's statement see *Cahiers*, No. 49 (1962), 240, and Kerr, *Cold War*, p. 49. The statement provoked a reply from 'Aflaq, announcing that Haurani had already been expelled from the party the preceding month. Haurani himself does not seem to have participated in the *Qutriyyun's* Regional Congress, but some of his associates like Riad al-Malki maintained close contact with them. The negotiations between the National Command and the *Quṭriyyūn* during May and June are described in detail in two lengthy Internal Bulletins that were distributed by the former in June and July 1962. The episode is also mentioned in 'Aflaq's crucial speech of February 18, 1966, reproduced in American University of Beirut, *al-Wathā'iq al-'arabiyya* ("Arab Documents") (1966), pp. 60–67, especially p. 65.

This circle was composed of ex-Ba'this and ex-Communists. 'Abd al-Karim Zuhur was born ca. 1920 in Hama and came to the Ba'th through Akram Haurani with whom he later quarrelled. Dr. Jamal al-Atasi, a native of Homs (1910) and a psychiatrist by profession, had been a veteran member of the Ba'th and in the late 1950s the owner of the party's organ *al-Jamāhīr*. Yasin al-Hafiz had been a "second rank" member of the Ba'th but is reported to have had Communist connections as well, and Elyas Murqus, a Greek Orthodox from Ladhiqiyya, was a disillusioned Communist. The significance of their circle's activity and publications lies in the introduction of Marxist doctrine into Ba'thi thinking. The group sought to transform what they considered the vague and romantic socialism of the Ba'th into a scientific and revolutionary doctrine, while maintaining the party's nationalist-unionist orientation. The scientific and revolutionary socialism they advocated, as expounded in their most important publication,[31] was a version of Marxism adapted, as it were, to the conditions of the Arab world. The ex-Communist members of the circle seem to have been disenchanted with the Syrian Communist Party's rigidity and subservience to Moscow,[32] while the Ba'this represented the development of a leftist current that had previously existed in their party, but had been submerged by the leaders' cautious approach to socialism.[33] This development is clearly illustrated by the transition from a mild leftist approach in an essay on socialism, which Dr. Jamal al-Atasi had published in 1960, to his renunciation of "Arab Socialism" and adoption of a virtually Marxist concept of socialism by early 1963.

Al-Atasi's 1960 essay, titled *al-ishtirākiyya tuḥarrir bi-an-niḍāl* ("Socialism Liberates through Struggle"), was published in the collection *Dirāsāt fī-al-ishtirākiyya* ("Studies in Socialism") issued by the Ba'th in 1960 in an apparent attempt to document the party's socialist orientation. The collection as a whole still reflected the

[31] *Fī al-fikr aṣ-ṣiyāsī* ("Concerning Political Thought"), 2 vols. (Damascus, 1963).

[32] Eliās Murqus, "Stalin and the National Question" in *Fī al-fikr as-siyāsī*, pp. 68–138, and *Ta'rīkh al-aḥzāb ash-shuyū'iyya fī al-waṭan al-'arabi*, and *cf.* Bassam Tibi, *Die arabische Linke* (Frankfurt am Main, 1969), pp. 40–41 and 43–45.

[33] The account "Left and Right in Our Party" (*al-Munāḍil*, July 1966) is indeed an attempt to show that there had always existed a strong leftist current in the Ba'th which had been suppressed by the "rightist" leaders.

Ba'th's traditional attitude and it explicitly rejected the notion of class struggle as the moving force in society. Atasi himself only mentioned the division which exists within the society. His major contribution to *Fī al-fikr aṣ-ṣiyāsī* is called *al-ishtirākiyya al-'arabiyya wa-ustūrat al-khaṣā'iṣ* ("Arab Socialism and the Myth of Characteristics") and in it he rejects 'Aflaq's fundamental position, the uniqueness of Arab socialism, and calls for "opening" towards Marxist thinking:

> . . . and the free opening towards the other human experiences and towards Marxist thinking in its broad framework is bound to generate an atmosphere of serious thinking from which it will be possible to develop an outlook or a theoretical guide for the liberating struggle and the socialist application in the Arab homeland.[34]

But the impact of these developments was not yet apparent in 1962 and early in 1963. The importance of the group seemed to be rather in its contribution to *al-Ba'th,* in which Atasi, Zuhur, and Hafiz took issue with Haurani and the Communists for their anti-unionism and cooperation with the bourgeoisie.[35]

Even though the *Quṭriyyūn* represented a radical opposition to the Ba'th's traditional leadership and were self-proclaimed advocates of social reforms, such leftists as Hafiz regarded them warily. The leftists took exception to the *Quṭriyyūn's* association with Haurani—whom Hafiz called a "petty feudatory"—to their lack of an ideological basis, and to their anti-unionist stance. While critical of Nasser's regime, Atasi, Zuhur, and Hafiz, in line with their rejection of the Separatist Regime, always stressed the unionist orientation of their ideology.

The ties that bound this intellectual circle to 'Aflaq's reconstituted party were loosened with the suspension of *al-Ba'th* by the Syrian authorities in October 1962. 'Aflaq's party was numerically small and composed mostly of university and high school students in Damas-

[34] *Fī al-fikr as-siyāsī*, p. 145. For the traditional outlook still characterizing the collection assembled in *Dirasāt fi al-ishtirākiyya* see in particular pp. 12–13.

[35] See Yasin al-Hafiz's articles reproduced in his *Ba'd qaḍāya* and Zuhur's attacks on Haurani in *Fī al-fikr as-siyāsī*, especially I, p. 67.

cus,[36] but it also enjoyed several advantages, being led by 'Aflaq, who was better known than his anonymous party rivals and, as the secretary-general of the National Command, controlled the party's nexus with its other branches. Bitar was not formally registered in the reconstituted party and he would only join after March 8, 1963, so that 'Aflaq seemed to be its unquestionable leader. Despite criticism directed at it from various quarters, it is clear that the Iraqi committee charged with supervising the reorganization of the Syrian party introduced new standards of disciplined and clandestine party work, with which the Ba'th in Syria had until then not been familiar.[37]

The usefulness of 'Aflaq's close relationship with Sa'di and the other leaders of the Iraqi Ba'th (such as Hamdi 'Abd al-Majid and Hani al-Fakiki) was more fully revealed after the February 8 *coup d'état* in Iraq. Carried out with 'Aflaq's foreknowledge and consent,[38] the *coup* brought the Ba'th to power in Iraq and it immediately changed the standing of 'Aflaq and his party on the Syrian political scene. This change also affected the plans and prospects of the officers preparing for the overthrow of the Separatist Regime.

THE MILITARY COMMITTEE AND THE COUP D'ÉTAT OF MARCH 8

The history of the military plot that preceded the *coup d'état* of March 8, 1963, in Syria is still a matter of uncertainty and conflicting accounts. Not only were the preparations clandestine by definition, but the underlying assumption that the authors of a *coup* have a right to participate in the government that it produces would motivate

[36] Safadi, *op. cit.*, p. 290, says the party had about 300 young members. Dr. Jamal al-Atasi in an interview with Eric Rouleau (*Le Monde*, October 13, 1966) said that in March 1963 the Ba'th had no more than 400 members.

[37] Razzaz, *op. cit.*, p. 113, and *Azmat al-ḥizb wa-ḥarakat 23 shibāṭ wa-in'iqād al-mu'tamar al-quṭrī al-akhīr* ("The Party's Crisis and the Movement of February 23 and the Convening of the Latest Regional Congress") (a brochure issued in Damascus in 1966), p. 43. On the organizational standards in the Iraqi Ba'th see P. Seale, "The Role of the Ba'th in the Ramadan 14 Revolution", *Middle East Forum*, XXXVII (1963), pp. 17–19.

[38] See *Maḥāḍir*, p. 33, for Sa'di's explicit statement that he came to Syria to obtain 'Aflaq's approval for carrying out his *coup*.

contenders for power in Syria to take credit for a major role in the *coup* and minimize that of their partners.[39]

Following their debacle early in 1962, the unionist officers maintained their loose organization and continued their preparations for toppling the Syrian government. Their position was doubtlessly weakened by the events of March and April which bred more tension and suspicion between Ba'this and Nasserites and resulted in the in the incarceration and retirement of several unionists like the Ba'this Hamad 'Ubaid and Muhammad Ibrahim al-'Ali, arrested in Aleppo, and the mild unionist Luayy al-Atasi, who was recalled from the United States and sentenced to prison. On the other hand, the arrest and retirement of such officers seem to have added to their and to their colleagues' determination and motivation. Very little is known about their activity between April 1962 and February 1963, except that they encouraged the exiled Nahlawi to try his hand at a comeback in January, hoping probably that in the ensuing confusion they would be able to carry out their own plans.[40]

The crucial turning point came with the establishment of a Ba'thi regime in Iraq following the *coup d'état* of February 8, 1963. The Iraqi Ba'th was then generally taken to be a unionist, if not a Nasserite force[41] and the prevailing feeling was that the Separatist Regime in Syria had been encircled. This spurred the military and civilian leaders of that regime to a last-minute effort to close ranks and to adopt more dynamic policies. But it also brought several senior officers

[39] The two fullest versions of the *coup* are the accounts given in the National Council of the Revolutionary Command's (NCRC) communiqué of May 19, 1963, and the anonymous booklet *Qissat ath-thaura fi al-'irāq wa-surya* ("The Story of the Revolution in Iraq and Syria") (Beirut, 1963). Zahr ad-Din in the last section of his memoirs brings out many details of the plot which preceded the *coup*, as does Sami al-Jundi. Occasional but important references are found in the protocols of the 1963 Unity Talks, in Salāmeh, pp. 29–31, and in several other sources.

[40] This was confirmed by Luayy al-Atasi, by then head of the NCRC at the Cairo Unity Talks; see *Maḥāḍir*, p. 126. Zahr ad-Din recorded in detail "Nasserite" conspiracies against the Separatist Regime in the latter half of 1962, in which several well-known Ba'thi officers (Muhammad 'Umran, 'Uthman Kan'an, Musa az-Zu'bi, and Salah Dulli) were reported to have been involved (pp. 281–305), but the account often seems dubious. See also Jundi, *op. cit.*, pp. 96, 97.

[41] That this was not the case should have been clear to those who read the Ba'thi statements carefully, as did Nasser who appears to have had no illusions in this respect. The Ba'thi orientation was explicitly stated by 'Abd al-Karim Zuhur in a

to cooperate with the consipiring unionist officers who seemed to hold the key to the country's political future. As a result, the balance of power in the army shifted in the direction of the unionist officers who on their own held very few of the key military posts. It is this change in the political atmosphere in Syria that largely accounts for the difference between the *coups* of April 2, 1962, and March 8, 1963.

The military group preparing for the overthrow of the Separatist Regime in February 1963 was composed of independent (headed by Colonel Ziyad al-Hariri, at that time commander of the Israeli Front), Nasserite (headed by Colonel Rashid al-Qutaini, the director of military intelligence, and Colonel Muhammad as-Sufi, commander of the brigade stationed in Homs) and other unionist, including Ba'thi, officers. There were very few Ba'thi officers on active service in the Syrian army at that time: Captain Salim Hatum, 'Uthmān Kan'an, Suleiman Haddad and Mustafa al-Hajj 'Ali. Nevertheless, they and their ousted colleagues had the advantage of affiliation with a well-coordinated Military Committee and with a political party (the value of an alliance with a political force must have become obvious by then to politically minded, ambitious Syrian officers). The re-emergence of the Ba'th as a major political force in Syria following its accession to power in Iraq seems to have given the Military Committee a standing vis-à-vis its non-Ba'thi partners that it could not have achieved on its own merits. This would be admitted later by the Ba'this themselves: "The March operation could have remained a mere military *coup* . . . had it not been preceded by the party-led revolution in Iraq. . . ." [42]

The true nature of the Military Committee at that stage has yet to be revealed. Evidently it was a close-knit and well-coordinated group that maintained contacts with civilian and military elements which

postscript that he hastily added to the first volume of *Fī al-fikr as-siyāsī* (pp. 203–208), seeking to explain the significance of the February 8 *coup* in Iraq that took place after the volume had been sent to the printer. In it he explained that following that *coup* there was no more need to tie Arab unity exclusively to Nasser's person (pp. 207–208). The postscript is also significant in that it again demonstrates the degree to which Ba'thi intellectuals have been overwhelmed by power and success. The volume itself deplored Ba'thi dependence in the past on "military bureaucracies", but Zuhur was obviously carried away by the *coup* of February 8 in which a "military bureaucracy" played a decisive role.

[42] *Resolutions of the First Regular Syrian Regional Congress*, September 1963, p. 4.

had at one time or another been associated with the Ba'th Party.[43] The Committee apparently coordinated the activities of all Ba'thi officers, but it is not known whether all of them realized at that time that they were dealing with an organized secret cabal with definite schemes and goals. The leaders of the Military Committee had been in touch with both 'Aflaq's wing and the *Quṭriyyūn,* and while they were opposed to 'Aflaq's leadership they had close ties with at least part of the *Quṭriyyūn.* But 'Aflaq's assets, his public image and reputation, his opposition to the discredited Separatist Regime and, since February 8, his presumed influence in Baghdad, made the Ba'thi officers prefer him and his faction as civilian allies.[44]

Conversely, 'Aflaq seems to have been aware of the pitfalls involved in entering such an alliance with an autonomous cabal, particularly when his own party had not yet been duly reorganized.[45] But this realization could not weigh against the fear that some other political force would forestall the Ba'th and replace the tottering Separatist Regime, that a unique opportunity would be missed. And so once again 'Aflaq was bidding for power in Syria against his better judgment.

Nothing definite is known about the pre-*coup* agreements and arrangements between 'Aflaq's Ba'th and the Military Committee and between the latter and its non-Ba'thi military partners. It appears that the independent officers involved in the plot, particularly Ziyad al-Hariri, were closer to the Ba'th than to the Nasserites, probably because they feared the latter, unlike the others, might sincerely seek a return to the Union. They appreciated the advantages of an alliance with a political party that was considered unionist and progressive and at the same time was also linked to Iraq.[46]

43 'Umran, *op. cit.,* pp. 19–21, and Jundi, *op. cit.,* p. 380.

44 Even the hostile Safadi grudgingly acknowledges the political value of 'Aflaq's reputation: "'Aflaq's reputation (*sum'a*) which he managed to surround with mystery and Sufism" (*op. cit.,* p. 380). The shift in the position of the Military Committee is indeed explained in the same manner in an Internal Bulletin issued by the National Command on December 22, 1965.

45 Razzaz, *op. cit.,* pp. 89–90, and 'Aflaq himself in his interview with Rouleau, *Le Monde,* March 20, 1963.

46 See Jundi, *op. cit.,* pp. 106–108, 117. Luayy al-Atasi was at that time in prison and Hariri was the unquestioned leader of the "progressive unionist" independent officers who cooperated with the Ba'th and the Nasserites.

At least the independent officers are thought to have agreed late in February to entrust the Ba'th with the civilian functions of government. Bitar is reported to have been invited at that time to head the cabinet upon the implementation of the *coup* and to have accepted.[47] With some hindsight it may also be suggested that the top military positions were distributed among the conspirators and their colleagues during those weeks and that it was agreed that the retired Ba'thi officers be returned to active military service.

During that period the cooperation of several officers who did not belong to the conspiring group was assured. Ziyad al-Hariri controlled the sizable forces stationed at the Israeli Front, not far from Damascus, Muhammad as-Sufi commanded the key brigade stationed in Homs, and Ghassan Haddad, one of Hariri's independent partners, commanded the Desert Forces. However, to assure the success of the *coup*, at least the tacit cooperation of the officers who controlled the units in the network of camps which surround Damascus was needed. Such officers as Colonels Nur ad-Din Kanj and Mahmud al-'Audeh and Lieutenant Ahmed Khattab were approached by the plotters. Sensing that the end of the existing regime was near, they agreed, in return for various rewards, to cooperate with the conspirators.[48] So demoralized were the leaders of the Separatist Regime that even though Hariri's designs were quite well known he was not prevented from carrying them out. He was to be transferred to Baghdad as Syria's new military attaché but that decision affected only the timing of the *coup*.

Early in March it was decided to implement the plan on March 9. On March 5, however, Rashid al-Qutaini and Muhammad as-Sufi informed Hariri and the Ba'this that they wished to postpone it, that given more time they could consolidate their hold on several units and stage a bloodless *coup*. It now seems that the Nasserites were preparing a *coup* of their own and wished to withdraw from their pact with Hariri and the Ba'this.[49] Presumably they realized that Hariri's close cooperation with the Ba'this was bound to relegate them to a position of minor partners. The last-minute desertion of Sufi

[47] Jundi, *op. cit.*, p. 111.
[48] Zahr ad-Din, *op. cit.*, pp. 416–426.
[49] See the NCRC's communiqué of May 19, 1963, and Jundi, *op. cit.*, p. 112.

and Qutaini delayed the *coup* for another day but hardly affected it otherwise. The operation started at night and early in the morning of March 8 its military phase was over.

The tottering Syrian government and its army put up little resistance to the conspiring officers and, by March 8, it was evident that a new political era had begun in Syria.

3 THE ESTABLISHMENT OF A BA'THI REGIME IN SYRIA

. . . There is also another point, my dear Salah. It seems that you have an Abdel Nasser complex and that I have a Ba'th complex (laughter) (Abdel Nasser to Bitar, Protocols of the 1963 Unity Talks).

The term Ba'thi Revolution (or *coup d'état*) as applied to the events of March 8, 1963 should be qualified in two respects. As our earlier account has shown, the *coup* itself was carried out with little direct Ba'thi participation, and most key positions in the army were held by independent and non-Ba'thi unionist officers. Secondly, those Ba'thi officers who helped engineer the *coup* and assumed important military and political positions and roles upon its implementation were not party members in the ordinary sense of the term. They belonged to a secret military organization, affiliated with the party but distinct from it. The relationship between the Ba'th and its partners was the major political issue of the new regime's first four months, a period that ended with the establishment of a purely Ba'thi regime in Syria. At the same time within the Ba'th itself new facts and patterns that would have a profound affect on the later history of the party and its regime in Syria were less perceptibly determined.

The helplessness of the Separatist Regime that had so facilitated the execution of the military *coup* accounted also for the smooth and rather rapid establishment of a successor regime. Leading politicians and army commanders of the ousted regime either were arrested or fled without trying to organize resistance.[1] Arab and international recognition was soon extended and life seemed to return to normal.

Cooperation between the Ba'this and their independent partners continued and may even have been strengthened by the last-minute desertion of the Nasserites, who nevertheless were treated as part of

[1] *Cahiers*, No. 51 (1963), p. 93. Lesser supporters of the overthrown regime were only gradually purged, and on April 6 General Luayy al-Atasi told Nasser that on March 10 there had still been 300 "secessionist" officers in the army; see *Maḥāḍir*, pp. 126 and 139. See also *Qissat ath-thaura*, p. 57, and *Chronology of Arab Politics* (1963).

the victorious coalition—their collaboration in controlling the army and the state was needed and there was no point in antagonizing Egypt at that delicate stage. With the help of the independent officers, headed by Hariri and by Luayy al-Atasi who had been freed from jail, Ba'thi retired and reserve officers were recalled to active military service. The Syrian radio station had been captured and controlled by forces under the command of the Ba'thi Captain Salim Hatum. On March 8, 1963, 8:40 a.m., the station broadcast a decree issued by the National Council for the Revolutionary Command that "for the restoration of justice" summoned back to service several Ba'thi officers who at that time were rather anonymous and held relatively junior ranks: Lieutenant-Colonels Muhammad 'Umran, 'Abd al-Karim Jundi and Salah J'did, Captain Hafiz al-Asad, and a number of others.

This having been accomplished, the Ba'this could dominate the new regime, forming the best-organized military and civilian faction and enjoying the cooperation of their party's regime in Iraq. They were, however, aware of their tenuous position in the army,[2] the weakness of their popular support, and the thorny dilemmas that any policy adopted towards Egypt was bound to raise.

The important positions held by non-Ba'this and the uncertainty about Egyptian reaction explain why the new regime was initially constituted as a generally "unionist progressive" rather than a Ba'thi one. The first communiqué broadcast at 6:45 a.m. in the morning of March 8 over Damascus Radio reflected at one and the same time this prudence and the Ba'thi bias of a victorious group.[3] It "extended a hand" to Cairo, Baghdad, San'a, and Algiers and thus sought to place the new regime in the Cairo-oriented orbit of a "liberated" Arab state. But while the Ba'th was not explicitly mentioned, its "trinitarian" slogan of "Unity, Liberty, and Socialism" was twice inserted in the communiqué, and Iraq featured in it more prominently than Egypt. Such nuances were carefully studied in Cairo, where Nasser frowned upon the preference given by the Syrian radio station

[2] The three top military positions were held by non-Ba'this as were many other sensitive posts.

[3] This communiqué as well as several other communiqués and documents pertaining to these events were reproduced by Hashshad. Jundi in his memoirs writes that the communiqué was meant to be ambivalent (p. 115).

'Ali Saliḥ as-Sadi (center) with members of his faction after having been exiled to Madrid in November 1963

Syrian troops in Damascus in the wake of the *coup d'état* of March 8, 1963

to the Iraqi telegram of support over that sent by the Egyptian prime minister.[4]

The warm relationship with fellow Ba'this in Iraq did not in itself signify a hostile attitude towards Nasser's Egypt. The new government constituted itself as a unionist regime in the sense that its leaders wanted to establish normal, perhaps even close relations with Nasser. One important lesson of the previous 18 months was that this had become a prerequisite for political stability in Syria. The Ba'th reorganized itself in 1962 on this premise, and some measure of rapprochement with Egypt was known to be desired by a considerable segment of the Syrian population. Nasser's conditions for a reconciliation were not yet known, but it appeared that cooperation with his Syrian supporters was one of them. Their participation in the government was naturally desired by the Nasserite officers and also by the independents, the latter seeking to counterbalance the Ba'th.[5]

In the best tradition of a military-controlled regime the National Council of the Revolutionary Command (*al-majlis al-waṭanī li-qiyādat ath-thaura*) (NCRC) was set up as the supreme authority in the state with the cabinet as its executive arm.[6] There are strong indications that the NCRC was originally conceived as a purely military body, composed of officers who led the *coup* and some of their colleagues, and that it was later altered to include civilians as well. As such it comprised ten officers representing the three major trends in the dominant military group: the "independent progressive" officers (Generals Luayy al-Atasi and Ziyad al-Hariri, Colonel Ghassan Haddad, and Lieutenant-Colonel Fahd ash-Sha'ir), the Ba'th (Lieutenant-Colonels Muhammad 'Umran and Salah J'did and Major Musa Zu'bi), and the Nasserites (Generals Muhammad as-Sufi and Rashid Qutaini and Lieutenant-Colonel Fawaz Muharib).[7] It was then

[4] *Maḥāḍir*, pp. 63–66, and Razzaz, *op. cit.*, p. 97.

[5] *Cf.* Kerr, *Cold War*, p. 61, and see *Mahadir*, p. 45, for Hariri's effort to convince Nihad al-Qasim to join the coalition government.

[6] The provisional decress establishing the NCRC were replaced on June 9, 1963, by a legislative decree defining its prerogatives. See *Arab Political Documents* (1963), pp. 284–285. Jundi (*op. cit.*, p. 116) notes that with political authority vested in the NCRC most cabinet ministers were in reality no more than secretaries-general of their ministries.

[7] Jundi, *op. cit.*, pp. 118–119, *Maḥāḍir*, pp. 27–28, *Cahiers*, No. 51 (1963), p. 91, *Ṣaut al-'urūba* (Lebanon), March 13, 1963, and *ad-Difā'* (Jordan), March 13, 1963.

decided to add ten civilian members. The Ba'th insisted that at least half of them be Ba'this, so that together with the three Ba'thi officers on the council and half the cabinet seats it was demanding, its control of the new governing institutions would be guaranteed.[8]

The Ba'thi officers and civilian leaders were obliged to negotiate all these points for about 14 hours with the representatives of three Nasserite groups. Of these the Socialist Unionists were closest to the Ba'th, while the United Arab Front (*al-Jabha al-'arabiyya al-muwaḥḥada*) and the Arab Nationalist Movement (*Ḥarakat al-qaumiyyīn al-'arab*) were clearly identified as Nasserites. The Arab Nationalists resembled the Ba'th in organization but were closely tied to Egyptian policy and at that time showed reservations with regard to socialism, considering it incompatible with wholehearted devotion to Arab nationalism.[9] Leaning on their rapport with Cairo, their considerable popular support, and the important Nasserite representation in the upper echelons of the army, the negotiators on behalf of the Nasserite groups rejected the demand of the Ba'th Party for a representation at least equal to their combined representation and assailed its position on the question of union. Ba'thi insistence on a "studied" (*madrūs*) and tripartite union, they charged (with a considerable element of justification from their point of view), was an evasive stance.[10] Material bargaining and ideological disputes were thus mixed together to make the negotiations complicated and protracted, and by the morning of March 9 only the composition of the cabinet was agreed upon.

It was probably the support of the independent officers which enabled the Ba'this to gain the upper hand in the new cabinet. Bitar was chosen premier and of the 20 ministers at least nine were identi-

[8] The details of this bargaining are obfuscated by conflicting reports and inaccuracies in the sources. See, for instance, *Maḥāḍir*, pp. 29 and 37, and Jundi, *op. cit.*, pp. 115–116.

[9] M. Suleiman, *Political Parties in Lebanon* (Ithaca, N.Y., 1967), pp. 155–158.

[10] *Maḥāḍir*, pp. 63–66. Interesting details on these negotiations are given in the manifesto published by the NCRC on July 22 (*Arab Political Documents*, (1963), p. 355), and in the letter sent by 'Abd al-Wahhab Haumad and Nihad al-Qāsim to Bitar and broadcast on Cairo Radio on May 10, 1963. For another anti-Ba'thi version see Maḥmūd 'Abd ar-Raḥīm, *Qiyādat ḥizb al-ba'th al-murtadda* ("The Apostate Leadership of the Ba'th Party") (Cairo, n.d.), p. 51.

fied as Ba'this.[11] Most key positions were held by Ba'this but the defence portfolio was given to the Nasserite General Muhammad as-Sufi. This appointment, together with that of Rashid al-Qutaini as deputy supreme commander, gave the Nasserites a marked presence in the army's supreme command. Still, such questions as the composition of the NCRC and, beyond it, the more profound difficulties rooted in the mutual distrust between the partners to the coalition and in their different attitudes to Egypt remained unresolved.

While the Nasserite unionists were less than successful at the bargaining table, they soon benefited from the strong popular pressure for an immediate return to union with Egypt, which at least some of them helped to build up.[12] The enthusiasm aroused by the seemingly unionist *coups* in Iraq and Syria was fanned by the more extreme Nasserites (*ghulāt* in Syrian parlance) and between the eleventh and thirteenth of March brought waves of demonstrators to the streets, demanding immediate union. On March 11 another episode occurred that still remains to be clarified. The Ba'this and their independent partners later claimed that the Nasserite officers headed by Sufi and Qutaini tried on that day to stage a *coup d'état,* presumably with the same forces they had originally planned to use when they withdrew from their pact with Hariri and the Ba'this on March 5. It is not known how serious this alleged attempt was; the Ba'this and their other partners preferred, however, to ignore it for the time being owing to the delicate situation, and they would only reveal it to the public on May 19, 1963, after having openly quarrelled with the Nasserites.[13]

The uneasy coalition was maintained but the demonstrations in Syria posed a certain dilemma for Cairo, as Haikal's article in *al-Ahrām* of March 15 demonstrated, and a much graver one for the Ba'th—breaking up the demonstrations by force was an odious solution for a regime trying to establish a close relationship with Egypt and having Nasserites in its coalition government. There is enough evidence to

[11] For the composition of the cabinet see Appendix A.

[12] See *Mahāḍir*, pp. 63–67, and *Chronology of Arab Politics* (1963), p. 58, for the activity of the Arab Nationalists and of such known Nasserites as General al-Jarrah and the former minister of the Auqaf, Yusuf al-Muzahim. There is no evidence that the activities of the various Nasserite factions were coordinated in any way.

[13] The communiqué issued on May 19 was published in the Syrian press of the 20th. A fuller version of this story is given by Jundi, *op. cit.*, p. 117.

suggest that the continuing demonstrations shook the Ba'this and strengthened the case of those among them who advocated a rapprochement with Nasser, despite the concessions the latter was likely to demand. The Ba'thi dilemma was explained by the party's leadership in an internal circular it distributed early in April in an attempt to allay the apprehensions of the rank and file, alarmed by real and apparent concessions to Egypt and the Nasserites:

> . . . But these basic conditions did not suffice to maintain the Party's leading position since the contest (with the Nasserites) had already turned into an open struggle in which Cairo played the role of the inciter; and the Party should not have been dragged into side battles as it had become clear since March 8 that the Party's positive attitude towards the unionist groups and its call for a national front of the unionist forces had had its results so that the Party began to regain its popular vanguardist position and its power among the masses and most popular bases came to adopt its slogans. It was clear to the Party that the aim of the campaign of incitement against it was to lure it into a side battle with the Nasserites calculated to enable them to block the Party's road to its unionist masses.[14]

President Nasser appeared to hold the key to the Ba'th's relationship with its potential supporters in Syria. It was in order to explore Nasser's conditions for a rapprochement with the new regime that the Syrian delegation to what came to be known as the Tripartite Unity Talks left for Cairo. But the need to contend with, even outbid, the Syrian Nasserites pinpointed the contradiction that was inherent in the Ba'thi position on the question of union since February 1962. The Ba'th had been able to assert its distinctiveness vis-à-vis Nasser and still be considered a unionist force as long as it had been in opposition to a regime whose fall was desired by Nasser as well. Now that the Ba'th was about to come to power in Syria, it had to make a choice between exclusive power and Nasser's goodwill.

The problem was further complicated by important differences

[14] Internal Circular titled "Analysis of the Current Political Situation" issued by the Syrian Ba'th early in April 1963. On the internal divisions among the Ba'this regarding these issues see 'Umran, *op. cit.*, pp. 20–22, and Razzaz, *op. cit.*, p. 97.

within the Ba'thi ranks over (among other things) this issue. For 'Aflaq, Bitar, and their brand of Ba'this, it was not a mere political issue. While they did not desire to return to a full union with Egypt and relinquish the power they and their party had just attained in Syria, they were anxious to receive Nasser's blessing in order to eliminate the shadow of illegitimacy hovering over a separate Syrian state or a Syrian-Iraqi axis. It could make the Ba'th a respectable partner in inter-Arab politics and satisfy a deeply felt emotional and ideological need. All this was far less important to younger Ba'this, who did not share the veteran leaders' profound concern with Arab unity but were suspicious of Nasser and his Syrian supporters and reluctant to share power with them. The difference in attitude is vividly borne out by an anti-'Aflaq source describing the results of the party's reconstruction in 1962:

> Most of the Syrian Party members who returned to it understood the slogan of restoring the Union as a tactic appropriate for organizing the masses against reactionary secessionism. But *al-majmū'a al-qaumiyya* [The Nationalist Group, namely 'Aflaq and his supporters] who were the most influential in the National Command, saw their goal as [really] restoring the Union, thus demonstrating that they were no longer capable of revolutionary development.[15]

These anti-unionist elements had not as yet achieved prominence in the civilian sector of the Ba'th. On March 13 a new Regional Command was set up for the Syrian Ba'th to replace the inadequate Temporary Regional Command that had been chosen by the Fifth National Congress in May 1962. The new Command was expanded to include 18 members representing a variety of orientations—'Aflaq could not afford to be choosy when he needed support from every possible quarter.[16] 'Aflaq was still the uncontested leader of the Ba'th but the military dominated the new regime and were granted a privileged position within the party. The Military Committee was

[15] Quoted from "The Latest Party Crisis" (in the appendix to *al-Munāḍil*, June 1966) and *cf.* Razzaz, *op. cit.*, pp. 97 and 110.

[16] Internal Bulletins of the Organizational Bureau *(maktab tanẓīmī)* of the Syrian Regional Command from May and October 1963.

formally recognized and was given exclusive and autonomous control over the (still nonexistent) military sector of the party and a guaranteed heavy representation in the Regional Command. The far-reaching consequences of these concessions are described below, but in March 1963 the Military Committee, and its allies opposing concessions to Nasser and his Syrian supporters, already possessed power and authority to obstruct them.[17]

An undated Internal Regulation (*niẓām dākhilī*) of the Military Organization (*tanẓīm 'askarī*) of the Ba'th from a somewhat later period defines the Military Committee as a "group of officers who under adverse conditions acted for the implementation of the party's principles in which they believed and so far had had great achievements in the military and civilian spheres". It then goes on to describe the Committee's function as "Secretly establishing an organization of military men believing in the Party's principles. The Committee will decide in military matters whatever it will deem necessary for ultimately turning the army into a defender of the Party's thought and will pass these decisions to the NCRC for their legal implementation".

The Military Committee was evidently seeking to institutionalize its control of the Syrian army. Following the *coup* of March 8, its individual members, Muhammad 'Umran, Salah J'did, Hafiz al-Asad, Musa az-Zu'bi, Ahmad al-Mir, 'Abd al-Karim Jundi, and their colleagues all assumed sensitive military positions. As a group their position was based on their role in preparing the *coup*, and the arrangement they devised had the advantage of preserving the original group and at the same time giving it a formal status. The Committee was, in effect, claiming supreme authority over all politically relevant decision-making with regard to the army. In March 1963 this was yet to be achieved, as authority in such matters was vested in the NCRC and the Officers' Committee in which non-partisan officers still played an important role.[18] The Ba'thi officers would, however,

[17] Jundi, *op. cit.*, p. 118, tells of an incident which illustrates the relationship between military and civilian sectors during the first days after the *coup* of March 8. When the NCRC met, the Ba'thi Shibli al-'Aisami proposed Bitar as candidate for the chairmanship; Luayy al-Atasi then said that the officers had decided that the chairman should be a military personage and he himself was soon elected to that post.

[18] See the statements by Luayy al-Atasi quoted in *Maḥāḍir*, p. 220.

Salah al-Bitar and the Syrian delegation to the Tripartite Unity Talks leaving Damascus on April 6, 1962

gain a practical vetoing power on some of the most crucial points in the negotiations that their colleagues and partners were going to hold with President Nasser.

SYRIAN-EGYPTIAN NEGOTIATIONS

The Ba'thi dialogue with Nasser in March and April 1963 took place on a number of levels—in the Unity Talks in Cairo, in the Cairo and Damascus press and radio broadcasts, and through political activity in Syria. The Cairo Unity Talks, held in three stages from March 14 to April 17, are of much broader interest as they offer a close and most instructive view of several aspects of contemporary Arab politics, but are treated here as part of this dialogue.[19]

While they were and still are called Unity Talks, the minutes of the 1963 Cairo negotiations clearly indicate that it was not unity and union proper that were on the minds of most of the negotiators. The touch of irony thus introduced is further underlined by the protagonists' obvious realization of each other's motives. President Nasser was aware that the Syrian (and to a lesser degree Iraqi) Ba'this were seeking his blessing to stabilize their shaky regimes, and he was trying to make them pay a price for it and thus accomodate his Syrian supporters. The Ba'this could hardly afford to acquiesce if they wanted to build a Ba'thi regime in Syria, nor could they openly say so, as long as they wished to maintain Nasser's goodwill. Nasser used this inherent weakness in the Ba'th position as well as his personal ascendancy and other political advantages to lord over the discussions and humiliate his Ba'thi rivals, only to find out in the end that they had carried out the very policy that he had described as their alleged design when the negotiations started.

Real bargaining only began over the Tripartite Union proposed for Egypt, Syria, and Iraq at the third stage of the sessions on April 6. At the previous meetings of March 14–16 and 19–20 it was mostly the past that was discussed, as both sides were sizing each other up and Nasser was trying, successfully, to embarrass his rivals. The

[19] For a full analysis of the Cairo Unity Talks and their internal dynamics see Kerr, *Cold War*.

Syrian Ba'th was but lightly represented in the first round of talks, by 'Abd al-Karim Zuhur, so that only when 'Aflaq and Bitar showed up on March 19 did the real issue emerge: Nasser had no confidence in the Ba'th and would endorse no regime in Syria dominated by it.

The treatment 'Aflaq and Bitar had received at Nasser's hands ought to have cooled whatever enthusiasm they still possessed and may have brought them closer to the position of the Military Committee, whose members did not care to take a significant part in the negotiations.[20] The limits of the Ba'thi readiness to endanger the party's control over the new regime had already been demonstrated on March 14 by the denial to prominent Nasserites, exiled in Egypt, of permission to re-enter Syria.[21] However, Nasser's aggressive line during the negotiations and the mounting pressure of his supporters during the latter half of March made it clear that resumption of the Cairo negotiations depended on some concessions to the Nasserites in Syria.

Bargaining with the Syrian Nasserites focused on the division of power in the NCRC, in the cabinet, and probably also in the army. The toughest stand was adopted by the leaders of the "United Arab Front", Nihad al-Qasim and 'Abd al-Wahhab Haumad. Qasim had already been a cabinet minister in 1954: during the UAR period he served as minister of justice in Syria and had since remained linked to the Egyptians. Haumad, who in the 1950s was associated with the People's Party, had a similar career. As no progress was made in their negotiations with the Ba'th, the two ministers resigned as a means of exerting pressure, but still refrained from making the announcement public. The Ba'this, in anticipation of charges of anti-unionism, began on March 24 to publish lists of "secessionist" leaders stripped of their civil and political rights. This was the first of several instances in which the fate of these politicians was affected by the vicissitudes of Ba'thi-Nasserite relations.

The Ba'this and their independent allies also took to the offen-

[20] 'Umran was the only member of the Committee who took even a minor part in the negotiations. See Razzaz, *op. cit.*, p. 97.

[21] Cairo Radio, March 14, 1963, 2:30 p.m. President Nasser referred to this significant incident in his speech of July 22, 1963. See *Arab Political Documents* (1963), p. 326.

sive in the press (when *al-Ba'th* attacked the Syrian Nasserites and even jibed at the Egyptian regime) and in public admonitions by Bitar and Luayy al-Atasi, chairman of the NCRC, who was closely co-operating with the Ba'th. The diatribe by Atasi was particularly acrimonious, denouncing the "opportunists and self-seekers" and threatening "to oppress mercilessly . . . those who try to falsify the true unionist slogans".[22]

On March 29 Haikal responded to the *al-Ba'th* article mentioned above, thus launching what after a short interval would develop into full-scale propaganda warfare between the Nasserite and Ba'thi regimes. Still more effective were the pro-Nasser demonstrations that again broke out in Aleppo and spread to Damascus. The crisis continued up to April 3, culminating in an announcement from Cairo that the six Nasserite ministers had resigned from the Syrian cabinet.[23] During the crisis the minister of the interior, Brigadier Amin al-Hafiz, was appointed deputy military governor (*nā'ib al-ḥākim al-'urfī*) with full powers. Hafiz, a native of Aleppo, was a veteran Ba'thi officer who had in the past been close to Haurani but was not considered one of his "men". He had not belonged to the original circle of the Military Committee but is reported to have been approached by it after the break-up of the UAR.[24] At that time he was transferred to Argentina as a military attaché, whence he was recalled by his fellow Ba'this following the *coup* of March 8. In handling the crisis Hafiz displayed the resoluteness which helped build his personal status within the regime. He was the one Ba'thi officer with charisma.

As during other similar crises, an Iraqi military delegation arrived to bolster the Ba'thi position. However, even though the Ba'this were able to quell the demonstrations by force, they realized that insistence on their demands would lead to the final resignation of the Nasserite ministers, to disruption of the Unity Talks, and to a confrontation with Nasser and with the considerable segment of the Syrian urban

[22] Radio Damascus, March 29, 1963, 2:15 p.m., and March 30, 1963, 7:15 p.m., and *al-Ba'th* (Damascus), March 27 and 28. For Nasser's later reference to the editorials of *al-Ba'th* see *Maḥāḍir*, p. 122.

[23] But *al-Ḥayāt*, better informed perhaps, wrote on April 2 that five Nasserite cabinet members resigned, referring to Sami al-Jundi's switch of loyalty. See below, p. 65.

[24] Jundi, *op. cit.*, pp. 88–89. Hafiz, according to this story, rejected the offer by the retired unionist officers to oppose his transfer to the Argentine.

population that appeared to support him.[25] This was a political price that they were not yet ready to pay; and during April 4 and 5 they made a number of concessions to the Nasserites, enabling the Cairo negotiations to resume on April 6.

The nature of these concessions was to become the subject of a bitter controversy in May and cannot be fully ascertained. The official communiqué, published by the four partners to the coalition government,[26] announced that they had agreed to act towards establishing a unionist front that would be represented and led by a Political Bureau (*maktab siyāsī*). In the future the front was to become the organized popular force on which the Revolution would be based. The establishment of such a front was in line with the Cairo negotiations, where unification of the "revolutionary forces" had been envisaged. But this was something to be achieved in the more distant future; in early April the Ba'th was merely seeking a formula that would make resumption of the Unity Talks possible, while the Nasserites wanted to erode Ba'thi political control and to break the principle of Ba'thi superiority. The incompatibility of their respective positions was probably clear to both sides in Syria as it was to Cairo, but at that stage all parties apparently believed they had more to gain than lose by continuing the negotiations.

Bargaining during the third round of negotiations (April 6–17) centred on two broad categories of problems: those pertaining to the nature of the eventual Tripartite Union and those having immediate political relevance. Prominent among the latter were the nature and length of the transition period leading to the Union and the composition of the political fronts, the establishment of which was envisaged in Syria and Iraq. While Nasser generally had his way on the constitutional questions, the Ba'th scored a political victory in extending the initial transition period to five months, supplemented by a further period of twenty months, before complete union was to be implemented.

This proved to be a rather meaningless achievement, as the Union Agreement and the tenuous deliberations between the Ba'th and

[25] The *Resolutions of the Syrian Regional Congress* (September, 1963), pp. 9–12, offer a Ba'thi analysis of the support given by Syrian peasants, workers, and students to Nasser. See below p. 91.

[26] Radio Damascus, April 5, 1963, 8:30 p.m.

Nasser soon collapsed. At what stage dialogue ended and strife began is moot; the two had been closely interwoven and the deterioration of relations was gradual. The ouster of pro-Egyptian officers from the Syrian army between April 28 and May 2 may possibly be regarded as the turning point. It was followed by the final resignation of Nasserite ministers, the emergence of a regime increasingly Ba'thi in nature, and, on July 18, a bloody break with Nasser and the Nasserites.

The ouster of the pro-Egyptian officers late in April may seem a strange step to have been taken by a regime that a fortnight earlier had signed an agreement that evoked so emotional a reaction. The Ba'this must have known that the purge was likely to undermine the April 17 Agreement, but the charges levelled by their adversaries that it all was a scheme premeditated by the Ba'th (or as implied by Razzaz, the Military Committee[27]), is too simplistic to be accepted. The showdown seems to have been inevitable in view of the irreconcilable positions of both sides, and it was precipitated by a combination of factors. As soon as the Federal Union Agreement of April 17 was signed, the Syrian Nasserites began demanding the implementation of the conditions agreed on on April 5 and they were supported by Cairo using the April 17 Agreement as a spur.[28] What had previously been an unpleasant eventuality now became an unavoidable choice. The Military Committee had all along been opposed to making essential concessions to the Nasserites and it had in the meanwhile strengthened the party's (and its own) position in the army (with Hariri's cooperation, it seems) by recalling Ba'thi officers (including supporters of Haurani) to service and by hastily converting other party supporters into officers. The Ba'thi military were probably more adamant in refusing the Nasserites' demands, but it seems that by

[27] See the allegation made by President Nasser in his speech of July 22 (*Arab Political Documents* [1963], p. 329), and Razzaz, *op. cit.*, p. 97. Razzaz's allegations against the Military Committee on this point, while possibly true, should be regarded with caution since besides his obvious bias against it, he had an interest, as an ideologist still preaching Arab unity, in proving that the 1963 Unity Talks did not fail for objective reasons.

[28] Kerr, *Cold War*, pp. 103, 110, 'Indani, *op. cit.*, p. 161, *al-Ḥayāt*, April 26, 1963, and Aḥmad Bahā' ad-Dīn, *Azmat ittifāqiyyat al-waḥda ath-thulāthiyya* ("The Crisis of the Tripartite Unity Agreement") (Cairo, 1963), pp. 67–69.

then 'Aflaq, Bitar, and their followers realized, too, that the time had come to make a choice.

Having secured its hold over the army, the Ba'th still tried for some time to maintain the illusion that nothing exceptional had happened, and to pursue the policies postulated by the April 17 Agreement. Thus, on May 1 the Syrian flag was replaced by the tristar flag of the Federation. At the same time the Ba'th was also preparing to ward off expected denunciations from Cairo. On the same day political seclusion (*'azl siyāsī*) was imposed on forty "secessionist" leaders and the pending trial of those held responsible for the secession from the UAR was announced. On May 2 a decree nationalizing the Syrian banks was published. What could be interpreted as a genuine first step towards establishing a socialist or at least state-controlled economy, seems rather to have been primarily designed to create that impression. It is interesting to recall, in this context, that during the Cairo Unity sessions, when being lectured by Nasser, Bitar was told that nationalization of the banks should indeed be the first revolutionary step to be taken.

The Ba'thi leadership, preoccupied with pressing political problems, had as yet no plans for introducing any sweeping social and economic changes. Bitar's policy statements of the period[29] conveyed a moderate and prudent approach to questions of economic development and social justice. The disharmony between this approach and the nationalization of the banks was well reflected in the confused explanation offered by 'Abd al-Karim Zuhur, the minister of the economy. Political, moral, and ideological reasons were lumped together in Zuhur's statement—the banks were too powerful and they controlled politicians and political activity; they had too little of their own capital invested and thus were exploiting the depositors; control of the banks was a prerequisite for a directed socialist economy. At the same time, to allay the fears of the Syrian bourgeoisie, whom the Ba'th did not wish to antagonize at that delicate stage, Zuhur promised that "the Revolution will protect and encourage all productive industrial sectors, which sincerely serve the interests of the people".[30]

[29] The text of the March 14 statement is reproduced in *Arab Political Documents* (1963), pp. 48–51, and excerpts from the one issued on May 19 are quoted *ibid.*, pp. 260–263.
[30] *Ibid.*, pp. 253–254.

As could be expected following the purge in the army, the resignations of the Nasserite members of the cabinet, pending since March 25, were again tendered and made public on May 6. The Nasserites made it clear that they would only withdraw their resignations if the changes in the army were reversed and their original demands met. Violent demonstrations again broke out in Aleppo and then spread to Damascus, but were sternly dealt with by Hafiz. Palestinian refugees reportedly played a noticeable role in these demonstrations[31]; having but a small stake in the status quo and looking hopefully to the establishment of an Arab union under Nasser, they ranked at that time among his staunchest supporters in Syria.

Ba'thi success in controlling the demonstrations did not solve the underlying political problems. The Ba'th first tried to split the ranks of the Nasserites and naturally concentrated its efforts on the Socialist Unionists, the former party members. Their success was limited. Sami Sufan and most other leading members were not attracted and only Sami al-Jundi, closely tied to his relative, Colonel 'Abd al-Karim al-Jundi, and to Muhammad 'Umran, left the ranks of the Nasserites to join the Ba'th.[32] The Ba'th then had no choice but to reshuffle Bitar's cabinet. Following a rather strange intermezzo, during which Sami al-Jundi tried to form a government acceptable to Cairo and the Nasserites, Bitar presented his second cabinet on May 13.[33]

The new cabinet was made up of Ba'this and independents with six portfolios reserved for a possible (though highly unlikely) reaccomodation of the Nasserites. There were a number of other significant changes in the composition of the cabinet. Hafiz was elevated to the post of deputy-premier, but he continued to hold the crucial

[31] Radio Beirut, May 9, 1963, 8:00 p.m., and Radio London (in Arabic), May 9, 1963, 10:40 p.m.

[32] Jundi's own account of these events is not very helpful. Sami Sufan issued a statement severing the Movement's ties with Jundi (Cairo Radio, May 9, 1963, 7:30 p.m.). On May 10, 1963, 4:30 p.m., the same radio station denounced the attempts by the Ba'th to set up a "front" with "unrepresentative elements". A description of the Ba'th's attempts to lure various Nasserites is given in *al-Ḥayāt,* May 11, 1963.

[33] On the attempt by Jundi to form a compromise cabinet see Kerr, *op. cit.*, pp. 107–110. The description of this episode by Jundi himself would corroborate the explanation given by Kerr (see Jundi, *op. cit.,* pp. 127–128). For the composition of Bitar's cabinet see Appendix A.

ministry of the interior as a more substantial source of power. Three prominent supporters of a unionist orientation—Dr. Jamal al-Atasi, 'Abd al-Karim Zuhur, and Dr. Sami ad-Durubi (a veteran Ba'thi, a professor in Damascus, and a former diplomat under the UAR regime)—all members of Bitar's previous cabinet, were absent from his second one. Personal reasons may have partially accounted for Zuhur's desertion, but it seems that all three did not believe in the prospects of a unionist regime at odds with Nasser (and for that matter of a party-led regime under the aegis of the Military Committee).[34] The new minister of planning, the independent General Ghassan Haddad, had previously held the key military position of director of officers' affairs. His transfer to the cabinet sinecure that he now held was an achievement for the Ba'this as Salah J'did took over Haddad's military post, which he would use for consolidating the Military Committee's (and his own) hold on the army. For the time being, however, Ziyad al-Hariri, the independent chief of staff, added the ministry of defence to his province.

THE CONFLICT WITH HARIRI AND THE FINAL BREAK WITH THE NASSERITES

In mid-May, following the formation of Bitar's second cabinet, the pro-Nasser demonstrations were finally quelled. Further attempts to reach a compromise with the Nasserites failed and the tension with Egypt and its supporters was primarily manifested by increasingly bitter propaganda warfare. It had already begun earlier, but was exacerbated by the Ba'thi entrenchment in power that the new cabinet signified. Cairo described the new cabinet with an ominous insinuation as an "unjustified blow to the Union's state",[35] and what the official Egyptian radio station only hinted at was vividly spelled out by the "unofficial" Voice of the Arabs, by the pro-Egyptian press in Beirut and occasionally by Egyptian newspapers.[36]

The Syrian press and radio retorted in kind, but less effectively;

[34] Kerr, *op. cit.*, p. 111, Razzaz, *op. cit.*, p. 98, and Ṣafadī, *Ḥizb al-ba'th,* pp. 296–297.

[35] Cairo Radio, May 13, 1963, 1:30 p.m.

[36] See, for instance, the article by Iḥsān 'Abd al-Quddūs in *Rūz al-Yūsuf,* May 20.

they were, moreover, careful to maintain the distinction between the unassailable President Nasser and those aides at whose doors the blame for sabotaging the Union could be laid more safely.[37] On the internal front the NCRC came out on May 19 with the detailed version of the *coup* of March 8 and its antecedents. This account was designed to justify the ouster of such Nasserite officers as Qutaini and Sufi from the army a fortnight earlier, and it therefore sought to prove that they had no creditable share in the success of the *coup* and indeed almost managed to abort it. Ziad al-Hariri and Luayy al-Atasi (who prior to the *coup* was in jail) emerged from the communiqué as the real heroes and *coup* makers. All the same, the official Syrian line remained that Syria adhered to the April 17 Agreement, this being the natural line to be taken by a government unwilling to bear the responsibility for breaking an agreement involving such deeply felt emotions.

The waves of pro-Nasser demonstrations that continued intermittently from mid-March to mid-May and which the government was only able to stop with considerable difficulty, underscored the weakness of the Ba'th's popular organization and basis of support. If it wanted to remain in power the Ba'th had to remedy this weakness; in order to do so it turned (with far-reaching consequences) to indiscriminate recruitment of unindoctrinated, often opportunistic, elements. This was later described with some perspective by the party's National Command:

> . . . The Party's weakness from a numerical and organizational point of view at the beginning of the Revolution . . . and its weakness in the street as against the strong enemies, bred during that phase a certain sensitivity to the need to expand the Party machinery and the Command resorted at that time to its expansion without having time to direct and instruct it.[38]

Later in May Ba'thi leaders began to meet with workers and students (the two groups from which most of the demonstrators seemed to come) in an effort to enlist at least their passive support.[39]

[37] Thus on May 24 they sharply denounced the Voice of the Arabs radio station.

[38] Quoted from an Internal Bulletin of the National Command from September 1965.

[39] For details of these benefits and gestures see *Cahiers*, No. 52 (1963), p. 237. The *Resolutions of the Syrian Regional Congress* (September 1963) described these

The first press reports on the Ba'th's intention to establish a para-military Nationalist Guard date, too, from the same period. The excesses committed by the party's Nationalist Guard in Iraq and possibly also the reluctance of the army (out of jealousy for its monopoly of armed power) account for the regime's hesitation to form a similar organization in Syria. As the need became more pressing and the Ba'thi character of the regime more pronounced, this initial hesitation was overcome. The Nationalist Guard (*al-ḥaras al-qaumi*) was formally created on June 30, 1963, but preparations had begun earlier and elements of the Guard were reported present at the ceremonies held when the Yemenite president, Sallal, arrived in Damascus on June 11.[40] The Nationalist Guard proved to be a very effective instrument for establishing Ba'thi presence where the party had virtually no popular support, and was to remain in various forms a permanent feature of the Ba'th regime in Syria.

The party's hold on the regime was further consolidated by the removal of Hariri and his supporters from the army, after an open struggle that lasted from June 23 to July 8. There had existed a latent tension betzeen Hariri and the Ba'thi officers, and it gradually surfaced after the common threat of the Nasserite presence in the army had been eliminated. Hariri's command of vital positions in the army was irreconcilable with the Military Committee's determination to have absolute control of the Syrian army in its hands. Among the Ba'thi civilian leaders, however, Bitar at least is known to have favoured him.[41] Presumably Bitar reckoned that Hariri's continued

measures: "During the months which followed the *coup* of March 8 the party was able to give the working class one proof after another showing its belief in the problem of the working class" (p. 11).

40 *Al-Ḥayāt* (Beirut), June 12, 1963. The first press report was published in *al-Anwār* (Beirut), May 21, 1963.

41 Following its victory in February 1966, the Syrian Regional Command issued a brochure titled *al-Taqrīr al-wathā'iqī li-azmat al-ḥizb* ("The Documentary Report on the Party's Crisis"). Though intended to blacken the faction defeated in the *coup* of February 23, it seems that the documents, facts, and quotations reproduced in the brochure are authentic (but often taken out of context). On p. 16 the authors charge that Bitar had been a rightist politician and cite his support of Hariri and his opposition to his banishment. On p. 43 the same brochure mentions that Hariri tried to divide the ranks of the Ba'this and to attract some of them to his side. See also Jundi, *op. cit.*, p. 130.

presence would serve to counterbalance the Military Committee whose growing power had already menaced his and 'Aflaq's hold on the party. The officers had their way in this matter, too, and as Hariri left for Algiers at the head of a high-ranking delegation, his supporters were transferred on June 23 from their sensitive military positions and he himself was ordered to proceed directly to Washington as the new Syrian military attaché to the United States.

On the same day a new Agrarian Reform Law was published in Syria, which abolished the 1962 law and considerably modified the original one of 1958. The new law placed new limitations on land ownership that varied from province to province but as a rule were more severe than those of 1958, and gave the peasants easier terms for the purchase of land.[42] The amending of the Agrarian Reform Law had been promised in Bitar's two policy statements, but the timing of its execution was probably fixed so as to serve the Ba'th in its struggle against Hariri. It is not known whether or not Hariri opposed the new law, but by publishing it in the midst of the conflict with him the Ba'th could hope not only to improve its "progressive" image and attract peasant support, but also to present Hariri's ouster as a matter of ideology and principle rather than a mere jockeying for power.[43]

Getting rid of Hariri proved to be a longer and more complicated affair than the Ba'th had assumed it would be. Instead of going to Washington Hariri returned to Damascus and marshalled his supporters. The overriding concern of both sides, however, was to avoid a violent collision between their respective forces. It had already been remarked with regard to similar circumstances in the 1950s[44] that "more often than not in Syrian conflicts both sides, whatever their threats, conspire to stop short of bloodshed", and this often proved to be the case with the Ba'th as well. Since neither the Ba'thi officers nor Hariri wanted to fight, it was a question of who would prove to have more military support and play his cards better. The Ba'thi officers were more powerful and resolute; Hariri lost, and

[42] *Chronology of Arab Politics* (1963), p. 148.

[43] The portrayal of the struggle in the Lebanese press (as summarized in the *Chronology of Arab Politics* [1963], p. 149) would indicate that the Ba'th achieved its purpose.

[44] Seale, *The Struggle for Syria,* p. 143.

on July 8 had to leave for Paris. He was accompanied to the airport by his independent partner Ghassan Haddad and by Bitar, the latter with tears in his eyes,[45] probably because he realized that once Hariri had gone he would have to contend with the unchecked powers of the Ba'thi officers. And indeed Hafiz took over both as a minister of defence and (acting) chief of staff.

The Nationalist Guard was fully activated in Syria for the first time on July 1, at the height of the crisis with Hariri. It was a precautionary measure against a possible attempt by the Nasserites, who at that time appeared as the only organized power capable of endangering the regime, to take advantage of the military's preoccupation with themselves. Colonel Hamad 'Ubaid, a rather unpopular officer, member of the Military Committee, who in April 1962 was one of Jasim 'Alwan's aides in Aleppo, was put in command of the Guard, whose most important function at that point was to combat 'Alwan and his fellow Nasserites.

The latter did, however, try their hand a little later, on July 18, the very day on which a delegation headed by General Luayy al-Atasi, chairman of the NCRC, left for Alexandria in an attempt to break the deadlock with Nasser. The abortive *coup* was led by 'Alwan, unpopular with the Ba'thi officers since April 1962, and was carried out by retired officers and some troops stationed in Damascus, mostly from the Signal Corps. Various sources have accused the Ba'this of encouraging the *coup* through their "agents provocateurs", and while this cannot be documented, the Ba'this themselves did assert that they had prior knowledge of the forthcoming attempt.[46] This would mean that the Syrian authorities preferred to have the Nasserites stage the *coup*, fail, and be publicly discredited as those who brought about the collapse of the Union. Unlike previous *coups* this one involved relatively heavy fighting and bloodshed and it was ruthlessly suppressed — 20 military and civilian participants were immediately executed. So engrossed were some of the Ba'thi officers in suppressing the *coup* that they wanted the state's television station to show the whole process of execution.[47] Those Nasserites who

[45] Kerr, *Cold War*, pp. 115–116. The *Documentary Report* ridiculed Bitar's weeping at the airport, referring (p. 16) to "his feigning to cry in front of him".

[46] Radio Damascus, July 18, 1963, 6:30 p.m.

[47] Jundi, *op. cit.*, pp. 131–132.

Amin al-Hafiz

were not arrested fled or went underground and ceased their political activity. Luayy al-Atassi disapproved the manner in which the insurgents were treated, and resigned. Perhaps he was pressed to do so by the Ba'this, who after the events of July 18 no longer deemed it important to have a nonpartisan as titular head of state. His place as chairman of the NCRC was taken by Hafiz, who thus completed the Ba'th's hold on all key positions in the regime and further enhanced his already considerable personal power.

The repercussions on Syria's relations with Egypt were immediate. Cairo launched a vituperative propaganda attack against the Ba'th and Hafiz, whom it labeled *as-saffāḥ* (the bloodshedder). On July 22 in his traditional Revolution Day address, President Nasser at last came out with a scathing denunciation of the Ba'th and then announced Egypt's withdrawal from the April 17 Agreement, blaming the Ba'th for it. As the Ba'this themselves privately admitted a few months later,[48] the Egyptian president succeeded in convincing the Syrian public. Similarly painful for the Ba'th was another theme that President Nasser stressed in the speech he delivered at Alexandria University on July 28 — the Ba'th was a party of irreligion and heresy (*ilḥād*). This accusation was particularly effective, since the Ba'th had been traditionally held in suspicion by devout Muslims, whose distrust of the party's secularist ideology was deepened by the presence of several minoritarians in the new ruling group. President Sallal of Yemen, an ally of Nasser, went even further and suggested that they were less than genuine Arabs. Picking on 'Aflaq's Christian name he stated: "What a strange name; we are genuine Arabs, what do we have to do with Michel?". The Ba'th's angry response indicates how telling such charges and insinuations were.[49]

Once order was restored in Syria a new cabinet, the third in succession headed by Bitar, was formed on August 4.[50] This time no vacant portfolios were left as a gesture to the Nasserites, and the

[48] *Resolutions of the Sixth National Congress of the Arab Socialist Ba'th Party* (October 1963), p. 58.

[49] For Sallal's insinuations see Abu Jaber, *op. cit.*, p. 77, and for the Ba'th's response to Nasser and Sallal see the editorials of *al-Ba'th* reproduced in *Niḍāl al-Ba'th*, VI, pp. 186–194, particularly one titled *ad-Dīn wa-as-siyāsa* ("Religion and Politics"). These points are discussed further below on pp. 114–115.

[50] The composition of the cabinet is given in Appendix A.

cabinet was composed of Ba'this and of cooperative "independent unionists". The role of the latter was to signify wider support for the regime and public participation of sorts in government. General Hafiz, abounding in titles and authority, left the cabinet, and the sensitive ministry of the interior was entrusted to Dr. Nur ad-Din al-Atasi, a physician from Homs and a representative of the younger, more radical, generation of Ba'this.[51]

The formation of the new cabinet concluded the Ba'th's gradual takeover; it was now in full control of the Syrian government. But the party also faced a set of difficult problems to which it had to turn its full attention — the heavy political offensive mounted by Egypt and the resulting need to forge a new Arab policy, the need to determine the orientation of the party and its regime within Syria, and the growing conflicts between rival factions of the Ba'th.

A natural reaction to the growing Egyptian hostility was to draw closer to Iraq. The notion of a Syrian-Iraqi Ba'thi axis had been discarded immediately after the *coup d'état* of March 8 as bound to antagonize Cairo and be branded by it as a "regional grouping" (*takattul iqlīmī*) — anathema to all adherents of Arab nationalist ideology. This notion, moreover, evoked the still fresh memories of Iraqi royalist designs on Syria in the 1950s and the "imperialist" context of these designs. But after July 18 when they were, anyway, vehemently denounced by Nasser, the Syrian and Iraqi Ba'this chose to close ranks and prepare the ground for a bilateral union by a series of partial unionist measures.

The open conflict with Egypt had disparate repercussions on the internal policies of the Ba'th regime in Syria. To counter Egyptian charges and to balance the severe measures taken against the Nasserite insurgents after July 18, the trial of the leaders of the "Separatist Regime" was begun on August 4. However, some Ba'thi leaders also felt that it was unwise to antagonize the urban middle classes, an important anti-Nasserite sector, which the "separatist" leaders still represented to some extent. This social stratum was also disconcerted by the irreligious image of the new regime and by fears of radical

[51] Nur ad-Din al-Atasi is a member of the prominent family of Homs, but it is not known from what branch of the family he comes nor how he is related to other bearers of this name, active in Syrian politics of the period (Jamal, Luayy) and in earlier years (Hashim, 'Adnan, and others).

social reforms that it was deemed likely to institute. It was to dispel these fears that Hafiz and Bitar devoted much of their public activity throughout the month of August, meeting with delegations from all parts of Syria. "Next to my belief in God I believe in Socialism", Hafiz told representatives of the chamber of agriculture, industry, and commerce from Homs. He described the Ba'this to them as "a group of people who believe in God and the people and who try to alleviate the troubles of the people".[52]

It is doubtful how effective such reassurances were, and in any case they were not meant to be more than a temporary expedient. The Ba'th had yet to decide on what regime it wanted to build in Syrian and to what segments of the Syrian public it wanted to appeal. This could be done only after the internal struggle for domination of the party, overshadowed until then by external conflicts, had been decided. That internal struggle was the overriding issue at the First Regular Syrian Regional Congress and the Sixth National Congress of the Ba'th, held in Damascus in September and October 1963.

[52] See, for instance, Radio Damascus, August 7, 1963, 6:15 a.m.

4 THE SIXTH AND SEVENTH NATIONAL CONGRESSES AND THE FALL OF THE BA'TH REGIME IN IRAQ, SEPTEMBER 1963 –FEBRUARY 1964

> . . . They are a number of intellectuals in the Ba'th Party . . . and they became familiar with the writings of Lenin and Mao Tse-tung too . . . and with the experience of (other) nations . . . and they lived their own experience and want to benefit from the experiences of the (other) nations and of the Arab nation and from their own experience ('Abd al-Karim Zuhur to President Nasser during the Cairo Unity Talks).

With the party congresses of September and October 1963 the period of transition and installation in power ended and the Ba'th turned to the long-delayed task of defining its orientation and the purpose of its rule. The Regional and National Congresses formally advanced new groups to the party's leadership and radically altered its doctrine. Partly as a result of these developments the Ba'th lost its position in Iraq and in the ensuing altercation the party's leadership, but not its doctrine, was again modified early in 1964. To evaluate properly these changes one should go back to the latent transformation that the Ba'th Party had undergone in the six months that followed its accession to power in Syria.

Upon establishing the party's regime in Syria the small membership of the Ba'th included three distinct components: (a) the rudimentary party organization reconstituted by 'Aflaq in 1962; (b) the Military Committee and its affiliates; and (c) sundry elements associated with the party in the past, who for various reasons did not join 'Aflaq in 1962, but did so after the party's rise to power. They included the Atasi-Zuhur-Hafiz group, the first two becoming ministers in Bitar's first cabinet, and some of the *Quṭriyyūn* like Yusuf Zu'ayyin, Muslih Salim and Ibrahim Makhus. On the fringes of the party were members of dissident factions (most of the *Quṭriyyūn*, Haurani's wing, the Socialist Unionists) who had been ousted from or had left the party but were not entirely dissociated from it.

The Broadened Regional Command chosen on March 13 included members from all three categories. The Military Committee was given a heavy representation in this Command while retaining exclusive authority over the embryonic Military Organization (or Section) of the party. During the following months the ranks of both the civilian and military sectors of the Syrian Ba'th were swollen with new members, most of whom had no previous connection with the party, only a few coming from the three dissident factions on its fringes. A source close to the Military Committee itself described, from the perspective of 1966, this process as it took place in the military sector:

> The initial conditions followings the *coup* and the difficult phase induced the urgent calling of a large number of reserve officers and NCO's, Party members and supporters to fill the gaps created by the purge of the enemies and to consolidate the Party's positions and its defence. This urgency made it impossible at the time to insist on objective standards in this operation, rather friendship, family relationship and sometimes mere personal acquaintance were the basis [of admission], which led to the infiltration of elements alien and strange to the Party's mentality and points of departure and—once the difficult phase was over—to the exploitation of this issue as a tool for pricking at the intentions of certain comrades (*rifāq*) and for casting doubts on them.[1]

Similar developments took place in the civilian sector of the Ba'th where a feeling of weakness and isolation led to a wide opening of the gates, which has already been alluded to above. During its first year in power the Syrian Ba'th grew fivefold in membership.[2] Such an influx of new members to an initially noncohesive party, whose leaders were preoccupied with the major issues of the regime's

[1] Quoted from *The Party's Crisis and the Movement of February 23 and the Convening of the Latest Regional Congress* (Spring 1966), pp. 20–21. It seems strange that this report, prepared by the group that emerged victorious in February 1966, vindicates charges raised against it by its rivals, but its frankness is to be explained by the political circumstances of the period and by the need to justify the expulsion of several members of the Military Committee. The reference in the last sentence of the quotation is probably to charges that certain 'Alawi and Druse members of the Committee packed the army with members of their communities.

[2] Razzaz, *op. cit.*, p. 110.

stormy first months, led to organizational anarchy and to a lowering of standards and was opposed on these grounds by several party leaders.[3] 'Aflaq and Bitar were among those who resented the hasty recruitment of members, which changed the party's make-up and converted their supporters to a minority. This development was closely related to the emergence of a group of young party militants, who were in control of considerable sections of the party's new organizational structure and in league with the Military Committee.

'Aflaq and Bitar, busy with the greater issues of the day, realized too late that routine organizational work carried out by humbler members of the party, who had once been their followers but did not belong to their intimate circle, gave the latter considerable political influence. Most prominent among these "aparatchiki" was the young Hamud ash-Shufi, a Druse from the Sweida region about whom little is known except that he was a former school teacher and under 30 years of age at the time. More is known about the earlier career of his colleague, Ahmad Abu Salih, a Sunni lawyer from Aleppo in his early thirties, who during the UAR period had been active in the National Union and was elected to the National Assembly. On March 13, 1963, Shufi was chosen to head the Organizational Bureau in the new Regional Command. A little later, Shufi and Dr. Nur ad-Din al-Atasi, both still considered loyal disciples of 'Aflaq, were added as members to the NCRC.[4] Shufi and his colleagues were young, radical, and ambitious and, moreover, devoid of the reverence felt by older party members towards the "founding fathers". The membership of what developed as Shufi's faction seems to have come from various origins—'Aflaq's reconstituted party, Marxists close to the Zuhur-Atasi-Hafiz group, and post-March 8 recruits.

At that stage these were natural allies for the Military Committee, long disenchanted with 'Aflaq and Bitar, and determined to hold

[3] Internal Bulletins of the Syrian Region's Organizational Bureau from May and October 1963.

[4] See *al-Ḥayāt*, October 29, 1963, and Michel Abu Jauda's article in *an-Nahar*, November 2, 1963. According to Sami al-Jundi's memoirs, it was 'Aflaq who first proposed that Shufi and Atasi join the NCRC. Jundi then remarked sarcastically (p. 129): ". . . and so two reverent disciples joined the Council . . . ready to please the master and implement his will. . . ."

Salah al-Bitar

Michel 'Aflaq

From left to right: Dr. Nur ad-Din al-Atasi, Salah J'did, and Dr. Yusuf Z'ayyin

sway in the party and the regime. The Military Committee had by then already assumed control of the Syrian army from behind the NCRC and through the Officers Committee inherited from the previous regimes, and it had also been given, as will be recalled, heavy representation in the Regional Command and full authority over the party's military sector. The combination of its power in the state and in the party with that of Shufi's faction gave them practical control of the Syrian Ba'th, where they were in continuous friction with 'Aflaq and Bitar's supporters.[5]

Nor could 'Aflaq and Bitar fall back again on Iraqi support through the National Command as they had done in 1962 and early in 1963. The Iraqi Ba'th too had split in the meanwhile into rival factions. 'Ali Salih as-Sa'di, Hamdi 'Abd al-Majid, and Hani al-Fakiki, 'Aflaq's former supporters, had adopted a new perspective on the policies best suited for maintaining the Ba'th in power in Iraq and on the authority that the National Command and its secretary-general should have over the regional branches. They now advocated radical policies and drifted away from 'Aflaq.[6] The latter was trying to convene the Sixth National Congress since May 1963 to mobilize support against the intra-party opposition in Syria, but with continuous Iraqi evasions the Congress was postponed several times.[7] When it was finally held between October 5 and 23, the Iraqi Ba'th was largely controlled by the radical faction opposing 'Aflaq.

The erosion of 'Aflaq and Bitar's hold over the party in Syria was painfully demonstrated in the Syrian Region's First Regular Congress held in Damascus early in September 1963 in anticipation of the Sixth National Congress which was to follow immediately. Unlike the highly irregular and fragmentary Regional Congress held in April 1963 (in preparation for the National Congress scheduled for May), the September congress proceeded according to the

[5] Razzaz, *op. cit.*, pp. 96, 106, and 109; *Organizational Report* of October 1963; *Report presented to the Extraordinary Congress on February 1, 1964,* and 'Aflaq's speech of February 18, 1966, as quoted in *al-Wathā'iq al-'arabiyya* (1966), p. 61.

[6] M. Khadduri, *Republican Iraq* (London, 1969), pp. 209–210, and International Bulletins issued by the National Command and the Syrian Regional Command during November 1963 on the situation in Iraq.

[7] Internal Bulletin submitted by the National Command to the Seventh National Congress, convened in February 1964.

party's "Internal Regulation", though the elections that preceded it were rigged by the military and their civilian allies.[8] The results of the elections held in the party's branches determined the composition and the outcome of the congress. The doctrinal and political resolutions reflected the radical approach of 'Aflaq's rivals, who also won all eight seats in the new Syrian Regional Command and the majority in the Syrian delegation to the Sixth National Congress. Shufi was elected secretary-general of the Regional Command, made up of five civilians and three military.[9]

In the Iraqi Ba'th, Sa'di's radical faction was opposed by a moderate group led by Talib Shabib and Hazim Jawad. A third group, as could have been expected, took an intermediate position trying to achieve a compromise. These factions were divided over issues of Iraqi politics, but the relations among them could not be isolated from the growing tensions in the Syrian Ba'th. Thus, the Shabib-Jawad faction stood close to 'Aflaq while Sa'di and his group now cooperated with 'Aflaq's Syrian rivals. Like their Syrian counterparts they advocated far-reaching changes at home and a strong anti-Nasserite stance, and they also shared their desire to shake off 'Aflaq's "tutelage".[10]

In mid-September a temporary compromise was reached in Baghdad whereby Sa'di's power was somewhat curtailed on the cabinet level but reinforced in the party. These developments coupled with the results of the Syrian Regional Congress determined the

[8] 'Aflaq, in his speech of February 18, 1966, blamed the military (*al-Wathā'iq al-'arabiyya* [1966], pp. 61–62), while a source close to the Military Committee, in the Organizational Report submitted to the next Regular Syrian Regional Congress, made Shufi the scapegoat: ". . . the Congress, which convened on September 5, 1963, witnessed for the first time the spirit of factionalism (*takattul*) and pre-arranged electoral procedures, carried out by the Organizational Bureau headed by Shufi" (p. 23).

[9] For the resolutions of the congress see below p. 82; for the composition of the new Regional Command see Appendix B.

[10] See n. 6 above. Tutelage (*wiṣāya*) is one of the terms directed by the opposition at 'Aflaq and Bitar as a derogatory allusion to their claim for "historic rights" as their share in founding and leading the party. Another term used in this context, paternalism (*abawiyya*), indicates even more clearly that to a considerable extent it was a conflict of political generations.

domination of the Sixth National Congress by 'Aflaq's rivals. He still commanded the support of some lesser branches, but the major delegations from Iraq (25 members) and Syria (18 members) were led by the opposition.[11]

THE SIXTH NATIONAL CONGRESS

Too little is known about the internal workings of the crucial and relatively lengthy Sixth National Congress of the Ba'th, but some light is shed on several of its aspects by three separate publications issued in its wake:

a. The "ideological report" (*at-taqrīr al-'aqā'idī*), approved by the congress with important modifications and published some time in 1964 together with an introduction by 'Aflaq under the title *Ba'ḍ al-munṭalaqāt an-naẓariyya* ("Some Theoretical Points of Departure").[12] It was one of the several reports that are normally submitted to major Ba'thi congresses by preparatory committees and serve as a basis for their work.
b. *The Resolutions of the Sixth National Congress.* This text consists of excerpts from the reports submitted by other committees, some of their recommendations, and several of the resolutions passed by the congress.

As the text itself states,[14] it does not contain several other resolutions, and there is also evidence to suggest that some paragraphs were interpolated or modified to suit developments that took place between the end of the congress and the publication of the

[11] See 'Aflaq's report to the Extraordinary Syrian Regional Congress in February 1964 as quoted in *Arab Political Documents* (1964), p. 30.

[12] It was first distributed to party members in brochure form and then published in *Niḍāl al-ba'th*, VI, pp. 232–291. The following quotations from this document refer to the page numbers in the brochure.

[13] The text was distributed to party members in brochure form and it, too, was reproduced in *Niḍāl al-ba'th*, VI, pp. 292–346, but with some significant omissions. The following quotations from this text again refer to the page numbers in the brochure.

[14] P. 62.

text.[15] A comparison of this text with the earlier *Resolutions of the Syrian Regional Congress of Arab Socialist Ba'th Party* (September 1963) shows that the former is very close to being a reproduction of the latter. Large portions of the two documents are almost identical, with the exception of minor changes introduced to account for obvious differences between Syria and Iraq, one significant omission,[16] and several fresh political resolutions passed by the National Congress. This points, no doubt, to the closeness in outlook of the radical wings of the Syrian and Iraqi Ba'th parties as well as to the persistently Syrian bias of the party's doctrine. More significantly still, the fact that the analysis of social and political forces in Syria could be so easily stretched to apply also to Iraq, indicates the general, nonspecific level of the analysis and most of the recommendations based on it.
c. The shorter communiqué published immediately after the congress under the same title, *Resolutions of the Sixth National Congress.*[17] It includes some of the resolutions as well as allusions to the reports submitted to the congress and to the doctrinal basis of the resolutions.

The texts and the occasional references to the congress in other sources reflect the two levels of political and ideological conflict that the congress witnessed. A coalition of the Syrian military with the radical wings of the Syrian and Iraqi party organizations dominated the congress: 'Aflaq was humiliated, his moderate line was often rejected, and only under threat of resignation (still a menace to the opposition) were some of his demands met. The balance of power in the party at that stage is illustrated by the following resolution that was submitted to the congress:

[15] *Ibid.* The text itself also refers to the "spirit of leftist adventurism" evident at the congress, a phrase that suits the 1964 polemics against Sa'di. Also, while Razzaz describes a resolution that was passed at the congress to negotiate with members of three dissident Ba'thi factions, the text mentions only two of them, omitting Haurani's group, negotiations with which did not materialize. See *ibid.*, p. 57, and Razzaz, *op. cit.*, p. 111.

[16] The resolutions of the Sixth National Congress, affecting Iraq as well as Syria, omitted the paragraph referring to Arab oil.

[17] The communiqué was published on October 27, 1963. For English translations of it see Abu Jaber, *op. cit.*, Appendix B, and *Arab Political Documents* (1963), pp. 438–44.

> Those comrades *(rifāq)* responsible for the opaqueness of the Party's thought and for the failure to take power in Syria prior to 1958 and for accepting the Party's dissolution and for staying in power despite its obvious deviationism since the early months of the Union and for similar mistakes that are still taking place now, should present the Congress with a written self-criticism.

The resolution was obviously calculated to humiliate 'Aflaq and Bitar whose political past it sought to disparage. But since 'Aflaq's rivals did not as yet wish to bring about his resignation, and as he had some support in the congress, the resolution was neither approved nor rejected but was transferred together with other "political recommendations" for review by the National Command.[18] Of the nine seats allotted to Syria and Iraq on the new National Command elected by the congress only three were won by moderates (including 'Aflaq but not Bitar), the other six members being definitely counted among 'Aflaq's rivals. It was only through the four representatives of the lesser party branches that 'Aflaq was able to retain a hold on the new Command whose secretary-general he remained.[19]

Not as conspicuous at that time was the division that surfaced in the ranks of 'Aflaq's rivals. The Syrian and Iraqi Ba'thi radicals were a heterogeneous group composed of (mostly Marxist) doctrinaire revolutionaries, of more visceral militants like the Iraqi Sa'di,[20] and of less principled opponents of the party's veteran leaders. Some of them were carried away by doctrine and impulse to adopt extreme

[18] See *Resolutions of the Sixth National Congress*, p. 58, *Arab Political Documents*, (1964), pp. 21–22 and 31, and Shimali, "Crucial Days", *ath-Thaura* (Damascus), November 17, 1968.

[19] For the composition of the new Command see Appendix B. 'Aflaq had the support of the two unnamed Jordanian delegates (who according to *an-Nahār* of November 2, 1963, were Munif ar-Razzaz and 'Abd al-Muhsin Abu al-Meizer) and of the two Lebanese members. The Iraqi moderate members Ahmad Hasan al-Bakr and Mahdi 'Ammash did not lend 'Aflaq unqualified support but tried to play an intermediary role.

[20] The violent emotionalism of Sa'di is illustrated by the telegram he sent to Hafiz in the aftermath of the abortive *coup* of July 18, 1963: "Crush the bones, the very bones, of all cringing mercenaries of reaction and all who traffic in slogans. Smite boldly and mercilessly those who lurk behind this vile conspiracy . . . " (*Arab Political Documents* [1963], p. 318). This was quite different from the style of such doctrinaire revolutionaries as Hafiz and Tarabishi.

and unrealistic positions that puzzled their more realistic military and other partners. The latter chose in such instances to side with the moderate delegates in checking the overenthusiastic revolutionaries. The intricate interplay of these three currents can be discerned in the work of the congress, as it tried to solve the problems that faced the Ba'th Party and regimes.

THE REVISION OF BA'THI IDEOLOGY

One such major problem was the long-felt need to reformulate the party's doctrines and bring them in line, as 'Aflaq's critics demanded, with the profound changes that had taken place since 1958. This need became painfully apparent during the 1963 Unity Talks. President Nasser, well versed in recent socialist thinking, kept lecturing the Ba'thi delegates, quoting freely from the Egyptian "National Charter of the Popular Forces" issued in 1962 and usefully serving him as an ideological catechism. When he stated that he saw no latter-day ideological contribution peculiar to the Ba'th and that the party's feud with him was purely personal and political, the Ba'thi delegates were at a loss to reply. Shibli al-'Aisami protested that Ba'thi doctrine had developed since 1943 but Nasser promptly replied: "Has this been announced, for instance? We for instance have announced our views clearly and frankly. Have you announced your views and in what newspaper or publication?"[21]

With the Egyptian publication of the *Maḥāḍir* in June 1963, and especially after Nasser's speech of July 22, the Ba'this realized it was politically even more imperative than before for their party to demonstrate that it did have an ideology distinct from that of Nasser if not superior to it. Since they could neither effectively dispute Nasser's leadership of Arab nationalism nor afford to speak for Iraqi and Syrian particularism, they felt they could only legitimize their conflict with him by convincing Arab public opinion that it was an ideological one. This theme had long been implicit in Ba'thi writings and since July 1963 it was being noticeably stressed by the party's organs. On August 8, a Ba'thi spokesman in Damascus told reporters that

[21] *Maḥāḍir*, p. 162.

the party was preparing a statement "in the form of a booklet of a hundred pages" explaining in detail "the difference in ideology and belief" (*al-khilāf al-'aqā'idī wa-al-madhhabī*) between the party and President Nasser.[22]

It seems that the Ba'thi spokesman referred to the "ideological report" that was being prepared for the Sixth National Congress. The original report was written by an "ideological committee", in which members of the party's small Marxist faction played a major role. The committee's make-up is not known, but the report's reliance on *Fī al-fikr as-siyāsī*[23] and its close resemblance to a later publication by Yasin al-Hafiz[24] strongly suggest that he was a principal contributor to it. With Jamal al-Atasi and 'Abd al-Karim Zuhur out of the party, Hafiz, Jurj Tarabishi, and other eloquent Marxists were the natural candidates to be picked by 'Aflaq's rivals for revising and updating the party's doctrine. This was the group whose writings attracted Nasser's attention which evoked Zuhur's reply to him as quoted at the head of the present chapter. Members of the group like Tarabishi had figured prominently earlier in the summer in theoretical debates on Socialism and Revolution with Egyptian spokesmen.[25]

The outlook and objectives of this group, adumbrated in its writings of early 1963 and further developed through the political role it played later in the year, were most explicitly stated in an essay published by Hafiz in 1965 under the instructive title *Ta'rīb al-marxiyya* ("The Arabization of Marxism").[26] The fall of Stalinism and developments within the Arab world, says Hafiz, prepared the way for the adoption of Marxism as the ideology of "the movement of the Arab masses". It should not be a mechanical borrowing of a general theory but rather its sophisticated application to the peculiar conditions of the Arab world. This was the only way in which the Arabs could bring about the synchronous scientific-secular and economic revolutions that they must undergo if they wished to

[22] *Chronology of Arab Politics* (1963), p. 256.

[23] See Chapter 2.

[24] *Ḥaul ba'ḍ qaḍāyā ath-thaura al-'arabiyya* ("Concerning Some Problems of the Arab Revolution") (Beirut, 1965).

[25] See *Maḥāḍir*, p. 141, and Baha' ad-Dīn, *op. cit.*, p. 105.

[26] Hafiz, *op. cit.*, pp. 271–279. A restrained version of this essay can be traced in the *Points of Departure*, pp. 22–25, where it serves as an introduction of sorts.

modernize. It was from this perspective that the "ideological report" submitted to the congress sought to criticize the doctrines and past record of the Ba'th Party's historic leaders, to present a political and socioeconomic programme for the Bath'i regime, and to assert the distinctiveness and superiority of the new Ba'thi ideology as against the Nasserite approach.

A comparison of the original report submitted to the congress with the text of the *Points of Departure* readily shows that the former was substantially modified. As a matter of fact its authors themselves complained about it in an interview they granted to the Yugoslav news agency, Tanyug.[27] The majority of the delegates were alarmed by the radical and idealist approach of the platform that was obviously divorced from actual conditions in Syria and Iraq and at several points seemed to menace their own interests. In the paragraph treating the question of the military's political role, for instance, important changes were introduced, probably at the insistence of the army officers present at the congress.[28] Seeking to achieve multiple and divergent aims, the original report was not a very coherent text and as a result of the substantial modifications it became even more incongruous. Furthermore, 'Aflaq succeeded in writing the introduction to it himself. Though not approved by the congress and thus lacking in legitimacy as compared with the revised version of the report, 'Aflaq's introduction is a reassertion of the party's traditional doctrines and of his own accomplishments.[29]

Nevertheless, the formal adoption of the revised version and the subsequent publication of the *Points of Departure* signify an important ideological turning point. Arab unity was relegated to a secondary position in the new Ba'thi doctrine; a significant element of Marxist-

[27] *Cf.* A. Ben Tsur, "The Neo-Ba'th Party of Syria", *Journal of Contemporary History*, III (1968), pp. 173-174.

[28] Another striking example is the deletion of the term *'almānī* (secular) that appears in Hafiz' 1965 essay but not in the corresponding paragraph of the *Points of Departure* (see n. 26 above). The majority at the congress probably realized what an adverse effect on Muslim opinion this term would have.

[29] In so doing 'Aflaq even uses the old term *inqilābiyya* for revolutionism, which in the meantime had acquired the pejorative connotation of signifying the outcome of a mere military *coup*, as distinguished from the substantial revolutionary change brought about by a *thaura*.

Leninist doctrine and terminology was integrated into Ba'thi thinking and with it a more radical concept of socialism. Marxism, however, was introduced through the back door, never mentioned explicitly, but referred to as a "revolutionary doctrine" or as the "ideological awareness and fine knowledge of the laws governing the transformation of societies and the bases of the course of history". Marxist concepts were grafted on traditional Ba'thi notions as the following example clearly indicates:

> The second characteristic of our Party is revolutionism, since the point of departure for the scientific, nationalist socialist thinking in social and economic analysis is a dialectical one. It starts from the affirmation of a contradiction in the national society and the existence of a struggle between the classes, which in turn is characterized by its tendency to achieve two simultaneous goals: national unity and the liquidation of exploitation.[30]

The reluctance to admit explicitly the Marxist origin of the ideas and terms grafted on the traditional Ba'thi ones seems to reflect the feeling of the congress that, despite Hafiz' assertions, such acknowledgment was or at least was likely to be regarded as a breach of loyalty to Arab nationalism. The majority of the delegates may also have realized that it was politically unwise for a party struggling to remain in power to blur its identity and radically break with its past.

Consequently, the *Points of Departure* gives an ambivalent review of the Ba'th's traditional outlook and its past accomplishments. While their former significance is duly noted (to maintain the party's reputation), so also are their limitations, and in a manner that would justify replacing the party's old leadership and doctrines. Thus the veteran leaders are credited with having bolstered the notion of Arab unity at a critical phase and with placing it under the custody of the popular rather than the upper classes, but they are also blamed for having given to it the primacy over the notions of socialism and freedom and for failing to develop it into a comprehensive theory.[31]

[30] *Points of Departure*, pp. 24 and 89.
[31] *Ibid.*, pp. 27–31.

But all this belongs to a bygone phase, say the authors; Arab unity is no longer in need of proof but a reality. The important task is to define its social content. This is followed by an apologetic attempt to show that striving for Arab unity is progressive in that it can only serve the interest of the masses and furnish the basis for a sound socialist economy. It is socialism that the *Points of Departure* presents as the central goal, while Arab unity is reduced to an instrumental role — "Arab unity is an indispensable basis for the construction of a socialist economy".[32] In 'Aflaq's teachings, too, Arab unity is an intermediate goal, but it stands at the centre, looming as an imminent vision much more potent than the ultimate, almost utopian goals. For the majority at the Sixth National Congress the immediate goal appeared to be the establishment of a socialist society, while Arab unity became a sacred slogan still deserving of proper respect.

Then, abruptly and tangentially, the discussion of Arab unity is geared to the pressing problems of the moment. Arab unity, it is stated, will be best achieved through a struggle conducted by distinct movements reflecting the residues of regional differences in the Arab world. The differences between such movements can only gradually be overcome by exchange of views and mutual criticism. Any attempt to force the pattern obtaining in one region on the others can only breed enmity between movements and obstruct the course of unity. Having thus defended and rationalized the Ba'th's overt feud with Nasser, the section dealing with Arab unity is crowned with an attempt to lay the ideological foundations for a bilateral Syrian-Iraqi union. Arab unity, says the text, will be implemented in stages; a partial union formed with good intention is a step on the road to an all-embracing union.[33]

The section of the *Points of Departure* dealing with socialism draws heavily on the contributions by Atasi and Hafiz to *Fī al-fikr as-siyāsī* but applies them to the new conditions obtaining in Syria after March 8, 1963. The traditional concept of "Arab Socialism" is rejected as implying a narrow-minded nationalistic attitude (*aṣabiyya*) and is replaced by the more appropriate "Arab road to socialism". The authors then strike at the heart of the problem — tra-

[32] *Ibid.*, p. 37.
[33] *Ibid.*, pp. 39–41.

ditional Ba'thi acknowledgment of private ownership as a natural right symptomizes a reformist *(iṣlāḥī)* approach, which seeks a resolution of class conflicts and attracts petty bourgeois elements into the party.[34] This must be radically altered, the "national bourgeoisie" and its allies should be toppled, and the petty bourgeoisie gently incorporated into the socialist sector formed through nationalization of the major branches of the economy (it was implied that small workshops and stores were not to be nationalized). In the process of nationalization the danger of state capitalism should be averted by the actual participation of the "toiling masses" in the direction of the economy (but it will in reality be directed by a "revolutionary vanguard of the organized people").

All this was quite different from the socialist programme of the Nasserite regime in Egypt, where a more benign attitude was taken towards "national" capital and capitalists and a more pragmatic spirit prevailed. The *Points of Departure* adopted a still more radical approach to the agrarian problem. It presents Agrarian Reform as insufficient since mere distribution of land creates a new bourgeoisie in the countryside. The human and economic revolution necessary for the peasants will only be achieved through the creation of collective farms.[35]

The "revolutionary vanguard" to direct these changes was already identified in an earlier section of the text, dealing with "the exercise of popular democracy", as the members of the projected, new, Leninist-like Ba'th Party. "Popular Democracy" is presented as an antithesis to the discarded Western parliamentary democracy that offers freedom only to the wealthy few and proved to be unsuited for the needs of the developing nations.[36] "Popular Democracy" will, on the other hand, guarantee freedom to those classes who constitute the true people[37] and ensure the country's rapid develop-

[34] *Ibid.*, pp. 77–79. *Iṣlāḥī* has become in Ba'thi (and other) parlance a derogatory term as contrasted with a revolutionary change.

[35] *Ibid.*, p. 85.

[36] *Ibid.*, pp. 52–54, and compare with Nasser's remarks in *Maḥāḍir*, p. 165. "Popular Democracy" is sometimes referred to in Ba'thi sources as "True Democracy".

[37] These classes are the workers, peasants, revolutionary intellectuals (civilian and military), and the lower-middle classes. This resembles the Egyptian concept, the difference being that the ultra-leftists in the Ba'th saw the alliance with the lower-

ment. The new regime will centre in the party, leading the popular organizations and councils and operating according to the principle of "democratic centralism".[38]

Despite its pronouncedly Leninist colouring[39] this section presents a relatively mild departure from Ba'thi thought and parlance as they developed through the years. The totalitarian elements in 'Aflaq's teachings had long overcome the liberal ones, and parliamentary democracy had been dismissed openly by the party's leading ideologists.[40] Leninist terminology and organizational concepts, too, had long been employed to some degree by the Ba'th (and others in the Arab world).[41]

The striking feature of the text is therefore not so much the marked Marxist-Leninist influence but rather its divorcement from the political realities of Syria and Iraq (even as they were portrayed in the "political report" submitted to the same congress). Though substantially revised by the congress, the "ideological report" remained sufficiently removed from reality to warrant a note of caution: "The road is not yet ready for the revolutionary government and contradictions may obstruct its course. It may be forced to accept certain temporary concessions or a necessary bargaining and some-

middle classes as a temporary arrangement. Article 7 of the communiqué published after the congress only hinted at this notion, but it was later spelled out by Hafiz (*Ba'ḍqaḍāya,* p. 31). He wrote that only in the second phase (of the Revolution) will the talent conflict between the "toiling popular masses" and the petty bourgeoisie become a basic contradiction.

38 *Points of Departure,* pp. 55–56. It seems that "popular councils" stands for "Soviets" in the original model.

39 *Cf.* Stalin's *Problems of Leninism* (New York, 1934) and *Foundations of Leninism* (New York, 1939) and especially Chapter 5 in the former.

40 M. Kerr, "Arab Radical Notions of Democracy", *St. Antony's Papers,* No. 16 (1963), pp. 9–40. M. S. Agwani, "The Ba'th: A Study in Contemporary Arab Politics", *International Studies,* III (1961), p. 11, quotes Bitar who told him in an interview that he would favour something like Sukarno's "Guided Democracy".

41 This is clearly evident in the long discussions on political organization during the Cairo Unity Talks. The term "democratic centralism" was first introduced in 1954. The percolation of Leninist organizational concepts into the Ba'th Party prior to March 1963 is illustrated by the collection of essays called *Abḥāth fī-at-tanẓīm al-ḥizbī* ("Studies in Party Organization") republished by the Syrian Regional Command in April 1963 but based on essays written in the 1950s and earlier in the 1960s.

times it may even be forced to retreat".[42] All this soon materialized as the time came for the practical resolutions to be passed.

RESOLUTIONS OF THE SIXTH NATIONAL CONGRESS

In similarity to the *Points of Departure* the resolutions adopted by the Sixth National Congress reflect the struggle of the three major trends among the delegates, but unlike it they rested on a more realistic evaluation of the numerical and political weakness of the Ba'th Party and regimes. An analysis of the social and political forces in Syria presented to and endorsed by both the Regional and National Congresses, pointed to the sway still held by President Nasser over many peasants, workers, and "revolutionary intellectuals" (though the Ba'th was said to have its own share of support among them) and by the "grande bourgeoisie" over the urban lower-middle classes.[43] At the same time an analysis of the rival political parties in Syria (and Iraq) indicated that none of them was a suitable ally for the Ba'th and that the Nasserites posed the gravest threat.[44]

There seems to have been general agreement at the congress about the gravity of the Nasserite danger but no such consensus with regard to the policy best suited to meet it. The argumentation of the resolutions implies that the moderate minority advocated an anti-Nasserite alliance with traditional right-wing politicians (and perhaps with Haurani too) that would have called for a milder approach to political and social changes. And indeed the first official bulletin issued by the congress that was released on October 14 stated that it was studying "the cooperation of the Ba'th Party with other political organizations

[42] *Points of Departure*, p. 70.

[43] *Resolutions of the Sixth National Congress*, pp. 29–32, and *Resolutions of the Syrian Regional Congress*, pp. 9–14.

[44] *Resolutions of the Sixth National Congress*, pp. 15–18. The traditional bourgeois parties were portrayed as still possessing considerable power that could bring them an important advantage in case of elections. The analysis presented to the Regional Congress failed to mention the Muslim Brethren, but during the Sixth National Congress a paragraph concerning them was added to another section of the resolutions (p. 53). This may have reflected anxiety over their renewed activity, leading to the arrest of their leader 'Isam al-'Attar on October 21.

in the government". This proposal, however, was strongly rejected by the majority, whose position was that such a policy would not only betray the party's ideology but was bound to fail. The "reactionaries", it was argued, were the Ba'th's natural enemies and the "popular masses" its natural allies, even if they temporarily followed Nasser. A "cease-fire" with the "reactionaries" would expose the regime to their plotting and would divert all popular support from the Ba'th into Nasser's fold. It followed from this analysis that the only way open to the party was to launch massive social and economic reforms that would outdo those of Nasser and guarantee the regime its popular basis of support. The *Resolutions of the Sixth National Congress* stated so explicitly:

> The nationalization of a large segment of this [industrial] sector had taken place on July 1961 and despite its shortcomings it brought about a deep transformation that Syria had not witnessed before. It brought a large portion of the workers to rally around 'Abd-ul-Nasser and it is possible that these workers will retain their loyalty to him, if the Party does not nationalize that sector. . . . It is at the same time a political necessity, so that the Party can attract those sectors of workers who are still loyal to 'Abd-ul-Nasser.[45]

What distinguished at that point the ultra-leftist delegates from the rest of the radicals was their insistence on the immediate implementation of such reforms. Some radical measures had already been taken; the governor of Aleppo, Hilal Raslan, a Druse confidant of Shufi, had nationalized the bakeries in the city during the summer. The controversial measure was reported to have been finally approved while the congress was still in session.[46] But the ultra-leftists were outvoted on most issues and the majority of the resolutions, especially in their public version, indicate an awareness of the regime's tenuous hold and the need to adopt measures suited for that delicate transitional phase.

While it decided against cooperation with other parties, the

[45] See pp. 31 and 49.

[46] The issue, however, was not settled at that. See *al-Ba'th* (Damascus), October 17, 1963, and *al-Ḥayāt*, February 4, 1964.

congress was for consolidation of the Ba'th's position in Syria by readmitting members of right- and left-wing dissident factions on an individual basis. Another decision taken with regard to the period of transition was to maintain a clear distinction between the party and the government and its apparatus. Though this was justified mainly on grounds of the need to bolster the party's "revolutionary dynamism", which might otherwise be absorbed by the daily governmental and bureaucratic routine, it was in fact a practical conclusion based on the recognition of the party's weakness at that stage. By announcing a distinction between party and government, the Ba'this were rationalizing a *de facto* situation[47] and giving themselves more room to manoeuvre. The government, though directed by the party, could be held responsible for failures, mistakes, and deviations from the party's doctrine.

For the longer range a general plan of social and economic reforms was drawn up. The plan was conceived as a general outline, whose elaboration into detailed programmes was left for a later stage, to be carried out in collaboration with the NCRC and the cabinet.[48]

Implementation of the Agrarian Reform was presented as the basic and initial step in the process of the envisaged "socialist transformation". A rapid progress of the Agrarian Reform, it was suggested, would furnish the regime with a wide basis of voluntary support and, by raising the standard of living in the countryside, would substantially change the prospects of economic development in Syria. But this sound analysis was followed, in keeping with the *Points of Departure*, by an unrealistic decision to dispense with routine "bureaucratic" land distribution and to set up collective farms. Though it was somewhat softened in the public communiqué,[49] the insistence on the establishment of collective farms at a time when the party had not yet seriously begun to organize the peasants was a victory for the extremists.

[47] See articles 3 and 4 of the communiqué published at the end of the Sixth National Congress. On p. 58 of the *Resolutions of the Sixth National Congress* the failure of party members to be admitted to teaching posts at the University of Damascus, supervised by a Ba'thi minister of education, is deplored.

[48] *Ibid.*, p. 34.

[49] It said (article 10) that the congress "considered the establishment of these farms a revolutionary goal aimed at by the Party".

A more prudent approach governed the resolutions relating to other aspects of the "socialist transformation". It was decided to nationalize all large and medium-sized industrial concerns but to do so only after an extensive study of the industrial sector and in a manner that would avoid the danger of state capitalism by entrusting industrial management to the workers. The communiqué published at the end of the congress was very ambiguous on this subject, tailored as it was to suit several ends. It contained no reference to the nationalization of industry (in order not to antagonize the "reactionaries" prematurely), but it did include a paragraph on the decision to entrust management of the means of production to the workers (so as to present a socialist programme more advanced than Nasser's). It was thus difficult to determine according to the communiqué what "means of production" the workers were to manage.[50]

Similarly cautious were the paragraphs dealing with the transformation of the state bureaucracy. In view of the realization that this was a long-term objective and that in the meanwhile the Ba'thi regime had to operate through the existing bureaucracy and not to antagonize it, it was announced that "the task is development and not amputation" and that "this plan will be dictated by human [itarian] considerations on the one hand and by faith in the conscience of the citizen employee on the other". The discussion of "popular supervision" of the bureaucracy at the congress was totally removed from the reality of growing military control of civilian administrative functions in Syria. The *de facto* situation had also been legalized by a decree of the NCRC which placed administrative departments in the provinces under military control. Some of the officers who thus amassed political power were nicknamed *mulūk aṭ-ṭawā'if* after the local princes in Islamic Spain.[51]

Perhaps most instructive was the group of resolutions dealing with "socialist policy in the domain of services". It included a decision to guarantee higher admission quotas, irrespective of scholarly standing, to prospective university students from "remote and backward provinces", a decision to institute free medical services (possibly

[50] See pp. 49–50 in the *Resolutions of the Sixth National Congress,* and article 8 of the communiqué.

[51] See Razzaz, *op. cit.*, p. 101, and *Chronology of Arab Politics*, (1963), p. 262.

through nationalization of medical practice), and several similar resolutions. However, more telling than the resolutions themselves was the acrimonious style of the text deploring the disparity between large cities and the countryside and the traditional exploitation of the latter by the former. It reflected both the depth of this gap and the relatively high representation of the "countryside and remote and poor provinces" in the ranks of the radical wing of the Syrian Ba'th. Genuine bitterness emerges from such paragraphs:

> Millions and millions of pounds are spent in the cities on bread to make it cheap, while most of the peasants do not eat flour throughout the year, but eat corn and barley during long periods of the year. And another form of exploitation is the attention given to some regions but not to others so that the country is divided into two parts: the spoiled and the neglected. This is another form of exploitation suffered by some regions that we will call backward and remote.[52]

Another set of resolutions concerned Arab policy of the Ba'thi regimes and especially their relations with Egypt. The gradual process whereby Syria and Iraq had been drawing closer since the eruption of the open conflict with Egypt culminated in a decision to establish a federal union between them within two months. This decision was announced while the congress was still in session and was so worded as to preserve Syria and Iraq's nominal adherence to the April 17 Agreement. While inviting Nasser to join this union on an equal footing, the communiqué published in the wake of the congress also denounced his "personal and dictatorial regime". The Ba'th then turned to Israel's plan, at that time nearing implementation, to pump water out of the Jordan River into its overland carrier. The project, declared the communiqué, constituted a direct military threat to all the Arabs. They, and in particular the UAR, were called upon "to action and solidarity for facing this danger with force, if the need arises".

The issue of the Jordan River waters had long been a source of friction in Arab-Israeli and particularly Syrian-Israeli relations. It triggered fighting along the Syrian-Israeli border in the 1950s and

[52] *Ibid.*, pp. 53–54.

the Ba'th regime would find it difficult to give in where its predecessors had stood firm. Furthermore, since the dissolution of the UAR the Israeli overland carrier became the topic of Syrian-Egyptian altercations. The leaders of the "Separatist Regime", harassed by Nasser, sought to undercut and embarrass him by displaying a more militant attitude towards Israel than he could afford to adopt. It was in accordance with this line that Haurani accused Nasser of colluding with the United States in an attempt to secure the peaceful implementation of the Israeli project. In daring Nasser to help them stop that project the Ba'this were following a pattern established by their "separatist" predecessors.

This issue was to occupy the centre of inter-Arab politics later in 1963, but in the meanwhile the congress was well aware of the fact that Nasser was having the upper hand in the propaganda war with the Ba'th and that Arab public opinion was blaming the latter for the failure of the Unity Talks.[53] It was also an issue of great internal significance, and several of the unpublished resolutions and recommendations passed by the congress were designed to improve the party's standing vis-à-vis Nasser; they called for intensified activity in the Arab world, strengthening of the propaganda apparatus, and the preparation of comprehensive studies of the 1958 Union and the 1963 Unity Talks.[54]

REPERCUSSIONS OF THE CONGRESS

The Regional and National Congresses of the Ba'th served to underline the political and ideological divisions in the party and to heighten the struggle between the rival factions both in Syria and Iraq. In Syria the Military Committee consolidated its position in two moves that were also calculated to restore a measure of internal balance among the leaders of the Committee. On November 11 Salah J'did, the éminence grise of the Committee, was promoted from lieutenant-colonel to major-general and appointed chief of staff, a position held by Hafiz since Hariri's ouster in July. J'did had competed for this

[53] *Resolutions of the Sixth National Congress*, p. 58.

[54] *Ibid.*, pp. 17–18, 57–59.

position against 'Umran and it was the support lent by Hafiz that secured it for him. The latter, it will be recalled, had not been an original member of the Military Committee and joined it as a prominent member only after the *coup* of March 8. The rivalry between Hafiz and 'Umran soon became apparent and the former chose to side with J'did against the latter.[55] J'did's promotion added the formal authority of the chief of staff to the considerable political power of the informal leader of a strong group of officers placed in key positions.

Hafiz and 'Umran became premier and deputy premier in the new cabinet, formed on November 12 after Bitar's resignation had been accepted. Bitar was reported to have resigned following the humiliation he had suffered at the Syrian Regional Congress, but the reshuffle was delayed until the completion of the National Congress. He was transferred to the comparatively insignificant post of deputy chairman of the NCRC.[56] 'Umran, commanding a politically crucial armoured brigade stationed near Damascus, was promoted, too, from colonel to major-general. The abnormal situation, in which the Syrian army had been controlled by relatively junior officers, was thus terminated. Besides the military character of its upper echelon, the one significant innovation in the composition of the new cabinet was the addition of more members of the radical wing, allies of the military, such as Dr. Yusuf Z'ayyin (a physician by profession and a native of Abu Kemal on the Iraqi border) and Dr. Mustafa Haddad (a native of Idlib and professor of botany in Damascus).

The changes in Syria were soon overshadowed by a rapid deterioration of the internal political situation in Iraq. There were sufficient internal factors that could lead the moderate wing of the Iraqi Ba'th to act against the radicals, but it seems that the crisis was also brought on by the consequences of the Sixth National Congress.[57]

[55] On J'did's appointment see Radio Damascus, November 11, 1963, 2:15 p.m. On the Hafiz-'Umran rivalry and the collaboration between the former and J'did see the very interesting details given by Jundi, *op. cit.*, pp. 129, 139–140.

[56] Radio Damascus, November 13, 1963, 7:15 a.m. For the composition of the new cabinet see Appendix A.

[57] One of the officers who played an active role in the *coup* is reported to have said (Khadduri, *Republican Iraq*, p. 212) that 'Aflaq had told him that the members of the Regional Command who had forced on the party wrong measures at the Sixth National Congress should be purged.

The moderates, led by Talib Shabib, Hazim Jawad, and Colonel Muhammad Mahdawi, staged a *coup* on November 11, forced the election of a new Regional Command, and tried to exile Sa'di and his supporters. But Sa'di was able to marshal sufficient support in the party, Nationalist Guard, and the army to create a deadlock. On November 13 the members of the National Command were summoned from Damascus in an effort to solve the crisis. On November 15 the National Command declared itself the supreme authority in Iraq as a temporary emergency measure, but it seems that by so doing it only served to aggravate the crisis. Some Iraqi officers were offended by what they regarded as outside meddling in their affairs and more particularly by 'Aflaq's presence and activity. Their resentment facilitated the success of the *coup d'ètat* staged on November 18 by President 'Aref and other non-Ba'thi officers in collaboration with some moderate Ba'this. Despite initial Ba'thi illusions, the new regime soon allied with Cairo and gradually assumed an anti-Ba'thi stand. The Ba'th lost its hold on Iraq and the events of November 18 were rightly referred to in Ba'thi parlance as the "November Setback".[58]

The failure in Iraq had important repercussions on the situation in Syria, some immediately discernible and others experienced only later. It placed the still fragile Ba'thi regime in Syria in an even more delicate situation. Not only were the Syrian Ba'this no longer able to lean on Iraq against Egypt, but they now found it necessary to fight Nasser on two fronts and Ba'thi Syria was entirely isolated in the Arab world. Hostile elements within Syria were most likely to be encouraged by the party's debacle in Iraq, and the regime would have to decide whether to soften or harden its attitude towards the opposition. The formulation of this policy was one of the important issues in the acrimonious debate that developed between the moderates in

[58] The initial optimism was based on the participation of such Ba'this as Tahir Yahya, Ahmad Hasan al-Bakr, and Hardan at-Tikriti in the new government. An optimistic statement of 'Aflaq's Lebanese confidant, Jubran Majdalani, was seized upon later by 'Aflaq's foes as a "proof" of his collusion with 'Aref, See Shimali, "Crucial Days", *ath-Thaura* (Damascus), November 19, 1968. The Arabic terms used by the Ba'this to designate these events are "an-naksa at-tishrīnīyya" and "ar-ridda at-tishrīnīyya".

the Syrian Ba'th and the ultra-leftists entrenched in and around the Syrian National Command.

Spokesmen for the moderate wing blamed the excesses committed by the Iraqi Sa'di and the extremist attitude shared by his Syrian allies for the party's debacle in Iraq. On the basis of the lesson learned in Iraq, the moderates advocated a more sensible and cautious policy in Syria.[59] The Syrian leftists, reinforced by Sa'di and his supporters living in exile in Damascus, accused 'Aflaq and his associates of triggering the squabble that led to the setback[60] and claimed that what had happened in Iraq only vindicated the line they were advocating. The failure to adopt a radical socialist policy and the soft attitude towards "the reaction" at home and towards Nasser, they argued, had deprived the party's regime in Iraq of its natural support and had given its enemies an opportunity to subvert it. The only way to guard against a recurrence of this process in Syria, they continued, was to carry out immediately the radical transformation they had advocated at the Sixth National Congress. Thus, an Internal Bulletin issued on December 27, 1963, by the Syrian Regional Command, still headed by Shufi, concluded with the following paragraph:

> This does not mean that one has to retreat from the socialist line in view of the opposition. On the contrary, the socialist transformation should be deepened. The failure to carry this transformation out in Iraq was one of the major causes for the failure. Only its implementation will guarantee the rallying of the toiling masses around the party and their desertion of Nasserism.

While the setback in Iraq thus exacerbated the already existing conflict with the ultra-leftists, whose detailed history will be described presently, it proved in the long run to have a moderating effect on rival factions in the Syrian Ba'th. The experience of witnessing a regime led by the party toppled by its enemies because of unrestrained

[59] Shimali, *op. cit.*, charges that 'Aflaq's supporters immediately launched "a hysterical campaign" in Syria, assailing what they called "crimes and deviations".

[60] This charge was only vaguely raised immediately following the event, but it was to be explicitly levelled against 'Aflaq at a later stage.

internecine squabblings, reinforced a penchant, noticeable earlier, to refrain from violent confrontation and to go only as far as the brink.[61]

Perhaps the most notable long-term outcome of the failure in Iraq was the virtual elimination of the notion of the Ba'th as a real pan-Arab power, a contender with Abdel Nasser for Arab leadership. The non-Syrian branches continued to play an important role in intra-Ba'thi politics and a section of the Iraqi Ba'th regained power in 1968 but the illusion of 1963 was not revived.

Over the objections of the ultra-leftists various measures were taken by the government in the second half of November and early in December to relax the atmosphere in Syria, calm the population, and secure the (at least passive) support of politicians such as Haurani. On November 21 Hafiz met with a delegation of Damascene businessmen and merchants headed by Hani al-Jallad, for whom he had a soothing statement. Jallad, too, was quoted to have issued an optimistic declaration following what he considered a successful encounter.[62] Deputy Premier 'Umran declared a few days later, in a statement directed both at Cairo and the home front, that the role of the new cabinet was to ease the tension in inter-Arab relations. Its policy, he said, could be summarized as "wisdom, stability, leniency and shunning of propaganda".[63]

Accordingly, such leading politicians as Nazim al-Qudsi were freed from jail and on December 5 the minister of information, Sami al-Jundi, came out with a public declaration, in which he confirmed that the "political isolation" imposed on lesser "secessionist" politicians was cancelled and that the death sentences imposed on participants in the abortive *coup* of July 18 were commuted. He denied, however, that this implied that the "March 8 Revolution" had turned back on its principles or that the cancellation of "political seclusion" was tied to "political agreements and bargains".[64] This

[61] This was recognized by the Ba'this themselves; an Internal Bulletin published by the Regional Command on September 11, 1965, stated that "the experience which our party had undergone in Iraq taught a lesson—that it knew how to use and it has so far defeated the enemies with all their conspiracies. . ."

[62] *Al-Hayāt*, November 24, 1963.

[63] *Chronology of Arab Politics* (1963), p. 391.

[64] Radio Damascus, December 6, 1963, 7:15 a.m.

was meant to be a refutation of the rumours alleging that the Ba'th was negotiating with Haurani and other politicians in order to include them in a new coalition government. Political detainees, both right-wing politicians and Nasserite militants, continued to be set free during December 1963 and January 1964.

The attempts at appeasement failed. At home, the Muslim Brethren, best organized of all the opposition parties and acting with the sanction of a religious fundamentalist ideology, tried to challenge the regime. As early as October, while the Sixth National Congress was still in session, 'Isam al-'Attar had agitated against the Ba'th. He did so again in a Friday sermon in December, which resulted in a clash between his supporters and the Ba'this and in his flight on December 18 to Lebanon.[65] In a related development, the city of Homs experienced unrest in mid-December stirred by conservative Muslim circles following an incident in which a Ba'thi teacher was reported to have torn a religious book. The incidents were effectively contained,[66] but they revealed the deep resentment felt by pious Muslims in Syria towards the Ba'th regime.

Similarly unsuccessful was the attempt to ease Egyptian pressure. The Ba'th responded by threatening to launch a "suicidal" attack against Israel's water-pumping project. The challenge to Egypt was obvious: failure to protect Syria even from the consequences of such an unsolicited attack would be very damaging to the prestige of the foremost leader of the Arab world. From late in November 1963 Syrian anti-Nasserite propaganda was hammering at Egyptian timidity on the issue of the Jordan River water,[67] and it seemed to be very effective because it confronted Egypt with a dilemma. But the Ba'this were surprised by another manifestation of Nasser's tactical genius. After preparing the ground for it through the Egyptian press, he came out with an invitation to the Arab heads of state to come to Cairo and devise plans for common action against the Israeli project. This meant that Nasser was contemplating a truce with the "reactionary" Arab regimes, which among other advantages was designed to

[65] *Al-Jarīda* (Beirut), December 19, 1963, and *al-Yaum* (Beirut), December 19, 1963.

[66] Details of the incident are given in *al-Ḥayāt*, December 19 and 20, 1963.

[67] See, for instance, *ath-Thaura*, November 25, 1963, and Radio Damascus, December 10, 1963, 7:30 p.m., December 15, 1963, 2:45 p.m., December 18, 1963, 2:45 p.m.

give him the moral and political support of all Arab states to contain Ba'thi Syria.

This major turning point in Egypt's Arab policy was brought about by a number of considerations[68] but was linked most intimately to the Syrian position and in turn made that position untenable. Syria now had to decide between making good its threats and taking single-handed action, doing nothing and boycotting the Cairo Summit Conference (which meant complete isolation in the Arab world), or losing face and attending the conference. After an internal debate the Syrian leaders decided to participate in the conference and to send a delegation led by the Syrian head of state, Amin al-Hafiz. Hafiz was isolated at the conference and had to accept the line supported by the others, which was, indeed, ambiguous enough for each side to claim victory. True, any direct offensive action on the Arab side was made dependent on long-term preparations, but these would have to be completed some day. Moreover, Arab diversion of the sources of the Jordan was bound to trigger some Israeli reprisal and a violent confrontation.[69]

While Hafiz could thus claim that he did not really deviate from the party's line, his position was strongly assailed at a meeting of the branch leaderships (*qiyādāt āl-furū'*) of the Syrian Ba'th summoned, upon the delegation's return from Cairo, on January 23. Shufi's supporters, strongly represented in the Regional Command and in the party's apparatus, denounced the concessions made by the government (*ḥukm*), which they considered unnecessary. Rather, this was, they argued, the opportunity to bring about a real revolutionary change in the whole region. An internal party circular issued by the Regional Command on January 26 passionately advocated a resort to violent action to achieve that expected transformation:

> What we have to do is push the whole Arab people into entering the battle with all its means, and through the fighting all these [moderating] considerations will be rendered useless and disappear . . . entering the battle on the diversion of the Jordan on this basis will not only save our country from a grave danger,

[68] For the other considerations see Kerr, *Cold War*, pp. 133–136.

[69] *Cf. ibid.*, pp. 140–156.

> that is bound to become still more difficult to handle in the future; it will also enable our masses to expose the regimes which are hostile to it and conspire with Imperialism in the Arab homeland .... Our masses' entry into this battle will enable them to find the formulas leading to their victory and to the establishment of an Arab socialist society ... and we believe that this battle is a great opportunity for truly achieving the aims of the people on the field of battle.[70]

The differences of opinion did not remain confined to closed party forums. At that stage the radicals were still entrenched in the Syrian state radio and accordingly a news commentary broadcast on January 18 expressed disappointment with the outcome of the Summit Conference in contrast to the declarations issued by Hafiz.

The obstructionist position adopted by the ultra-leftists with regard to Syria's Arab policy was followed by a blow struck at Bitar (which in fact may have been supported also by some of his less radical foes). They seized upon an interview with Bitar published on January 9 by the Beirut newspapers *an-Nahār* and *al-Kifāḥ*, in which he strongly denounced Sa'di, and on January 24 the Syrian Regional Command decided to expel Bitar from the party's ranks.[71]

The ousting of one of the party's cofounders was more an indication of the transformation it had undergone than of the strength of the ultra-leftists. As a matter of fact, late in January 1964 preparations had almost been completed by a new coalition of 'Aflaq's supporters and the Military Committee for a party congress designed to rid it of Shufi and his faction.

[70] *Cf.* Shimali, "Crucial Days", *ath-Thaura*, November 21, 1968.

[71] According to *an-Nahār*, Bitar said that Sa'di and the members of the Nationalist Guard in Iraq should be denounced because they were responsible for a deviation from and a *coup* against the party's tradition and principles. He protested against the "infiltration of adventurous elements to the front ranks ... they leaped to the head of government and Party machineries ... and applied quasi-Stalinist principles. ...". The decision to expel Bitar was included in a *ta'mīm* (circular) issued by the Regional Command on January 24, which added the interview to a long list of previous "sins". The decision was not publicly announced, reportedly because 'Aflaq threatened to resign in such an event.

THE SYRIAN REGIONAL CONGRESS AND THE SEVENTH NATIONAL CONGRESS

The rapprochement between 'Aflaq's group and the Military Committee was brought about by the dangers and the embarassment that the power held by the ultra-leftists had actually caused, especially since the setback in Iraq. Together they were able to sway the Extraordinary Syrian Regional Congress and the Seventh National Congress, both convened and held hastily in the first half of February 1964, and to oust the leftists from their positions on the regional and national level and ultimately from the party. They were, however, firmly enough established in their positions to compel 'Aflaq and his provisional allies to resort to irregular procedures in order to manipulate both congresses.[72]

Over the objections of Shufi and his supporters in the Syrian Regional Command and in the Commands of several branches in Syria the Syrian Regional Congress was summoned to an extraordinary session on February 1, following a joint session of the National Command and the Syrian Regional Command.[73] Once the congress convened it was realized that its membership (as compared with the Regular Congress in September 1963) had been expanded by at least 16.[74] These included the secretaries of nine new branches of the party's military section, which had been set up since September, and other delegates whose right to take active part in the congress was acknowledged.[75]

[72] Much of the literature about these congresses is devoted to polemics and apology concerning their legality. 'Aflaq, who could not afford to admit that he had resorted to irregular procedures, ultimately fell back on such arguments as the National Command's right to suspend any article of the Internal Regulation (Internal Bulletin on the Seventh National Congress issued by the National Command on February 22, 1964). 'Aflaq also claimed that what had been done did not contradict the "spirit" of the party's statutes. Such arguments were a double-edged weapon and would later be employed against 'Aflaq himself.

[73] Internal Bulletin of February 22, 1964.

[74] This is the number admitted by the National Command; the leftists claimed it was 28. Their arguments are contained in a very interesting document issued by the National Command of February 29, 1964, in which it added its replies to the complaints and misgivings of the leftists.

[75] Internal Bulletin of February 22, 1964.

This was the formal side of the congress. The underlying political reality was the cooperation between 'Aflaq, bestowing the legitimacy, and the Military Committee, supplying the political muscle. Once this became evident, the expansion of the congress was approved; the leftists were outnumbered and outvoted and could be purged according to the regular legal procedure. Their ouster was preceded by a debate on the responsibility for the party's failure in Iraq, which indeed was less an argument about the past than an attempt by both sides to vindicate their present positions. The congress did not reverse the resolutions of the recent Regional and National Congresses, but it did prepare the ground for their revision. The decision to "combat personal opinions coming from the outside" could thus be seen as justifying the elimination of Marxist-inspired views and of unwanted resolutions adopted previously. The most significant action taken by the congress was the election of a new Syrian Regional Command, composed of eight civilians and seven military and headed by Hafiz.[76]

The civilian wing of the new Command was made up of a minority of 'Aflaq's men and a majority of the Military Committee's supporters and included none of the ultra-leftists. While the latter were thus completely purged, 'Aflaq and his group now found themselves with a Regional Command dominated by the military and their protégés. It is not easy to tell the latter apart from Shufi and his small faction, since they seem to have come from similar origins and backgrounds. Nur ad-Din al-Atasi, for instance, had collaborated with the military together with Shufi prior to the Sixth National Congress and was elected to the Regional Command that Shufi had dominated, but he chose not to antagonize the military in 1964. Unlike Shufi and the firebrands who followed him, Atasi and his colleagues were more realistic, less doctrinaire, and willing to serve as docile partners of the military. The dangerous implications of this development were clear to 'Aflaq at the time and he tried to resist it, but unsuccessfully. Not only did he realize that there was a price to be paid for the military's cooperation in ousting the leftists, but he also knew that the military were the most important constituent of a regime that depended on them for its survival. Under the circum-

[76] For the composition of the new Command see Appendix B.

stances the Military Committee as a group could dictate its will to the civilian party leaders. The latter could resist and make the military pay a political price for such coercion, but in the delicate situation of February 1964 'Aflaq chose to succumb quietly.[77]

The issue, however, was to remain dormant for some time, overshadowed as it was by other developments. The immediate task was to deal with the sources of power that the leftists still possessed: the support of several party branches in Syria, a number of seats in the National Command, and the radical mood of a significant section of the Lebanese Ba'th. As soon as the Syrian Regional Congress was over, on February 6, 'Aflaq attempted to convene the Seventh National Congress and complete the purge on the national level, while Sa'di and his Syrian allies were trying to obstruct him by voting against this move in the National Command and by mobilizing support in Lebanon.

They were again outmanouevred and the congress was summoned on February 12 by 'Aflaq in his capacity as the party's secretary-general. Authority to convene a National Congress normally rests with the National Command; 'Aflaq had the support of five members (the others objected or were unavailable), but he relied on the precedent he himself had set in 1959 when convening the Third National Congress. The procedures employed in the congress revealed how artificial the national organization of the Ba'th tended to be. Membership in the congress was inflated by flooding it with obedient representatives from Syria and from semi-fictitious branches. Thus the party's branch in Yugoslavia, which could not have been an impressive one, was represented by no less than five delegates.[78] These probably were Syrian students dependent on their government and correspondingly reliable.

As in the preceding Syrian Regional Congress, the major activity at the Seventh National Congress revolved around procedural matters and the election of new Commands (a National Command and a new Regional Command for Iraq). The composition of the new National Command is not fully known, but it did include the three

[77] For 'Aflaq's own description of this episode in his speech of February 18, 1966, see *al-Wathā'iq al-'arabiyya* (1966), p. 62, and *cf.* Razzaz, *op. cit.*, pp. 110–111.

[78] See the document of February 29 quoted in n. 74 above.

most prominent members of the Military Committee and none of the ultra-leftists.[79] The latter were expelled from the party (or had their membership suspended) immediately after the congress.

These measures proved sufficient to terminate the role played by the radical leftists of the Sa'di-Shufi-Hafiz school at the centre of Ba'thi and Syrian politics. However, the schism, like the previous ones, was painful and it further disturbed the stability of Syrian politics at the time. Also, the impact of the "Shufi Era" on the Syrian party organization could not be eradicated at once and his continued sojourn in Damascus together with his friends slowed down the process of purging and reorganizing the party. The Sa'di-Shufi group, or as they came to be called "the seceders" (*munshiqqūn*), were even able to organize a clandestine Seventh National Congress of their own in a private home in Damascus in August 1964. They then split as Sa'di formed his own party and tried to mend fences with Nasser. Others joined various factions of the Ba'th. Hafiz and Tarabishi finally settled down as independent leftist writers considered by themselves and others as prominent spokesmen for the Arab New Left.[80] Their continued influence is illustrated by the apologetic bulletins that the Regional Command had to issue late in April 1964 defending its "moderate" policies against radical criticism.

But in immediate and politically more decisive terms the cardinal outcome of the congress was indicated by the make-up of the new Regional Command. The function and role of Shufi's faction at the centre of Syrian politics was, it will he recalled, taken by an apparently similar civilian faction. It shared the radicalism of Shufi's ousted group, its leftist terminology, and the hostility it felt towards the party's veteran leaders, but its radicalism was mitigated by a practical and realistic approach, which made its members better suited and more subservient allies to the military. It was a subtle but still a very significant difference.[81] The new alliance became an essential

[79] This is based on the details included in what seems to be a reliable account of the congress in *al-Anwār* (Beirut), February 28, 1964.

[80] See Tibi, *op. cit.*, *passim*.

[81] The replacement of Shufi's faction by a new group as the civilian allies of the Military Committee is a phase in the history of the regime that both 'Aflaq and the Military Committee tend to play down in their accounts. For 'Aflaq and his sup-

feature of the Syrian political scene but its full manifestation was delayed for a few months by the violent confrontation between the Ba'th regime and a large section of Syria's urban population in the spring of 1964.

porters the change did not make a real difference, and rather than dwell on their share in purging the leftists, they telescope the distinct struggles against Regional Commands led by Shufi and Z'ayyin into one struggle. The Military Committee and its new civilian allies were anxious to obliterate their role in cooperating with 'Aflaq against the leftists, and their semi-official account of the period (by Shimali) presents the purge as solely the work of 'Aflaq and his faction.

5 THE "HAMA REVOLT" AND THE POLITICAL CHANGES OF SPRING 1964

An ideological army is one that exercises its right of debating the country's policies in congresses and popular assemblies and of delegating the execution of that policy to a political leadership, which the people and its organized military and civilian vanguards have chosen (from Salah al-Bitar's cabinet statement of May 23, 1964).

Since July 1963 the Ba'th had been in sole control of Syrian government and politics. Ba'thi domination of the army, the crushing of the Nasserites, and the organizational weakness of most other opposition parties and groups had virtually confined significant political activity in Syria to the inner councils of the Ba'th Party. But while their rule was not being seriously menaced by any efficient opposition, the Ba'thi leaders were aware of their tenuous hold over Syria and of the hostility of the country's urban population. The incidents stirred by the Muslim Brethren and the Hafiz government's attempts to placate mercantile and religious circles late in 1963 already indicated the acuteness of the problem and the understanding on the part of the government that its policy must take it into account. But its true dimensions were only revealed by the series of events which between February and May 1964 evolved into a major crisis, producing changes in the structure of the Ba'th regime and in the nature and course of Syrian politics.

On February 6, the last day of the Extraordinary Syrian Regional Congress, the Damascus chamber of commerce presented Dr. George To'meh, the minister of the economy, with a note deploring the deteriorating economic situation and seeking to explain it. It listed the nationalization of the banks as one of the major reasons for economic stagnation.[1] Two days later Ba'thi and conservative students clashed in the coastal city of Banyas on the fringe of the 'Alawi region. The incident had strong confessional (*tā'ifī*) overtones, as it seems that most Ba'this involved in it were 'Alawis while their opponents were Sunni Muslims. The authorities were able to contain the incident and publicized it only when they realized that rumours based on information from outside sources were even more harmful to their interests.

[1] *Chronology of Arab Politics* (1964), p. 76.

The official government version, once it was published, did not try to hide the confessional aspect of the incident but rather chose to emphasize it in an attempt to prove the "reactionary" nature of the opposition. Thus the bulletin issued by the minister of the interior on on February 17 charged that "it came out in the inquest that a group determined on sowing sectarian dissension was encouraged by several professional politicians and tribal leaders whose steps have been narrowed by the Revolution which terminated their exploitation of the people". The same themes were further pursued by the Syrian press and radio commentaries.[2]

Possibly related to the events in Banyas was the commercial strike that broke out in the central Syrian city of Homs on February 22, the sixth anniversary of the formation of the UAR.[3] That date had not been particularly dear to all Syrian merchants in the past, but their perspective had changed after a year of Ba'thi rule and the atmosphere had been prepared by Nasserite agitation and activity.[4] The government's reaction was prompt. The minister of interior, Nur ad-Din al-Atasi, himself, it will be recalled, related to the city's most prominent landowning family, announced the formation of an Emergency Military Court, which as early as February 23 imposed heavy penalties on five leaders of the strike.[5] Another group was sentenced on February 24, and it seems that while the severity of the penalties provoked some reactions in the Homs and Hama areas it had a deterring effect in other parts of the country and order was restored by February 26.

The government now resorted again to gestures and reassurances designed to appease the urban middle classes. In what was obviously a reply to the note of February 6, Dr. To'meh defended the nationalization of the banks and defined the situation as difficult but not critical. He blamed capital smuggling and the drought for these difficulties. Realizing that the ferment reflected dissatisfaction with the

[2] See Radio Damascus, February 17, 1964, 7:15 p.m., and the editorials of *al-Ba'th* and *ath-Thaura,* February 18, 1964. *Cf. al-Ḥayāt,* February 11, 1964.

[3] *Al-Jarīda* (Beirut), February 20, 1964, reported that the ferment spread from Banyas to Homs and Ladhiqiyya (it will be recalled that Ladhiqiyya itself is not predominantly 'Alawi).

[4] See *al-Jarīda,* February 25, 1964 (this issue also carried an interview with Sami al-Jundi in which he spoke about cooperation with the private sector).

[5] Radio Damascus, February 23, 1964, 7:15 a.m. and 7:15 p.m.

political as well as the economic situation, Hafiz, in his Revolution Day address on March 8, announced the decision to draft a "revolutionary constitution" that would define the people's political rights. On March 10 he received another delegation representing "economic circles" in Damascus, which raised various demands.[6]

These measures were, however, hardly sufficient for assuaging the persistent ferment in the Syrian cities. After a relatively quiet month Nasserite agitators carried out a series of sabotage activities in Aleppo and organized demonstrations that forced the authorities to impose a curfew.[7] But the major phase of the political crisis started in Hama on April 5. The long-accumulating tension was released, as in many similar instances, by a minor incident. A high school student erased a Ba'thi slogan written by his teacher on the blackboard and was arrested. Agitation among his fellow students spread and was amplified by the city's *imāms,* who in their Friday sermons launched an all-out attack against the Ba'th. Some of them were reported to have covered themselves with shrouds, thus indicating that the struggle against the Ba'th had become a *jihād* (holy war).[8] On April 11 security forces clashed with high school students and by killing one of them triggered the declaration of a commercial strike in the city on April 12.

Hafiz tried to appease the population of Hama. During a visit to the city he ordered that indemnities be paid to the parents of the slain student and he promised to allot money for the city's economic development. But on April 14 violence broke out again and on such a scale that the army decided to shell the Sultan Mosque killing dozens of protesters. By taking exceptionally strong measures, the government was able to prevent the strikes and demonstrations from spreading to Homs.[9] A number of companies were nationalized in Aleppo and Ladhiqiyya and it was announced that the nationalized

6 *Al-Jarīda,* March 11, 1964. For excerpts from the speech by Hafiz see *Arab Political Documents* (1964), pp. 77–79.

7 *Al-Ḥayāt,* March 25, 1964. On April 6, 1964, 2:15 p.m., Radio Damascus quoted Colonel Mamduh Jabir, the governor of Aleppo, who announced the capture of "the terrorist gang" operating in the city.

8 *Chronology of Arab Politics* (1964), p. 179, and *al-Ḥayāt,* April 17, 1964.

9 For details on the height of the crisis in Hama see *al-Ḥayāt,* April 16, 17, 18, 1964, and Radio Damascus, April 15, 1964, 2:15 p.m. and 9:15 p.m., April 19, 1964, 7:15 a.m., and April 20, 1964, 7:15 a.m.

companies were to be managed by the workers. This, however, was hardly a step on the road to socialism but rather a punitive measure that affected allegedly bankrupt companies.[10]

The government now pursued a policy that sought to accomplish three major objectives. First, it took the severest measures and precautions against any recurrence of passive or active opposition. Accordingly, the Nationalist Guard was reported to have forcibly opened on April 28 stores that were closed in Damascus once the strike spread to that city. On April 29 ten persons were sentenced to death by the Emergency Courts. Other stores were sealed by the authorities in Damascus on May 4. Second, the government tried to organize its supporters to action. On April 20 demonstrators in support of the regime marched in Damascus, expressing the views of what the government termed "the real Syria".[11] On May 2 a second pro-government procession was organized in Damascus, in which the participants carried anti-Nasserite slogans and listened to a speech by Hafiz. Third, while the authorities stamped out every sign of opposition they continued their efforts to mollify the dissatisfied population. Hafiz, 'Umran, and Atasi met with several delegations and on April 25 Hafiz announced the details of a new constitution.[12] On April 29 'Umran promised that general elections would follow the promulgation of the constitution, and during the next few days death sentences were commuted and credit arrangements were promised for small merchants.

Tension began to subside in the second week of May and then a series of political and constitutional changes was introduced. On May 9 Bitar was entrusted with the formation of a new cabinet. On May 13 Hafiz was promoted to lieutenant-general (*farīq*) and made the head of a newly constituted Presidency Council composed of five members. Bitar became its deputy chairman and the other three members were Nur ad-Din al-Atasi, 'Umran, and Mansur al-Atrash, son of the Druse leader Sultan al-Atrash and a confidant of 'Aflaq. On the same

[10] *Al-Ḥayāt,* April 15 and 19, 1964, Radio London, April 18, 1964, 10:45 p.m., and Radio Damascus, April 20, 1964, 7:15 p.m.

[11] *Al-Ḥayāt,* April 29, 1964, and Radio Damascus, April 30, 1964, 7:15 a.m. and 2:15 p.m.

[12] *Ibid.* The constitution went into effect on May 18. For an analysis of it see below p. 117.

day the composition of the cabinet was made public and on April 14 it released its policy statement.[13] On May 27 Shibli al-'Aisami, also a Druse and associate of 'Aflaq, became secretary-general of the Syrian Regional Command, replacing Hafiz.

These were important changes indicating the depth of the political crisis that Syria and the Ba'th regime had faced between February and May 1964. The scope and variety of the groups who played an exceptionally active role in the events of this period provide an interesting view of the social and political conditions in Syria of the mid-1960s.

It was most natural for the urban higher-middle classes of Syria to oppose the Ba'th regime and to try to topple it at a moment of weakness and internal division. After all, the regime had openly declared these classes to be its enemies and their political and economic interests had been damaged by it. The Ba'th had correctly assessed the weakness of the parties traditionally representing these classes[14] but failed to realize how strong their social power still was in 1964.

There is little knowledge of the social structure of the Syrian cities and towns in the mid-1960s, but what is known suggests that the traditional structure of commerce and small-scale industry had undergone relatively few changes; traders and owners of workshops were closely tied to more prominent merchants and middlemen, who provided a nexus to the modern world.[15] The latter still retained economic and social leadership not only over the lower-middle classes but also over the employees of these small-scale establishments, still feeling closer to the owners rather than to "fellow workers".[16]

This was well known to the Ba'this and, as shown above, had served to moderate their policies late in 1963. But they hoped to eventually break the traditional social controls and did not expect such an open show of active and violent opposition. The outburst is to be attributed to a combination of factors. To begin with, there was a

[13] Radio Damascus, May 14, 1964. For the composition of the cabinet see Appendix A.

[14] See above, Chapter 3.

[15] This description is based on D. Chevallier, "De la production lente à l'économie dynamique en Syrie", *Annales* (1966), pp. 59–70. Chevallier opens his article with a quotation from an ambitious Ba'thi programme of introducing changes and then goes on to show how the guild system persisted in Syria down to our period.

[16] See Nabulsi, *op. cit.*, pp. 351–354. He characterizes these workers (in 1958) as spiritually still belonging to the guilds.

marked deterioration in the economic situation, caused by reluctance of domestic and foreign investors to risk capital in view of the political instability and the uncertainty about the government's future policies, by capital smuggling abroad, and by the drought.[17] The middle classes were profoundly disturbed by the prospect of further nationalization and of radical social and economic changes, and it seems that no soothing declarations could relieve their anxiety.[18]

The bitterness of these largely pious (Muslim) circles was intensified by what they at least regarded as Ba'thi atheism and the prominence of Christians and heterodox Muslims in the new ruling group. Traditional orthodox Muslim distrust of the Ba'th[19] was deepened by the party's one year of rule. While Nasser was successful in preaching an Arab Socialism that had strong Islamic overtones and in harnessing the religious establishment in Egypt to a policy that appealed also to devout Muslims,[20] the Ba'th failed dismally in this respect. Its socialism was construed by the observant Muslims as an alien anti-Islamic importation, all of which served to nurture the antagonism of the large conservative sectors in the Syrian cities and towns.

Closely linked with these grievances was the irritation felt by Sunni Muslims with regard to the Christian and heterodox Muslim origin of so many Ba'thi leaders and officers. It has already been explained above why numerous minoritarians had been attracted to the Ba'th in earlier years. The number of 'Alawis, Druses, and Isma-

[17] The government's version was that the economic hardships were caused by a siege designed to strangle "the progressive regime" in Syria. This explanation was included in a circular issued by the Cultural Bureau (*maktab thaqāfī*) of the Syrian Regional Command on July 15, 1964.

[18] This was later realized by the Ba'this themselves as the circular quoted above indicates.

[19] See above p. 11. An interesting instance in this context is a circular issued by the Regional Command in June 1965 warning party members against using such terms as "the holy Ba'thi trinity" (namely Unity, Freedom, and Socialism) that are exploited by the enemies. Probably these "enemies" pointed to the Christian religious connotation of the term "trinity".

[20] *Cf.* P. J. Vatikiotis, "Dilemmas of Political Leadership in the Arab Middle East: The Case of the U.A.R.", *American Political Science Review,* LV (1961), pp. 103–111. It is interesting that the Syrian scholar Salah ad-Din al-Munajjid in his *at-Taḏlīl al-ishtirākī* ("The Socialist Delusion"), Beirut, 1965, attacks only President Nasser's socialism, realizing that the socialism of the Ba'th does not appeal to devout Muslims and that there is no real need to warn them against it.

'ilis in the party and particularly in its Military Organization was swollen as they recruited friends and relatives following the *coup* of March 8, 1963. Not only were the Sunnis aware of the large number and high proportion of top posts in the party and the state held by members of these communities,[21] but they often had to confront them in closer, more personal positions of local authority. All this aggravated both religious and social prejudices traditionally held by urban Sunnis against the largely rural heterodox minorities.[22] The population of Banyas, so close to the 'Alawi region, was probably the more aroused, but its feelings were shared to some degree by Sunnis in other areas. Under these circumstances the harsh suppression of the insurrection in Hama, a mostly Sunni city surrounded by minoritarians, was attributed to a sectarian blood revenge (*tha'r*) taken by the Druse Colonel Hamad 'Ubaid.[23]

Many Syrians were also alienated by the failure of the Ba'th regime's Arab policy and by its feuds with Egypt, Iraq, and indeed most Arab states. While still belonging to the formal bodies established in the Summit Era in inter-Arab relations, Syria remained isolated in a period of relative thaw.[24] Most Syrians, it seems, did not desire a return to a union with Egypt, but they did want closer relations with her and the other Arab states rather than the feeling of seclusion, which they felt resulted from the character and policy of the Ba'th. The Nasserites did not take an essential part in stirring up the Syrian

[21] Prominent minoritarians among the party's civilian leaders were the Christian 'Aflaq and the Druses 'Aisami and Atrash. The names of most 'Alawi and Druse officers were hardly known to the public, but the more prominent and colourful among them, like the 'Alawis J'did and 'Umran, the Druses Salim Hatum and Hamad 'Ubaid, and the Isma'ili 'Abd al-Karim al-Jundi, were well recognized.

[22] Social contempt felt by urban Sunnis towards the generally poorer and often backward 'Alawis is reflected by the expression "les fils des domestiques" (*Le Monde*, October 16, 17, 1966). *Cf.* the circular of July 15, 1964, quoted in n. 17.

[23] See Safadi, *Ḥizb al-Ba'th*, p. 341, and *al-Ḥayāt*, April 24, 1964. *Cf.* also Weulersse, *op. cit.*, p. 86. When at the Second Regular Syrian Congress in February 1965 a demand to divide the party's branch in Hama into two branches—one for the city and one for its outskirts—was raised, it was rejected (*Organizational Report*, p. 31) as likely to be interpreted as motivated by sectarian considerations.

[24] Full-fledged attacks on the Ba'th from Cairo began only late in April 1964 and culminated with Nasser's speech of May 1. It seems that the renewal of attacks from Cairo was also brought on by developments within Syria.

population against the regime, but they contributed their share through those militants who remained in Syria.

The major role in organizing active resistance to the Ba'th was apparently played by the Muslim Brethren. They had a relatively strong organization, especially among the lower-middle classes,[25] and a number of advantages. The Friday sermon in the mosques furnished them with a traditional and still very effective instrument for mobilizing large masses and agitating them to action.[26] They were the right party for exploiting disaffection on religious and confessional grounds, and, unlike secular right-wing politicians, they did not appear to represent merely personal and material interests. At a period when Socialism and Revolution had been incorporated into the ideology of Arab nationalism and opposition to them implied Reaction, the *Ikhwān* (Brethren) had the important advantage of speaking in the name of another, still as respectable and potent, ideology.

The Ba'th had its own potential and passive supporters, but while the opposition was able to muster and lead numerous adherents in active resistance, the regime could not mobilize sufficient public backing to counter the political consequences of the demonstrations and strikes. Its efforts to form "front organizations", to express the support it did command or could manipulate among those who did not side with the opposition, were at a rudimentary stage. At the height of the crisis the first attempts were made to set up the National Union of Students, and at the same time the Ba'th found it necessary to purge the uncooperative leadership of the important Teachers' Union.[27] The two demonstrations held in Damascus in support of the regime could not change the impression of a government controlled by a minority party alienated from the majority of the population.[28]

But the key factor remained the regime's unshaken ability to

[25] *Cf.* Seale, *op. cit.*, pp. 93, 97, for a description of the troubles the *Ikhwān* were able to generate in the 1950s.

[26] B. M. Borthwick, "The Islamic Sermon as a Channel of Political Communication", *Middle East Journal*, XXI (1967), pp. 299–313.

[27] Radio Damascus, April 27, 1964, 11:30 a.m., and *al-Ḥayāt*, April 15, 1964.

[28] This could explain why on October 7, 1964, when the new Command appointed for the Suburbs' Branch (*far' al-aṭrāf*) in Damascus addressed the members it stressed the importance of the branch as being close to Damascus and encompassing numerous peasants. It was largely from among those peasants that pro-government

control physically even the troubled cities. With the assured support of the army (and the Nationalist Guard) the regime was in no real danger; still, realizing that they could not break the political deadlock by coercive means alone, the Ba'thi leaders decided after a close internal debate[29] on a number of concessions, which without changing the nature of the regime were to make it more acceptable to the urban population.

POLITICAL AND CONSTITUTIONAL CHANGES

The concessions made by the Ba'th regime were embodied in a series of political and constitutional changes, that were introduced in May 1964 and were also influenced by intra-party rivalries and certain long-term tendencies.

The new Syrian constitution portrayed the structure of government as contemplated by the Ba'th but not yet ready for implementation. It vested legislative and supervisory authority in a broadened NCRC that was to include, besides its original members, an unspecified number of "representatives of the classes of the people".[30] Since the Ba'th had not as yet been able to form or manipulate the "popular" and professional organizations, whose representatives were to man this legislature, the NCRC was not expanded in May 1964, and the original secretive Council remained for the time being the supreme legal authority in the state. Executive power (and for the time being some legislative authority) was vested in the newly created Presidency Council and in the cabinet.

Another important group of articles laid the legal foundations for the establishment of a socialist economy and society in Syria. These, however, were general principles and with deference to the sensibilities of the middle classes they were worded in a nonalarming manner. Moreover, private ownership and the right of inheritance

demonstrators were mobilized. On the history and social composition of the Quneitra Branch, carved out of the Suburbs' Branch, see A. Ben-Tsur, "Composition of the Membership of the Ba'th Party in the Kuneitra Region", *Hamizrah Hehadash,* XVIII (1968), pp. 269–273.

[29] According to a circular issued by the Regional Command on October 7, 1964, the NCRC decided to introduce these changes by a one-vote majority.

[30] Article 33. The text of the constitution is available in 'Indani, *op. cit.*, pp. 223–233.

were recognized by the constitution and defined as inviolable (against expropriation but not against nationalization in return for compensation).

In earlier Syrian constitutions it was stated that (a) the religion of the head of state is Islam, (b) Islamic jurisprudence is the principal source of legislation.[31] That formula was repeated in article 3 of the new constitution with one important change—Islamic jurisprudence was no longer "the principal source" but "a principal source" of legislation. This article demonstrates, nevertheless, how useful the insistence on a strict distinction between the Ba'th Party and the government of the state proved to be. The constitution of the party did not mention Islam, but on the state level the Ba'th had (and could afford) to compromise its principles in order to avoid another confrontation with the devout Muslims.

The establishment of a Presidency Council and the other political changes of May signified a reduction of the power held by Hafiz coupled with a partial restoration of that of 'Aflaq and Bitar's faction. The latter obviously benefited from the political failure of their intra-party rivals, but their (temporary) come-back should also be seen against the background of the social forces and political orientation they represented. The available information is too sketchy to permit a conclusive comparison of the social origins of the rival Ba'thi factions. Yet it is evident that the supporters of 'Aflaq and Bitar were older and tended to come from the ranks of the intelligentsia in the larger urban centres, while the military tended to be backed by (educated) younger men from smaller towns, from the provinces, and from the countryside. The former were considered more moderate and acceptable to the urban population and to the unionists and their reinstatement could be seen as a conciliatory measure.

In a regime dominated by the military the political fortunes of civilian factions could not be divorced from latent developments among the army officers. 'Aflaq and Bitar were close, as it were, to 'Umran and the advantages he drew from the failure of his rival Hafiz affected their position as well. While Hafiz was criticized by 'Umran

[31] For the controversy that surrounded this article in 1950 see von Grunebaum, *op. cit.*, p. 289.

on the one hand, he was also attacked by radical elements who favoured a harsher treatment of the insurgents rather than the attempts to mollify them. In the speech he delivered on April 21 while opening the National Congress of Syrian Students, Hafiz defended his policy against such radical, impatient critics. "There are those who raise demands and I appreciate their sincerity", he said, "but being older than them and perhaps even more experienced I advise as a brother . . . that we do not follow emotions . . .".[32]

Even more important was the fact that criticism of the Military Committee and its handling of the crisis spread to the ranks of the Military Organization to which the Committee was ultimately responsible. The little that is known about this episode is that in the wake of the "Hama Revolt" a congress was held by the secretaries of the party's military branches, at which opposition to the Military Committee surfaced. The Committee emerged victorious but the evidence of internal opposition to it is significant and at that time may have shaken the self-confidence of the military leaders.[33]

Nor was Hafiz successful in his efforts to accommodate Akram Haurani and his followers.[34] Hafiz desired this because he was close to Haurani, lacked a strong personal basis of support in either the military or civilian wings of the Ba'th, and could consolidate his position by the adhesion of this kindred faction. The events in Hama, where Haurani enjoyed strong support, underscored his political value[35] but other factors counted against his accommodation. He was

32 See also Razzaz, *op. cit.*, p. 115. Shimali in *ath-Thaura*, November 24 and 25, 1968, raises charges against both Hafiz and 'Umran, whose conduct encouraged the insurgents. These accusations were probably inflated for political purposes but nevertheless seem to reflect criticism levelled at that period.

33 The only reference to this congress is in a circular issued by the Military Organization on August 16, 1964.

34 Radio London, April 26, 1964, 6:00 a.m., quoted Hafiz' statement in a press conference held on April 25 in which he is reported to have said that a new cabinet was soon to be formed and to include "leftist unionists" and "socialists, supporters of Haurani".

35 It would later be claimed by the common rivals of Haurani and Hafiz that the former played a role in provoking the troubles in Hama (circular of the Regional Command of October 26, 1965, and Shimali in *ath-Thaura*, November 25, 1968), but what is known about the "Hama Revolt" suggests that while Haurani did not help the Ba'th and tried to profit from the crisis, he and his supporters did not actively oppose the party.

too closely identified with the Separatist Regime and his participation in the government could be used to denigrate the Ba'th. Several members of the Military Committee, who had been persecuted in the Separatist Period, bore a strong personal grudge against him.[36] Haurani himself, an experienced politician, would not agree to a mere symbolic representation that would benefit the Ba'th alone. Finally, the very fact that Hafiz wanted Haurani's inclusion in the government was sufficient for his rivals, fearing a too powerful Hafiz, to oppose it.

While representatives of Haurani's faction were thus not added to Bitar's new cabinet, it did include a considerable number of independent unionists, a fact which irritated the hard-core Nasserites who labelled them "weak souls".[37] The cabinet as a whole represented a tendency towards more moderate policies and towards a detente with Egypt and the other Arab states. This trend was underlined by Bitar's policy statement and a number of other declarations and gestures that followed it. On yet another level the structural and personal changes of early May 1964 served to diffuse authority and power within the Ba'th regime. In the party organization the Military Committee and its civilian allies remained paramount, but they still had to contend with the residues of Shufi's power, while the election of Shibli al-'Aisami as secretary-general of the Syrian Regional Command gave the 'Aflaq-Bitar group a vantage point from which it could try to regain its influence on the Syrian party. Bitar and his supporters were uppermost in the cabinet but the Military Committee had the majority in the Presidency Council and despite some changes in the NCRC it controlled that body as well.[38]

BITAR'S ALTERNATIVE AND ITS FAILURE

Upon assuming the premiership Bitar had the initial advantage of stepping in where his rivals had failed; they now were obliged to let

[36] Ṣafadī, *Ḥizb al-ba'th,* pp. 348 ff., explains the relationship between Haurani and several Ba'thi officers. There was deep antagonism between him and 'Umran, whom Haurani called *Bāṭinī,* referring both to his slyness and 'Alawi origin.

[37] *Ibid.,* pp. 376–377.

[38] It was not announced at that time, but some of the National Command members were added to the NCRC (according to the *Political Report* submitted to the Second Regular Syrian Regional Congress in February-March 1965, p. 69).

him try his hand at what they could not achieve: reconcile the Syrian middle classes, Egypt, and the Nasserites to the Ba'th regime. Under the slogan of *al-infitāḥ 'ala al-jamāhīr* (opening to the masses), signifying a less exclusivist and more benign concept of the party's rule, he offered an alternative group, namely his and 'Aflaq's supporters.

Bitar's plan of action was outlined in the lengthy policy statement of his new cabinet, issued on May 23.[39] In several respects this statement was, and indeed was generally accepted as, an attempted refutation of the October 1963 *Points of Departure*.[40] It was most natural for an ideological party like the Ba'th that one faction should vindicate its return to power by reasserting its doctrinal position, but it was also a measure of Bitar's tenuous position that this was done through the government (*ḥukm*) and not through the party.

The policy statement returned the point of gravity to Arab Unity, declaring that "the foremost revolutionary objective is unity: it forms the soil in which all other objectives can grow". Socialism remains the only road open before Syria, but the socialism advocated by Bitar is entirely different from the militant Marxist-like doctrine of the radical leftists. The Revolution, according to the statement, can accomplish its aims "in accordance with a revolutionary scheme that does not call for a class war but can resolve class differences peacefully".

Bitar had less to innovate where concrete policies were concerned. The regime was to remain Ba'thi and others could participate through "front organizations" that would be represented in the broadened NCRC and through local "popular councils". This was not very different from the "Popular Democracy" of the *Points of Departure* only more benign and devoid of revolutionary rhetoric. The same could be said about the short paragraph sketching the cabinet's policy towards Egypt. While announcing its intention to refrain from responding to propaganda attacks, the new cabinet made it clear that the Ba'th had no intention of relinquishing its (actually exclusive) leadership in favour of "certain other unionist groups".[41] This meant a refusal to give the Syrian Nasserites a share of real power in return for an Egyptian endorsement of the Ba'thi regime.

[39] *Arab Political Documents* (1964), pp. 184–194.

[40] Political Bulletin issued by the Regional Command on July 10, 1964.

[41] *Arab Political Documents* (1964), p. 186.

The major portion of the statement dealt with economic issues, which according to Ba'thi estimation had played such an important role in provoking the recent crisis. Bitar was walking the tightrope of having to lull the urban middle classes without exposing himself at the same time to intra- and extra-party charges of stepping back from socialism and assuming a rightist position. Not surprisingly, he adopted a line of compromise. Syria was to continue on the road to socialism, but while the public sector would be developed as the major sector of the economy the existing private sector would not be nationalized during the first stage. The state as a rule, read the statement, does not consider nationalization "a magic invocation" but rather one of several means for the implementation of socialism.[42] The same spirit of compromise was evident in the decision to establish a "common sector" in which the government would purchase 25 percent of the property and would be represented accordingly in the management. The resolution adopted by the Sixth National Congress to establish collective farms on land distributed through the Agrarian Reform programme was watered down by a decision to establish such farms on "certain lands" side by side with cooperative farms and standard land distribution.

In line with these principles Bitar set out, during May and June 1964, to generate a "new atmosphere" in Syria—this is how the minister of the interior, Fahmi al-'Ashuri, defined the goal of the new cabinet following a conference of provincial governors.[43] Several declarations and gestures directed both at the general urban population and the Nasserites were issued and made during these weeks. High-handed members of the Nationalist Guard were disciplined, agitators arrested in the wake of the "Hama Revolt" and a number of Nasserite prisoners were set free, confiscated prints were returned to their owners, and the civil rights of several politicians were restored.

It was certainly an achievement for the regime that there was no resurgence of the civil disturbances of the February-May period, but whether this was an outcome of Bitar's new policy is a moot point.

[42] *Ibid.*, pp. 192–193. It is significant that this is presented as the view of the state, implying that the party holds another view.

[43] Radio Damascus, June 2, 1964, 1:15 p.m., and *Chronology of Arab Politics* (1964), p. 188.

Bitar, moreover, had in mind objectives more ambitious than merely pacifying Syria. His major efforts were directed towards convincing non-Ba'thi, mainly unionist, elements to join the broadened NCRC. This would endow the regime with a quasi-parliamentary legislature and create the semblance of a "unionist progressive front" while retaining actual power and control in Ba'thi hands. This is what a Ba'thi spokesman meant when he referred a few weeks later to "a popular summoned council 60 percent of whose members would be Ba'this and 40 percent would be unionists who command the confidence of the [present] council from a nationalist and Arab point of view. Its activities would consist of advising, directing, and preparing plans".[44] Hopefully, integration of Nasserites and other unionists into the framework of the regime could also soften Nasser's attitude towards the Ba'th.

Bitar may have thought that Nasser and his supporters would be less recalcitrant now that the regime had been in power for more than a year and had demonstrated that it could not be easily dislodged. Personally he may have been willing to offer more for a rapprochement, but he had to consider the mood of the strong anti-Nasserite elements in the Syrian Ba'th whose stirrings were already evident. It was in response to criticism against the release of Nasserites, levelled by such elements, that the Cultural Bureau of the Syrian Ba'th issued a circular on June 24. Among other things the circular explained that "some of the measures carried out by the government as rapid solutions for certain dangerous crises tended to present the Revolution as indulgent towards the Reaction while the weakness of our propaganda apparatus made it difficult to confront charges of terrorism and Fascism". The wording of the paragraph reveals also the Ba'th's preoccupation with possible denunciations by Nasser and the usefulness of the distinction between party and government for shifting responsibility from the Regional Command to the cabinet when "nonrevolutionary measures" had to be explained away.

Under these circumstances what Bitar could offer did not satisfy the Nasserites. Their experience had taught them the futility of a "national front" with the Ba'th and they would settle for nothing less than a substantial restructuring of the regime and the military com-

[44] *Rūz al-Yūsuf* (Cairo), September 14, 1964.

mand.[45] These respective positions were obviously irreconcilable and the negotiations failed.

Even earlier on Nasser had confronted Bitar with a rebuff when he signed on May 26 a Coordination Agreement with Iraq which underscored the isolation of the Ba'th in the framework of the Summit Policy.[46] No less embarrassing to the Syrians was Egyptian intervention with the Algerians, which resulted in Algerian cancellation of the previously announced visit of a Ba'thi delegation headed by 'Aflaq to Algiers. It was all the more painful as the Ba'this had, since the party's reorganization in 1962, fancied Algeria as an alternative to Egypt: progressive, revolutionary, and friendly to the Ba'th.[47]

By this time, however, Bitar retained little actual power. 'Aflaq's planned trip to Algeria was, as a matter of fact, the first step in a self-imposed exile, which owing to circumstances was spent in Germany (where his brother lived) and lasted till November 1964.[48] 'Aflaq decided to leave Syria early in July when he realized that Bitar's return to power was illusory, and that the Military Committee and its civilian supporters were strengthening their hold on the Syrian party organization at the expense of his and Bitar's wing.

The new trend had not become evident immediately. In May the Military Committee was still under the impact of the recent crisis and regarded Bitar as an important element in the reconsolidation of the regime. The opposition Bitar confronted at that stage came from the rear-guard of Shufi's faction, still entrenched in the leadership of certain party branches in Syria, in the Nationalist Guard, in the Trade Unions Federation, and in Dar al-Waḥda, the government's publishing house.[49]

[45] For a presentation of the Nasserite position see *Kull Shai'* (Beirut), June 20, 1964. See also *an-Nahār,* June 26, 1964, and *al-Jarīda,* June 28, 1964.

[46] The feeling of the Regional Command that the party's rank and file in Syria were disturbed by the effects of the Agreement is indicated by the circular issued on July 15, in which an attempt was made to show its worthlessness.

[47] On July 18 the Regional Command had to issue another circular attempting to whitewash this debacle and to minimize its impact. It also tried subtly to shift the blame for what could not be hidden to the National Command.

[48] The episode is treated in detail in 'Aflaq's speech of February 18, 1966. See *al-Wathā'iq al-'arabiyya* (1966), p. 62.

[49] For details see below p. 128. The *Organizational Report* presented to the Second Regular Syrian Congress in February-March 1965 (p. 22) accused the

It was the need to eliminate the impact of these radical elements on the Syrian Ba'th that the Regional Command cited in order to justify its request from the National Command to suspend the party's Internal Regulation for six months. The request was granted on June 16 at a joint meeting of the National and Regional Commands.[50] The Regional Command thus achieved absolute authority over the party organization in Syria and set out to reorganize and mould it according to its concepts and interests. Shibli al-'Aisami and Walid at-Talib, representing the 'Aflaq-Bitar wing, played a minor role in this process; it was the Military Committee and its civilian allies, members of the Regional Command and functionaries in the party apparatus, who remoulded the party and in the process came to dominate it completely. 'Abd al-Karim al-Jundi, Marwan al-Habash, Mustafa Rustum, and several of their colleagues were in charge of the reorganization and those among them who had been virtually unknown in Syria earlier in 1964 were powerful political personalities by the end of the year. Habash, a former school-teacher from a small village near Quneitra, offers a striking example of a local party militant who thus rose rapidly in the party's hierarchy. Salah J'did found him to be a loyal and reliable supporter, made him the Quneitra branch's secretary, and in 1965 would have him elected to the Regional Command.

Late in June 1964 the shock caused by the political crisis of the February-May period had subsided and Bitar and the National Command were no longer deemed vital for reconsolidating the regime. The military did not cherish the veteran leaders and their group nor did they share their concept of the party's rule. Through the party's reorganization they were seeking to build a new instrument of power serving them and operating according to their concept of what a revolutionary party

Nationalist Guard of playing "a special role in protecting certain factionalists". The punitive measures taken early in June 1964 against unruly elements in the Guard in Homs and Der'a may therefore have been linked to intra-party struggles as well as to the effort to mollify the urban population (see Radio London, June 8, 1964, 6:00 p.m., and *Chronology of Arab Politics* [1964], p. 190). Later on Muslih Salim, director of Dār al-Waḥda, and Isma'il 'Urfi, editor of *ath-Thaura*, were dismissed (*Kull Shai'*, July 4, 1964, and *al-Anwār*, July 8, 1964).

[50] Bulletin of Regional Command from July 8, 1964, and Razzaz, *op. cit.*, p. 111.

ought to be. It is to 'Aflaq's credit that he sensed the trend of these developments at an early stage and tried to carry his friends to a confrontation with the Regional Command. However, they were apprehensive and he decided to leave Syria as a means of exerting pressure on both his friends and rivals. 'Aflaq would describe to his listeners on February 18, 1966, how some members of the National Command recoiled from the struggle: "The Command was afraid that what had happened in Iraq might happen in Syria and indeed this was correct to a certain extent".[51]

While 'Aflaq, therefore, left in protest, Bitar remained in Syria and in office to expend his energy in an uneven struggle with the Military Committee and its civilian supporters for another three months.

[51] *Al-Wathā'iq al-'arabiyya* (1966), p. 62.

6 THE HEGEMONY OF THE MILITARY COMMITTEE AND THE REGIONAL COMMAND

This is, comrades, how legitimacy in the Party was trampled and torn. Seven out of nine civilian members of the dismissed Regional Command joined the Party after the Revolution and those who dominated it were from that regionalist (*quṭrī*) faction which had seceded from the Party. And it was this Command which brought the leaders of this faction into the positions of leadership in the government and in the Party (Michel 'Aflaq in his speech of February 18, 1966).

The reorganization of the Syrian Ba'th Party in the latter half of 1964 brought it under the almost complete control of the Military Committee and its civilian associates and substantially altered the composition of its membership. Related to it was the reformulation of the party's social and economic outlook in an attempt to bypass those classes and groups that it considered irreconcilable to its regime. These developments combined to produce profound changes in Syrian and Ba'thi politics which seemed to be consolidated by the Second Regular Regional Congress of the Syrian Ba'th held in March and April 1965. But these changes were soon to be overshadowed and partially undone by an exacerbation of the conflicts between the Military Committee and the veteran Ba'thi leaders and within the Committee itself, which was in turn intimately connected with the reorganization process initiated in the summer of 1964.

The reorganization carried out by the Regional Command and its bureaucratic apparatus was aimed at turning the Ba'th Party in Syria into a loyal and efficient political machine. While far from being wholly successful these efforts still sufficed to establish the Regional Command's firm control over the party. In mid-June the Regional Command, it will be recalled, was granted extraordinary powers for purging the Syrian party organization of the vestiges of Sa'di and Shufi's influence. Relying on these powers the Command dispatched to the various branches ad hoc committees that re-evaluated the membership status of whole branches and in several cases reshuffled their Commands. During the summer, as it turned out, the eradication of Shufi's influence became a secondary goal and the ad hoc committees were pursuing other ends. Shufi himself had already been ousted from the party and the expulsion of seven of his close associates was decreed in June. Most prominent among them were Yasin al-Hafiz, the group's ideologist, and Khalid al-Hakim and Ahmad Abu Salih, former members of the Regional Command and influential among the party's Trade Unionists.[1] Another five members were expelled following the clandestine version of the Seventh National Congress in which they participated in mid-August.[2]

The Seceders (*munshiqqūn*), as Shufi's faction came to be called in Ba'thi parlance, were by that time significantly represented by active supporters in only four out of the party's 13 civilian branches in Syria: Damascus, Deir az-Zor, Suweida, and Hasakkeh.[3] The line taken by the Regional Command and the committees it delegated was to combat those who persisted in their association with the Seceders but to tolerate their passive sympathizers. The latter, in turn, found it easier to reconcile themselves to a party adopting an increasingly leftist orientation.

A politically more consequential aspect of the reorganization process was the admission to the party, on a large scale, of the 1962 *Quṭriyyūn*, often at the expense of their counterparts the *Qaumiyyūn* (Nationalists), those who in 1962 had joined 'Aflaq's reconstituted party. Part of the *Quṭriyyūn* had already returned to the Ba'th at various stages since March 1963, but in the summer of 1964 the gates were opened wide for them while many of those whose membership was terminated happened to be 'Aflaq's supporters.[4] Razzaz' accusations to this effect are corroborated at least in part by the Organiza-

[1] According to the *Organizational Report* submitted to the Second Regular Regional Congress and published among its resolutions (p. 39). The resolutions of this congress and the reports submitted to it were reproduced and published in a lengthy booklet distributed to the party members after the *coup* of February 23, 1966. Obviously, the Regional Command considered the document a good presentation of its case against the National Command that had been ousted by the *coup*. As for Hakim and Abu Salih, they continued for a number of weeks to agitate against Bitar. See *Chronology of Arab Politics* (1964), p. 297, and Radio London, August 20, 1964, 6:00 p.m.

[2] See above, p. 107.

[3] *Organizational Report*, pp. 28, 31–32, 36, and 37.

[4] Razzaz, *op. cit.*, p. 111. The process of purging was carried out under the banner of "evaluation of membership", a procedure regulated by articles 99 and 100 of the

Ḥafiz al-Asad

Muḥammad 'Umran

Syrian delegation arriving at Cairo. From left to right: Dr. Ibrahim Makhus, Dr. Yusuf Z'ayyin, General Ahmad Sweidani, Colonel 'Abd al-Karim Jundi, Egyptian Premier Sidki Suleiman

tional Report submitted to the Regional Congress in February 1965. Thus, in the numerically small branch of Deir az-Zor in northeastern Syria, which numbered less than 100 members, 107 *Quṭriyyūn* applied for admission. Some of them were admitted by the committee sent from Damascus and directly placed in positions of leadership and empowered to decide later on the applications of their colleagues. The same report mentions the "*Qaumiyyūn-Quṭriyyūn* issue" as a source of friction in two branches and relates how the provincial governor (*muḥāfiẓ*) of Idlib in northwestern Syria, feuding with the party's local leaders, accused them of "Sa'dism" (*sa'diyya*) and was in turn charged by them with siding with Bitar's faction (*at-takattul bi Salāḥ al-Bitār*). Supporting Bitar, it was implied, became in the eyes of the Regional Command a deviation equated with supporting Sa'di. Another incident recounted in the report indicates that the National Command tried to use its authority as the party's highest Command to help its supporters. After the Regional Command had deposed the leaders of the Raqqah Branch, the latter complained to the National Command which stripped the Regional Command of its authority with regard to that particular branch. Such measures, however, were obviously ineffective,[5] since the National Command lacked the effective means to enforce its decisions in the Syrian party organization.

The terms *Quṭrī* and *Qaumī* represented not only the names of two party factions originating in 1962; they also referred to supporters of the Regional and National Commands in 1964. It so happened that the *Quṭriyyūn* became the supporters of the Regional Command, while 'Aflaq maintained a modicum of influence in Syria through the National Command. Thus, the terminology could be used to indicate both a current political position and its historic antecedent.

Changes like those which took place in the Deir az-Zor Branch occurred also, though possibly on a smaller scale, in other branches, and by the end of 1964 had transformed the infrastructure of the Syrian Ba'th. The newly admitted *Quṭriyyūn* shared the Regional

party's Internal Regulation. According to the *Organizational Report* (p. 40), the Regional Command ordered the branches to admit the former *Quṭriyyūn* as full members and not as "supporters" (*anṣār*) as the Internal Regulation required.

[5] *Ibid.*, pp. 17, 29–30, 36.

Command's hostility towards ʿAflaq and Bitar, and they too advocated social and economic changes that would lend the party popular support and maintained a very reserved stance towards Nasser and the Syrian Nasserites. This affinity and community of interests led the *Quṭriyyūn* to amalgamate with the supporters of the Regional Command, and together they came to dominate the party's hierarchy and most of its branches.

The fierce feuds between rival political factions combined with a variety of other factors to reduce the party machinery to a most disorderly state. The attempts to overhaul this machinery and forge it into an efficient instrument of power and control constituted the other important facet of the reorganization process begun in June 1964.

Between July 23 and 25 the branch secretaries of the Syrian Baʿth were summoned to a conference which, in a long series of resolutions, laid the basis for further reforms. It reasserted the role of the Regional Command as the supreme political authority in Syria and proceeded to set three major goals for the party: (a) to bring it to the level of orderly operation in accordance with its own by-laws; (b) to consolidate the party's hold on the governmental bureaucracy by manning the latter with party members whenever possible; and (c) to solve the contradictions between the party and the "front organizations" (*al-munaẓẓamāt al-wājihiyya ash-shaʿbiyya*) and to assure the party's control over them.[6] This last resolution referred to the Baʿth's failure to set up and manipulate solid professional and other "popular" organizations, the absence of which had been so clearly demonstrated and acutely felt during the February-April crisis. Moreover, the party's representatives in the existing organizations, whether leftists of the Shufi school or others, had not yet been brought under the control of the Regional Command.

The resolutions of the conference reflected the lessons learnt by the Regional Command from the crisis of the spring. The party had failed to penetrate the Syrian population and to mobilize sufficient

[6] Circular issued by the Regional Command on July 26, 1964. A marked difference is noticeable between these resolutions and those of the Sixth National Congress. The party no longer wished to be an elitist vanguard uninvolved with governmental routine but seems to have come to the conclusion that control of the bureaucracy was a source of power that the party could not dispense with.

popular support and it now set out to remedy these weaknesses. The overhauled party machinery, the reformed front organizations, and the party-controlled bureaucracy were to consolidate Ba'thi rule in Syria.

It was the Command's awareness that the success of such an orientation depended on the party's ability to recruit more of its membership from the popular classes that led it somewhat later to employ the concept of "dual organization" (*at-tanẓīm al-muzdawaj*). The party, according to the scheme released in mid-August, was to divide its branches (*furū'*) into subbranches (*shu'ab* and *firaq*) based on either a regional or sectorial/professional criterion. In accordance with the latter criterion, workers, traders and craftsmen, women, university and high-school students and teachers were to be registered in separate subbranches while maintaining their affiliation with the regional ones.[7] The scheme was obviously designed to enable the Ba'th to pervade Syrian society and, by becoming an efficient instrument of control, to consolidate the regime's hold over the country.

This rather ambitious plan was far beyond the actual capabilities of the Ba'th at that stage (and even later too) and was indeed never implemented.[8] Its significance rests rather in its indication of the Regional Command's long-term intentions. Still, while failing to implement this grander plan, the Regional Command was able to raise the organizational standards in the party that it now closely controlled and could use against its rivals.

THE CONFRONTATION WITH THE NATIONAL COMMAND

These changes were incompatible with the personality of Salah al-Bitar and with the outlook he represented, and pressure was building up during the summer to oust him from the premiership and to change the nature and composition of the cabinet. It seems that the decision to do so was postponed only because of the approaching

[7] Bulletin issued by the Regional Command on August 17, 1964.

[8] A bulletin issued by the Regional Command on June 7, 1965, confirmed that this project was not implemented.

Second Arab Summit Conference held in Alexandria between September 5 and 11, 1964. After all, the formation of Bitar's cabinet had also been conceived as a gesture designed to improve Syria's relations with the other Arab states, and it would have been unbecoming to dissolve it on the eve of the conference. The Second Summit Conference did not produce the strong intra-party tensions that the first one had, but it revealed the difficulties involved in relying on the radical elements at home while trying to pursue a more realistic policy abroad. In the aftermath of the conference the Regional Command felt the need to issue an apologetic circular addressed to the party members attempting to justify Syria's cooperation with the "reactionary" regimes.[9]

Once the conference was over, the Regional Command decided on September 25 "to withdraw its confidence" from Bitar's cabinet and to replace it with one headed by Amin al-Hafiz.[10] The explanation given to the party members included a denunciation of Bitar's soft line towards the internal "Reaction", the rightist orientation of his cabinet, and his failure to interact with the party. It was also claimed that by uniting the functions of premier and chairman of the Presidency Council in one person, all potential risks of the contradictions between the two executive bodies would be eliminated.[11] What these explanations amounted to was an assertion that the extraordinary circumstances that had resulted from the "Hama Revolt" no longer existed and that the structural and political changes introduced in its wake could be revoked. The governmental structure was now shaped to suit the trends outlined by the party in July and August.

Bitar and his associate Mansur al-Atrash resigned from the Presidency Council and were replaced by General Salah J'did and Dr. Yusuf Z'ayyin. Thus the Council came under the complete control of the Military Committee and the Regional Command. The Council

[9] Undated circular issued by the Cultural Bureau of the Regional Command "On the Second Arab Summit Conference".

[10] *Organizational Report* submitted to the Second Regular Regional Congress (p. 26). For the composition of the new cabinet see Appendix A.

[11] *Ibid.*, pp. 26–27, the *Political Report* presented to the same congress, p. 69, and the bulletin issued by the Regional Command on October 7, 1964, under the title "Concerning the Formation of the New Cabinet".

was more firmly established in a supervisory capacity over the cabinet as its members were each put in charge of a certain sphere of governmental activity.[12] The new cabinet was formed on October 3 and the Regional Command saw fit to emphasize that this cabinet (unlike its predecessor) was almost exclusively composed of party members.[13] In previous cabinets non-party members were included so as to demonstrate a broader basis of support for the regime; this time it was deemed more important to show that the party was in actual control of the government. The new minister of labour, it was also emphasized, came from the ranks of the Trade Unionists, an indication of the party's intention to consolidate its position in that sector.

The same bulletin informed the party members that some of the new ministers were former *Quṭriyyūn*, defined as "other elements from among former members whose return to the party had been prevented by certain special circumstances". This illustrated how deep was the transformation that the Syrian Ba'th had undergone during the summer of 1964—newly readmitted members were almost immediately given cabinet posts.

The same orientation was evident in the unpublicized platform of the Hafiz cabinet.[14] It affirmed that it was the party that ruled Syria in theory and practice, and proposed to set up rapidly a General Peasants Union and to reform the existing Workers Federation. The new government, it declared, would seek to speed up the implementation of the Agrarian Reform and to "deepen" the experiment of nationalization and self-management. The platform took a noncommittal stance towards Egypt, possibly because of the negotiations with President Nasser that were held during the visit of a Ba'thi delegation to Cairo, where it had gone to participate in the Conference of Nonaligned Nations.[15]

The cabinet, in cooperation with the Regional Command, proceeded to carry out these policies. On October 8 a second congress of branch secretaries was held in Damascus and they were particularly urged to submit practical recommendations regarding the agrarian

[12] *Chronology of Arab Politics* (1964), p. 405.

[13] Regional Command's bulletin of October 7.

[14] *Ibid.*

[15] This platform was echoed by the new minister of information, Mash̲hur Zaytun, speaking on October 4 to newsmen (*al-Ba'th*, October 5, 1964).

problem in their respective regions. In mid-October the General Workers Federation decided to hold a general congress in Homs at the end of that month. But the impetus of this organizational activity was temporarily halted by the new turn that the internal struggle in the Ba'th had taken.

Weakened as 'Aflaq and Bitar were in Syria, they still held their position in the National Command and with it extensive sway and the moral advantage of speaking in the name of the party's supreme authority. The ruling party rivals had to acknowledge their status as long as they wished to rule in the name of a pan-Arab party. The ability of 'Aflaq and Bitar to translate these advantages into concrete political assets in Syria depended on circumstances. In the summer of 1964 they were helpless against a solid front of the Military Committee and its civilian associates, but the subsequent exacerbation of the conflict between Generals Hafiz and 'Umran enabled them to reassume an active role in Syrian politics in November-December of that year.

The Military Committee had never been a homogeneous body, and divisions and tensions in its upper ranks had already surfaced on a number of occasions.[16] Late in 1964 these centred on the rivalry of Hafiz and 'Umran. The two officers competed for the leadership of the army and, beyond it, the regime. 'Umran, coming from a poor 'Alawi family,[17] had some advantages over his rival. As one of the founders of the Military Committee and for some time its most prominent member, he built a strong personal faction, and as the ex-commander of an armoured brigade he still had supporters in key military positions. More than any other 'Alawi officer 'Umran was identified with the policy of mass recruitment of fellow 'Alawis and their placement in sensitive offices.[18] But after failing to secure for himself the post of chief of staff 'Umran had little formal authority. As deputy premier in charge of industrial affairs he was politically neutralized and personally unsatisfied.

[16] See above, p. 118.

[17] Vernier, *op. cit.*, p. 144, states that 'Umran is an 'Alawi from the Homs Plain whose father was a gendarme and that he had been a teacher prior to joining the Officers Academy. But in "Le rôle politique de l'armée en Syrie", *Politique Etrangère* (1965), p. 466, Vernier says that his mother was a servant and that his father had to sell his cow to support his son's education.

[18] Razzaz, *op. cit.*, pp. 116 and 187–189.

Amin al-Hafiz, on the other hand, was a newcomer to the Military Committee and since he had not held an active command post for several years he did not have a well-placed military faction (*kutla*) of his own supporters. But he enjoyed the extensive authority vested in the office of commander-in-chief and in the other positions he held, and he had two other important advantages. He was an urban Sunni (from Aleppo), the only prominent one among the regime's military leaders. The regime also benefited from the charismatic quality that Hafiz seemed to possess—he was elegant, suave, ruthless, and spoke in a traditional style that still appealed to most of the population.[19] His popularity was an asset that the regime could hardly afford to lose.

The circumstances in which Hafiz left for a private visit to Paris, where he underwent an operation (October 26 to November 12), seemed to indicate that 'Umran had the upper hand in the personal struggle between the two military leaders.[20] However, in due course, Hafiz returned from the trip and with Salah J'did's help was able to isolate 'Umran. It was typical of Ba'thi politics that the struggle was kept indoors with neither side trying to resort to violence. Whoever commanded more military support won tacitly and there was no need to display the might of the respective camps in public and to risk the very existence of the regime.

The whole episode pointed also to the limits of confessional solidarity as a determining factor in Syrian politics of the period. Confessional solidarity had played an important role in bringing 'Umran, J'did and Hafiz al-Asad together, but it did not prevent the latter two 'Alawis from supporting the Sunni Hafiz against 'Umran when their personal and factional interests pointed in that direction. 'Umran was accused by his 'Alawi rivals of "sectarianism" (*ṭā'ifiyya*)

[19] Shimali in *ath-Thaura,* November 20 and 21, 1968, in an attempt to discredit Hafiz, says he used to speak like a Bedouin Shaykh and that he never read anything beyond Arabic literature. But perhaps what seemed so distasteful to young party ideologists appealed to more traditional elements of Syrian society.

[20] Hafiz' kidney trouble had been reported some time before that (*al-Usbū' al-'arabī* [Beirut], June 1, 1964), but the tension that shrouded the military manoeuvres held on the eve of Hafiz' departure and the appointment of 'Umran as his temporary substitute gave rise to the feeling that Hafiz had been defeated. See *Arab Political Documents* (1964), pp. 435–436 and 537–538, and Radio Damascus, Octover 27, 1964, 9:15 p.m., and October 28, 1964, 7:15 a.m.

and he was indeed associated in the public mind more than other 'Alawi officers with fostering communal loyalty in the process of building his personal faction. During this crisis Asad, by then commander of the airforce and a political figure in his own right, played for the first time an overt political role.[21]

Defeated in the military sector, 'Umran turned to 'Aflaq and Bitar and offered his cooperation. His move was hardly surprising as he was closest to them and to their outlook among the military. In 1962 he had collaborated closely with the Nasserites and he later supported the readmission of the Socialist Unionists to the Ba'th, conducted the negotiations with them, and when they failed, he reportedly objected to the mass readmission of the rival *Quṭriyyūn*. 'Umran was generally believed to advocate moderate policies at home and a reconciliation with Nasser.[22] His rapprochement with 'Aflaq and Bitar had begun earlier in 1964 but it turned into political cooperation only after his defeat at the hands of Hafiz and J'did in November. He himself was a member of the National Command and he now strengthened the status of that body as representing the moderate wing of the Ba'th. 'Umran, moreover, brought with him into the alliance some military support and inside information. Only upon hearing 'Umran's account, says Razzaz, did the National Command comprehend how far-reaching the ambitions and designs of the Military Committee had been.

The reinforcement his supporters had gained through the adhesion of 'Umran seemed promising enough for 'Aflaq to terminate his self-imposed exile in Germany and return on November 23 to Damascus.[23] Soon afterward a joint meeting of the National and

[21] Razzaz, *op. cit.*, p. 138. On the position of Hafiz al-Asad see Radio Baghdad, Dec. 17, 1964, 9:00 a.m., and *Arab Political Documents* (1964), pp. 525–526.

[22] Jundi, *op. cit.*, pp. 141–144 and 147–148, and *Documentary Report*, pp. 34–42 and 63–64. The *Report* quotes Hafiz, who at that time accused 'Umran of being "Cairo's man", of maintaining private contacts with the Egyptians, and so forth. During the "Hama Crisis" 'Umran tried to pursue a conciliatory line, for which he was denounced by various rivals. Shimali in *ath-Thaura*, November 20 and 21, 1968, accused him of being altogether ready to desert the party during those difficult days.

[23] Razzaz, *op. cit.*, p. 115. 'Aflaq in his February 18, 1966, speech, and 'Umran, *op. cit.*, pp. 23–24, in his unreliable account of this episode do not relate 'Aflaq's return to the newly formed alliance between 'Umran and the 'Aflaq-Bitar wing, but it can hardly be explained otherwise.

Regional Commands was held, at which 'Aflaq and his supporters confronted the Regional Command with 'Umran's revelations in an attempt to embarrass it and regain the political initiative. Far from being intimidated, the Military Committee brought the Regional Command to pass a resolution stripping 'Umran of his party functions and banishing him from Syria. It was the occasion for 'Umran's rivals to settle their accounts with him and to list all his "sins" going back to his conduct during the period between March 28 and April 4, 1962.[24] In response, the National Command held a lengthy session (December 4–14) attended alternately by nine or 11 of its members and adopted a series of momentous resolutions.

Asserting its position as the supreme legal authority in the Ba'th Party, the National Command stated that the measures taken by the Regional Command against 'Umran were illegal and should be ignored. The Regional Command was reprimanded for adopting them and was suspended by the National Command which decreed that, pending the next Regional Congress, the Syrian party was to be led by a National Committee (*lajna qaumiyya*).

This *coup* was accompanied by several other resolutions designed to solve radically the problem of the relationship between the military and civilian sectors of the party. The National Command ordered that the Military Committee be replaced by a Military Bureau (*maktab 'askarī*) that was to be one of the several bureaus of the Regional Command. The Bureau would coordinate the party's military branches as well as a projected network of "Politruks" (*muwajjihūn siyāsiyyūn*). Furthermore, the military were given a month to choose between their military positions and their state and party functions. A party member would be allowed to occupy only two prominent offices simultaneously (but the National Command granted Hafiz temporary immunity from this rule, perhaps in an attempt to win him to its side).[25]

The National Command's action was completely out of touch with reality. Not only did the Military Committee possess sufficient martial power to force its will, but it did not even have to resort to it.

[24] Razzaz, *op. cit.*, p. 130.

[25] This account is based on a circular issued by the National Command in mid-December 1964 and on Razzaz' version (*op. cit.*, p. 116).

By December 1964 its control of the Syrian party organization was so complete that it could immediately mobilize it in support of its position. When the National Command demanded that the branch secretaries be convened, hoping to find support among them against the Regional Command, it failed utterly. The National Command could not even document its claim that it was supported by the rank and file. 'Umran had to leave Syria as ambassador to Spain and the Military Committee and the Regional Command emerged victorious.[26] But this was not merely a passing episode. The divisions in the ranks of the Ba'thi military produced by the struggle with 'Umran were not healed but developed into a consequential schism that 'Aflaq and Bitar were again to exploit, this time with a greater measure of success.

THE SOCIALIST MEASURES OF JANUARY 1965

The implementation of the programme drawn up by the Regional Command and the Hafiz cabinet was hardly interrupted by the December crisis. It seems rather that the confrontation with the moderate wing of the party convinced the Regional Command that it ought to hasten those projects that were designed to consolidate its hold over Syria. Thus, the party branches were urgently requested in the second week of December to submit lists of candidates for the General Peasants Union, and a decree establishing the Union was published on December 14. On December 16 two more decrees were issued, the first amending the Agrarian Reform Law by simplifying the process of land expropriation, and the second confining the exploitation of Syrian oil to the state and thus nationalizing it in advance, so to speak.[27] Still, the series of decrees early in January 1965, which nationalized practically all Syrian industry, came abruptly

[26] *Ibid.*, pp. 116–117, and an Internal Bulletin issued by the Temporary Regional Command on March 1, 1966, in which it reviewed the conflict which led to the *coup* of February 23, 1966. The National Command's surprise at the outcome of the confrontation is also illustrated by the optimistic announcement of its spokesman who on December 16 promised that its resolutions would soon be published. They were not.

[27] The decrees and their respective serial numbers are mentioned in the *Economic Report* submitted to the Second Regular Regional Congress, pp. 148–149.

and gave rise to the charge by the National Command and its supporters that their promulgation was an improvised political manoeuvre designed to present the Regional Command as the "leftist" and "progressive" side in its quarrel with the National Command.[28]

It does indeed seem that the timing of these nationalization measures, known later as "The Ramaḍān Socialist Decrees", was to a considerable extent determined by such political considerations. They were obviously prepared in a hasty manner so that among the 114 companies nationalized on January 2 and 4 several workshops were included that by size and nature did not belong in the category of industries; they were indeed returned later to their owners. The Regional Command's party rivals even charged that the lists were prepared according to the telephone directory. The government claimed it was misled by false information supplied by the owners, but this could at best mean that their statements were not properly checked.[29] The political overtones of the nationalization decrees were also indicated by the calls published on the pages of the government newspaper *ath-Thaura* on January 5 and 12 for "Arab leftists" to rally in support of the regime, thus implying that it was struggling against rightist opponents.

But while such tactical considerations may have accounted for the timing of the nationalization decrees, they did not play an important role in the decision to pass them in the first place. This decision was a natural outcome of the political and economic conditions created by earlier nationalization measures and of the line pursued by the Regional Command since early in the summer of 1964, and had been adumbrated in the unpublicized platform of Hafiz' new cabinet written in the first week of October. The explanations offered by the

[28] Razzaz, *op. cit.*, pp. 104–105 and 116–117, 'Umran, *op. cit.*, pp. 344–346. 'Aflaq, in a speech he delivered at the National Command's meeting on December 19, 1965, said that the nationalization decrees were also a manoeuvre designed to hide a crisis and compared them to Nasser's nationalization measures in July 1961 (*Documentary Report*, p. 21).

[29] Bulletin issued by the Regional Command on January 5, *al-Ḥayāt,* January 20, and *Arab Political Documents* (1965), p. 17. According to the official statistics, the nationalized companies had a capital of over 243 million Syrian pounds and employed over 11,780 workers.

Regional Command to its own supporters point to some of the considerations that motivated it to nationalize Syrian industry and several other sectors of the economy.

The piecemeal nationalizations carried out since May 1963 had by the middle of 1964 created a small public sector and had given the government a more important role in directing the economy. More specifically, the government had nationalized the banks, insurance companies, and nine mercantile companies, and had acquired a quarter ownership in 15 other companies. By accelerating the execution of the Agrarian Reform the government had introduced another important economic change. Such a degree of nationalization and intervention could in principle agree with the policy of détente which Bitar had initiated with some measure of economic success[30] in May 1964, but it certainly was out of tune with the increasingly leftist line adopted later in 1964. The middle classes were frightened into smuggling out whatever capital they still had in Syria[31] or at least into freezing it and abstaining from even minor investments. The government, on the other hand, did not sufficiently dominate the economy to be able to combat effectively the economic deterioration. The situation, complained the Regional Command, had "all the evils of a liberal regime without its advantages".[32] Therefore, while the nationalizations of January 1965 and their sequels could be explained on economic grounds, they were in reality brought about by broader considerations.

It seems that once the leadership of the Syrian Ba'th started the process of consolidating its hold over Syrian society it was bound to discover that Nasser had been right in telling the Ba'thi delegates repeatedly during the Cairo Unity Talks that this could not be done without controlling the economy. The events of the spring exposed the weakness of a regime that could not mobilize wide support in the

30 J. De Buck, "Les nationalisations en Syrie", *Correspondence d'Orient,* VII (1965), pp. 61–67.

31 Official Syrian sources suggested the fantastic figure of 800 million Syrian pounds as the total sum of the capital smuggled into Lebanon and Switzerland (*Chronology of Arab Politics* [1965], p. 67), but among themselves the Ba'this admitted they had no specific data (*Economic Report,* p. 137).

32 Regional Command's bulletin of January 6, 1965.

country, and one of their consequences was the resurgence of Bitar and the alternative he offered—reconciling the middle classes to the regime. That solution was unacceptable to the military and their civilian associates who now came out with an alternative of their own. Rather than reconcile the bourgeoisie, the Regional Command sought to take economic power into its hands in order to dispense with the upper-middle classes and to accomodate the lower-middle classes who were supposed to abjure political ambitions and power. These considerations emerge clearly from the explanations that the Regional Command offered to party members immediately after the nationalization and a few weeks later during the Second Regional Congress of the Syrian Ba'th.

The high bourgeoisie, it was claimed, was an implacable enemy: "[the private sector] knows that this regime (*'ahd*) is not its regime, whatever assurances it gives, and that the interests of the business owners would be guaranteed only if the government were in the hands of that class".[33] Since it was useless to try to come to terms with this class, it was better to terminate its economic (and political) power and to transfer it to the government, even if this was bound to produce political tensions in the short run.[34] The profits of trade and industry, 500 million Syrian pounds yearly according to Ba'thi calculations, would moreover be made available to the government. As for the lower-middle classes, government control of the major branches of the economy would make small-scale traders and artisans dependent on it rather than on the traditional middle men. Along with this level-headed argumentation there are some indications of a strong "anti-bourgeois" sentiment among radical military and civilian party members, which may have generated a political climate suitable for the leftward turn but does not seem to have directly motivated it. Such sentiments moved several Ba'thi officers to insist that the conservative agitators sentenced to death in January 1965 be executed (they were not). Unlike their predecessors of late 1963, the Ba'thi radicals of 1965 were firmly under control.

The nationalization measures of early January were supplemented during the first half of 1965 by government takeover of the import and

[33] *Economic Report*, p. 137.

[34] *Ibid.*, pp. 148 and 138 (written perhaps with a measure of hindsight).

export trade and of the major branches of wholesale commerce to make the public sector dominant in the Syrian economy.[35]

Opposition to the nationalization decrees in January was rather ineffective. Attempts were made throughout January to strike shops in Damascus and to incite the crowd at Friday prayers, but the results were far from resembling the crisis of February-May 1964. In January 1965 the opposition encountered a Ba'thi leadership that was more resolute, better established, and certainly not surprised by the show of resistance. Strikers and demonstrators were sternly dealt with: struck shops were seized and several agitators were sentenced to death by the reactivated Emergency Courts (and later reprieved).

More significantly, perhaps, the events of January revealed that the Ba'th regime had in the meanwhile been able to gain some influence even over the Islamic religious hierarchy. Following a call on January 24 by a group of *'ulamā'* urging the people to strike, a decree was issued on January 28 giving the Presidency Council legal authority over the religious hierarchy.[36] According to the decree, all powers pertaining to the supreme and regional *waqf* councils were transferred to the Presidency Council. The latter body was empowered to appoint and dismiss *imāms* (preachers) and other religious functionaries. A more acquiescent grand mufti, Shaykh Ahmad Kaftaru, had already been appointed and on February 7 he headed a delegation of *'ulamā'* that came to express its support of the regime.[37]

A shift to the left at home need not, but in fact often will, be followed by a change of orientation in a country's foreign relations. Thus the events of January 1965 were to some degree instrumental in the deterioration of Syria's relations with the West and in the corresponding strengthening of its ties with the Soviet Union. The trials of the anti-regime agitators arrested in January were coloured by revelations about alleged American financing of the latest anti-Ba'thi plot.[38] Syrian negotiations with West Germany on German aid

[35] B. Hansen, *Economic Development in Syria* (Rand Corporation, Santa Monica, Calif., 1969), p. 5.

[36] The decree was broadcast by Radio Damascus on January 28, 1965, 9:15 p.m.

[37] *Chronology of Arab Politics* (1965), p. 72.

[38] See for instance Radio Damascus, January 31, 1965, 07:15 p.m. This was followed by more concrete charges levelled at the American embassy in Damascus during

in building the Euphrates Dam were complicated by Syrian refusal to grant oil concessions to the German firm Concordia that had already invested in oil prospecting in the Jazira Province.[39] The change in Syria's international orientation and its relation to the leftward swing within the country were explained in the "political report" presented to the Regional Congress in March. It apologized for relinquishing the party's traditional line of nonalignment and justified it by stressing Western hostility to the Ba'th regime and by pointing out the affinity between it and the socialist states—". . . also, the socialist road which we follow is part of the human heritage of the socialism followed by the states of the socialist camp. . . ."[40]

Except for 1957–58, the Soviet attitude towards the Ba'th had been at best skeptic[41] and became even more so with the Ba'thi persecution and massacre of Iraqi Communists early in 1963. This attitude began to change in 1964 both as a result of developments within Syria and of a revision of the Soviet approach to "the radical petty bourgeoisie".[42] The nationalization measures adopted since January 1965 further facilitated this change and were hailed by the Soviets and by the local Communist Party.[43]

To the extent that these measures were related to the intra-Ba'thi struggle they did embarrass the 'Aflaq-Bitar wing whose leaders could not afford openly or directly to criticize the implementation of

the espionage trial in February 1965, which resulted in the execution of a Syrian officer and a Syrian-born naturalized American. See *Arab Political Documents* (1965), pp. 61–65.

[39] See *ibid.* (1965), pp. 15 and 53–54. The above-mentioned decree of December 16 nationalizing, so to speak, Syria's oil resources may have been linked to these negotiations. See also Shimali in *ath-Thaura,* November 23, 1968, for a post hoc "leftist" criticism of the negotiations with West Germany.

[40] *Political Report,* p. 80.

[41] "Soviet Opinions on Syria and the Ba'th", *Mizan,* VIII (1966), pp. 73–79.

[42] *Ibid.*, p. 79. According to N. Safran, *From War to War* (New York, 1969), p. 231, shipment of Soviet armaments to Syria was renewed late in 1964.

[43] "Soviet Opinions", pp. 81–82, and *Resolutions of the Extraordinary Regional Congress of the Syrian Ba'th in March 1966*, p. 16. For evaluation by Syrian Communist leaders of the nationalization measures of 1965 see Kh. Baghdache, "La Syrie sur une voie nouvelle", *Orient,* IX (1965), pp. 109–128, and M. Salibi, "Syrian Communists in the Fight for Social Progress", *World Marxist Review,* VIII (1965), pp. 76–78.

socialism. In his public pronouncements of the period 'Aflaq chose, therefore, to offer an implicit criticism of the January decrees and he somewhat adapted his terminology to suit the seemingly fashionable leftward trend. Thus he referred to the "Arab path to socialism" rather than to "Arab Socialism", stressed the need to benefit from the experience of other nations (a demand raised in the past by leftist Ba'this), and tried to belittle the significance of the Ba'th's past quarrels with the Communists. Still, as he had done earlier in his introduction to the *Points of Departure,* 'Aflaq defended the Ba'th's heritage and original contributions as well as his own role.[44] In private discussions during that period, he spoke differently and accused the Regional Command of *iqlīmiyya* (provincial nationalism) like that of the PPS. Such insinuations may have been specifically directed at Salah J'did whose brother, Ghassan, it will be recalled, had been a PPS militant and, accused by the Ba'this of engineering the assassination of 'Adnan al-Maliki, was killed by Syrian agents in Beirut.[45]

'Aflaq's public and private arguments of the period were tied to the elections held in preparation for the Second Regular Regional Congress which had begun early in January. The decision to hold the elections was passed by the Regional Command on January 4 and the elections themselves took place between January 10 and 24. As earlier developments had indicated, the party's hierarchy was firmly controlled by the Regional Command and short of polemics there was little that 'Aflaq could do by way of preparation for the congress.

THE SECOND REGULAR REGIONAL CONGRESS, MARCH 18–APRIL 4, 1965

The weakness of the 'Aflaq-Bitar wing and its inability to intervene in the Syrian party branches did not turn the elections for the Regional Congress into a routine procedure and a matter of course.

[44] See 'Aflaq's interview with the Ba'th's organ in Beirut, *al-Aḥrār,* January 6, 1965 (*Arab Political Documents* [1965], pp. 5–6), his statement of January 12 (*ibid.*, pp. 8–9), his address on the second anniversary of the Ba'thi Revolution in Iraq (*ibid.*, pp. 42–45), and *Arab Political Documents* (1965), pp. 44–45.

[45] See *Documentary Report,* p. 16.

There were other issues and differences to divide the membership, and a survey of the irregularities which accompanied the elections in several branches vividly illustrates some aspects of the everyday reality of party life in the Ba'th. The *Organizational Report* submitted to the congress by the outgoing Regional Command complained of "organizational factionalism" (*takattul tanẓīmī*), as electoral blocs were formed in certain branches along the division between "city and countryside, natives of the area and outsiders, [residents of] one region and [residents of] another region".[46] In some cases, complained the same report, the governmental authorities (*'anāṣir as-sulṭa*) intervened to secure the success of a candidate or even a whole list of their liking[47] as against another local faction. Perhaps most embarrassing was the discovery that the Ba'th was not fully insulated from the traditional segments of society it was expected to transform. Outside forces were reported to have meddled in the intra-party elections; in one case it was a tribal shaykh who championed a particular list in one of the branches, transported voters in his car, and closely followed the results of the elections.[48]

The Regional Command's overwhelming victory in these elections did not blind it to the weaknesses and defects thus revealed. One of the major issues in the ensuing Regional Congress was, indeed, the effort to rationalize and solidify the party's organizational structure. Though affected by the confrontation with the National Command in December 1964 and by several other urgent political problems, the congress was relatively free of the crisis atmosphere that characterized most previous and later party congresses, and the Regional Command could therefore devote more time and attention to long-range cures for the party's ills.

The congress decided that such structural and political weaknesses as were exposed by the latest elections were to be corrected by a reform of the party's organization in Syria. The number of the Regional Command's members was reduced to 11, six of them free

[46] *Organizational Report*, p. 43.

[47] *Ibid*, In another section of the report (p. 34) a case in point from the Raqqah Branch in northern Syria, is cited to illustrate the nature of such interventions. A peasant member is reported to have revealed to the Regional Command that he had been given a list of candidates and had been sworn on the Quran to vote for them.

[48] *Ibid.*, p. 44.

from any other duty so that they could devote their full time and attention to party work (in the party jargon they were called *a'aḍā' mutafarrighūn*). Each of these six was put in charge of a party bureau responsible for a certain aspect of the party's activity, such as the Peasants Bureau or the Cultural Bureau. In the branches the same pattern was followed; a minimal number of *mutafarrighūn* was set for branches and subbranches, and the same bureaus were to be established in each branch to deal with the same issues on the local level.[49]

In order to raise the standards of membership it was decided to reduce the ratio of new admissions and to expand the ranks of those who were merely organized party supporters and candidates for membership—the *anṣār*. The distinction among degrees of membership had been instituted in order to guarantee wide support for the party without flooding it with unsuitable new members. Owing to the party's feeling of weakness and to factional struggles these distinctions had lost much of their significance in 1964 and 1965, as new members were rapidly promoted to full membership and to leadership roles. With the relative consolidation that was felt to have been achieved in the spring of 1965, it was decided to regulate the organization of the *anṣār* so as to continue the process of penetrating Syrian society without further subjecting the party to the ill effects of rapid expansion. Related to it was the decision to expand the popular and professional mass organizations that would formally be independent of the party but in reality be controlled by it.[50]

A social and economic report was submitted to the congress, which surveyed and explained the latest nationalization measures and recommended future policies. The congress did not have the time to review the lengthy report but it passed several resolutions on social and economic issues and decided to reconvene for a later extraordinary session. For that session a comprehensive programme of social and economic policies called *al-minhāj al-marḥalī* (The Temporary Programme) was to be prepared.

A number of important resolutions concerned the regime's constitutional structure. Spurred by the events of December 1964, the

[49] *Ibid.*, pp. 46–47 and 232.

[50] *Ibid.*, pp. 45, 76–78.

Regional Command set out decisively to establish its superiority over the National Command with regard to Syrian affairs. The congress commended the Regional Command for its conduct during "the latest crises", thus implicitly reprimanding the National Command, and it clearly designated the Regional Command as that level in the party's leadership which should lead the government. The congress could not go further than that in reducing the National Command's authority without pushing 'Aflaq into overt opposition, which his rivals could not as yet afford.[51]

In more specific terms it was decided that the Regional Command, as elected by the Regional Congress, would nominate the members of the Presidency Council and the premier. The regional secretary would ex officio be chairman of the Presidency Council. Since Amin al-Hafiz, who was to hold these two positions, was at that time the Syrian premier, it was explicitly stated that all these positions could be held simultaneously.[52] The congress then decreed that the time had come to implement the broadening of the NCRC into that quasi-parliamentary body that the Temporary Constitution of April 1964 had promised. This was to be another measure of consolidation and normalization.

As had been the case with the previous Regional Congresses, the Second Regular Congress was to be followed by a National Congress, the Eighth, originally scheduled to meet in August 1964 but postponed for a number of reasons. Preparations for the congress were naturally affected by the struggle between the National and Syrian Regional Commands. Powerful as the latter had become in Syria, it was hardly able to influence party organizations abroad, whose loyalty to 'Aflaq and Bitar was strengthened by the secession and ouster of leftist supporters of Sa'di. The Regional Command, through the machinery of the Syrian government which it controlled, tried to manipulate support in non-Syrian branches, but with little success at that stage.[53]

[51] *Ibid.*, pp. 54–55 and 57–58. Politically the Regional Command's posture seemed also to be strengthened by the decision of the "Seceders", led by Shufi himself, to apply for readmission into the Ba'th.

[52] *Ibid.*, p. 73. The statement probably referred to the prohibition by the National Command of such an accumulation of powers in its resolutions of December 1964.

[53] On August 30, 1964, the National Liaison Office of the National Command (whose task was to maintain the Command's contact with the regional branches) warned

Through the incumbent National Command and its non-Syrian supporters, ʻAflaq and Bitar could thus be expected to be strongly represented at the Eighth National Congress, even though the 11-member Syrian delegation chosen by the Regional Command would be composed of the latter's supporters. This prospect worried the Regional Command and several pages of the report on the results of the Regional Congress echo its anxiety lest the December crisis between it and the National Command be discussed at the National Congress. ʻAflaq and Bitar were almost powerless in Syria, but should a National Congress rally to their support, the Regional Command ruling in the name of the party would be politically embarrassed. Moreover, the Military Committee and the Military Organization were in the midst of a crisis of which the other sections of the party were hardly aware. That crisis and its impact on the Regional Congress should be properly viewed against the background of whatever meager information is available on the history of the Syrian Baʻth's Military Organization.

The clandestine Military Committee, which after the *coup* of March 8 was recognized by the Baʻth as the supreme authority in military affairs and was thus made an official though still secretive body, set out gradually to expand its ranks and consolidate its position. Its leaders realized that they had to adapt their organization to the new conditions obtaining since the party's assumption of power; what had been good enough for a conspiratorial group was no longer sufficient for one seeking to perpetuate its rule. The solution they devised was to organize a separate Military Organization in the Syrian Baʻth, to which all reliable officers would belong and which the Military Committee would continue to lead. This may have seemed to them a good way of retaining some of the characteristics of the original clandestine group while expanding its ranks and institutionalizing it.

the party branches outside Syria not to trust any person not carrying documents issued by the National Command itself, even if that person was a certified Syrian official. The Regional Command in turn would later charge that the elections preceding the National Congress were rigged by the National Liaison Office (Internal Communiqué issued by the Temporary Regional Command on March 1, 1966).

During 1963 that Military Organization was set up with 12 branches resembling their civilian counterparts. Eight of the branches were hastily established in the period between August 1963 and February 1964 as the need arose to counter Shufi's influence on the party organization.[54] The Military Organization was led by a Central Committee (*al-lajna al-markaziyya*) representing the Military Committee. Its leaders sought to insulate it from the civilian sector of the party (in order, it seems, to prevent civilian factions from meddling in its affairs), and the two sectors of the party were joined only at the regional and national levels through the Military Committee's participation in the Regional and National Congresses and Commands.

The Military Organization maintained the secretive ways of the original Military Committee. Its sworn members committed themselves to secrecy and discipline and they were continuously warned not to divulge the existence of their Organization to other officers. The Military Committee felt that this Organization, expected as it was to guarantee their control of the army, should not be exposed and endangered.

There was a modicum of democracy within the Military Organization. As will be recalled, the Military Committee's leadership was contested in a congress held by the Organization's branch secretaries following the "Hama Revolt" and it never regained unanimous confidence. It may have been the divisions in the ranks of the Organization's leaders which encouraged some of its junior members to oppose them. This opposition, in turn, explains at least in part the Military Committee's decision in June 1964 to accept no new members into the Organization. Demands raised at that period to convene another Military Congress (as the congress of the branch secretaries was called) were evaded by the Military Committee.[55]

Little is known about the sources of internal strife in the Military Organization, but several allusions to it indicate that the majority of its rank and file were dissatisfied with the leaders of the Military Committee who rose to the highest ranks and amassed authority and

[54] Internal Bulletin on the Seventh National Congress issued by the National Command on February 22, 1964.

[55] Razzaz, *op. cit.*, p. 142.

power. Some of the original members of the Committee and fellow Ba'thi officers, among them the few party members who had taken an active part in the *coup* of March 8, held sensitive command posts, but unlike the leaders of the Committee were not promoted to the highest military ranks and were not appointed to high party and state positions. Some of them were nicknamed "the Band of Majors" (*majmū'at ar-ruwwād*) and most prominent among them were the wild-tempered Druse Major Salim Hatum and Majors Salah Dulli and Muhammad Rabah at-Tawil. Apparently these officers envied not only the leaders of the Military Committee but also civilian party militants who enjoyed an elevation of rank and status while they themselves had only a share of anonymous power which not everyone is able to enjoy and appreciate. Such tensions are sometimes inevitable but in this case they seem also to have resulted from a failure of leadership. Busy in party and national politics, Hafiz, J'did, and others like them neglected the daily chores of leadership that must be performed if one is to maintain the loyalty of his subordinates, and lost personal contact with several peers of yesterday. The tensions among the military were later explained by the party itself:

> Considering the leading role played by the first "Military Committee" following the Revolution and the many roles and functions it filled in the Party, army, and government, and the certain position thus acquired by its members, all this created a certain sensitivity between these comrades and other comrades holding lower ranks who had carried arms on the eighth of March, and between them and other comrades of various ranks who for a number of reasons preceding the Revolution could not carry arms. This tension grew daily and the Military Committee's neglect of the Organization's affairs and its preoccupation with the affairs of government and its entry into the endless struggle which existed in the leadership of the Party and the Revolution and its seclusion from the military rank and file deepened that sensitivity. . . .[56]

[56] *The Party's Crisis and the Convening of the Latest Regional Congress* (issued by the Regional Command in spring 1966), p. 21. For the activities of "the Band of Majors" see Jundi, *op. cit.*, pp. 127, 142 and 149, and *cf. al-Ḥayāt,* May 4, 1965.

These tensions seem to have been intensified by the struggle that broke out in the Military Committee late in 1964 and reached its peak in 'Umran's ouster. A few weeks later some of the dissatisfied officers presented a petition to the Regional Congress in which they stated their complaints against the Military Committee. The petition was suppressed before such observers as Munif ar-Razzaz could grasp its full significance.[57] The Military Committee, however, was aware of the danger to which such an internal division exposed its position, and it seems to have decided to re-form the structure of the Military Organization and its relationship with the civilian sector of the party in a manner that was intended to reduce both internal and external opposition to its power.

According to the resolutions passed at the Regional Congress, the Military Organization was placed under the direction of the Regional Command as represented by a Military Bureau headed by one of the Command's military members. The Military Committee was acknowledged as representing the Military Organization at the present congress; as for the next congress, it was decided that it would be represented by the secretaries of the military branches and other functionaries whose number would not exceed 25.[58] In the future the Military Committee was to limit its activities to what pertains to "military [as distinct from party] affairs". The Regional Command and its Military Bureau were to issue a new Internal Regulation for the Military Organization. It was decided that all members of the Military Committee would join the broadened NCRC once it was established. The congress invested the political authority nominated by the Regional Command (namely the Presidency Council) with the power to appoint the commander of the army and all those holding sensitive military positions. It was emphasized that these arrangements were made for four years and that once the regime was fully consolidated different patterns were to be set that would reduce its military bias.[59]

These reforms, which bear a superficial resemblance to those decreed by the National Command in December 1964, were in reality

[57] Razzaz, *op. cit.*, p. 132.

[58] According to another version, it was not to exceed 15.

[59] *Resolutions of the Second Regular Regional Congress*, pp. 50–52.

designed to leave real power in the hands of the leaders of the Military Committee. More authority was given to the Regional Command but it was now securely though indirectly controlled by the Committee; the latter had also agreed to reduce its representation in the Regional Command to three out of 11 (as compared to seven out of 15 in the previous Command). The Military Bureau, even though but one of the Regional Command's several bureaus, was carefully controlled by the Military Committee (it was to be headed by Hafiz). The Committee was no longer to be the exclusive representative of the Military Organization at party congresses but it would retain control of the Organization and of all politically relevant military affairs such as appointments, dismissals, and transfers (this is what "what pertains to military affairs" really meant).

Thus, though some concessions were made to the internal military opposition and the regime as a whole was given a more respectable civilian facade, Hafiz, J'did, and their colleagues emerged from the Second Regular Regional Congress as the real holders of power in Syria. They had yet to contend with ‘Aflaq and Bitar on their own ground at the Eighth National Congress and to deal with a graver resurgence of opposition within the Military Organization.

7 DISCORD AMONG THE MILITARY, THE HAFIZ-J'DID RIVALRY—APRIL TO SEPTEMBER 1965

The Liwā' [major-general, namely Salah J'did] is an artillery officer who weighs and makes an exact calculation of angles before firing his shot; as for the Farīq [lieutenant-general, namely Amin al-Hafiz], he is an infantry officer, valiant and brave, but he just shouts "at them" and charges with his sword (Lieutenant-Colonel 'Abd al-Karim al-Jundi as quoted by Munif ar-Razzaz).

The Eighth National Congress of the Ba'th held in the first part of April 1965 and the events subsequent to it revealed the extent to which the Military Committee had been hampered in its conflict with the 'Aflaq-Bitar wing by the opposition in the Military Organization. These developments contributed to the conflict between Generals Hafiz and J'did, which then became the focal point of all major issues of Ba'thi politics and ultimately led to the *coup* of February 23, 1966. However, despite the turmoil generated by the political struggles during the spring and early summer of 1965, the Ba'th regime was able later in the summer to carry out its long-delayed plans to set up a quasi-parliamentary legislature and to issue an official programme of action.

The Eighth National Congress dealt with a variety of subjects but the underlying issue was the attempt to reach a compromise between the 'Aflaq-Bitar group and the Military Committee. This was made possible by developments that had taken place on both sides. The Military Committee desired a reconciliation as it felt that it could not afford another confrontation with the National Command when its own house had yet to be put in order. Possibly it also evaluated that some of the measures adopted during the latest Regional Congress facilitated such an agreement. On the other hand, there appeared a strong current of opinion among 'Aflaq's non-Syrian supporters who regarded their master's position as untenable.[1]

[1] Razzaz in his memoirs (*op. cit.*, p. 199) wrote that as early as December 1964 he had asked 'Aflaq to explain the National Command's measures which to him (Razzaz) seemed hasty. Razzaz' description and analysis of this and the ensuing episodes

Considering the dangers to the regime and the military's strong position, these delegates to the congress would rather try to reach a settlement with them than attempt in vain to dislodge them from what seemed to be a secure position.

The conciliatory mood of 'Aflaq's supporters was facilitated by the absence of Bitar, a staunch opponent of the military. Bitar did not participate in either the Regional or National Congress and was away in Africa at the time. His membership status at that point is vague; he had been expelled from the party in January 1964 and it is not known when and in what way he rejoined its ranks.

The attitudes adopted by both sides created a certain balance at the congress. 'Aflaq insisted on "exposing the crisis" but was held back by his own supporters who realized the futility of such a debate. The incumbent National Command had prepared an "ideological report" with which it wanted to replace the *Points of Departure,* a thorn at 'Aflaq and Bitar's side. The report was not totally rejected but referred together with the delegates' comments to the next National Congress. The *Points of Departure* was thus retained as the manual of the party's doctrine though its legitimacy was somewhat affected.[2] The same balance was evident when the National Command was able to increase its authority generally through a modification of the party's Internal Regime, but the Regional Command secured the insertion of a stipulation that should the National Command decide to dissolve a Regional Command it would then have to convene a Regional Congress and justify its action.[3]

The most significant compromise concerned the report on the "the Party's relationship to the government". The original report submitted to the congress was felt to be superficial and inadequate and a four-member committee, composed of 'Aflaq, Razzaz, Hafiz, and J'did, was appointed to revise it. The revised version was indeed an attempt to solve the dispute between the National Command (as representing the 'Aflaq-Bitar group) and the Military Committee.

must be viewed with caution. This is the point at which he began to play an active, and sometimes decisive, role and he is naturally inclined to justify his position.

2 Public communiqué on the results of the Eighth National Congress published by the National Command on May 4, 1965, in Damascus, p. 7.

3 *The Internal Regulation* (with the amendments approved by the Eighth National Congress), p. 28.

Being apparently acceptable to its authors, the new report was naturally endorsed by the congress.[4]

It confirmed the measures taken by the Syrian Regional Congress with regard to the Military Organization and the Military Committee, and it affirmed the position of the National Command as the supreme authority in the Ba'th Party with a right of supervision (*ishrāf wa-murāqaba*) over the Regional Command and the executive authority. More significantly, the National Command was for the first time given specific power to exercise its supreme authority. Thus, the resolutions of the Syrian Regional Congress were modified and the power to nominate the premier, the chief of staff, and the members of the Presidency Council was transferred to a joint session of the National and Regional Commands. A new organ called the Political Bureau (*al-maktab as-siyāsī li-'al-ḥukm*) was to be established and to include the members of the Presidency Council, the secretary of the National Command and his deputy, the deputy regional secretary, the premier and his deputy, and the chief of staff. The national secretary was given the right to contact party members on whatever level he wished to.

Even though he participated in drafting the report that proved acceptable to the majority of the delegates, 'Aflaq refused to abide by the compromise it outlined. He had lost his confidence in the military and did not believe that any arrangement with them was viable. Or was he also aware of the depth of the crisis besetting the Military Organization and wanted to use the opportunity for a confrontation with the Military Committee? At any rate, 'Aflaq demonstrated his dissatisfaction by refusing to serve as the party's national secretary (vacating the post for the first time since 1947) and he was elected to the new National Command over his own objection. Munif ar-Razzaz was elected to succeed 'Aflaq as the national secretary and he was in many ways a good choice. Though a veteran associate of 'Aflaq and Bitar, he was not totally identified with them as were some of their other confidants such as Shibli al-Aisamī or Jubran Majdalani;

[4] The report was distributed by the National Command on April 21, 1965, under the title *The Temporary Pattern (ṣīgha) of the Party's Relationship with the Government Approved by the Eighth National Congress.* The work of the committee is described by Razzaz, *op. cit.*, pp. 120–122.

as a Jordanian of Syrian descent he was sufficiently remote to be considered personally harmless and yet not as antagonizing as a complete outsider might have been to many Syrians.[5]

Razzaz himself admitted in his memoirs that 'Aflaq's leaving the national secretary's post, though voluntary, was in itself an achievement for the Military Committee. They could regard this change in the long run as weakening the National Command's ability to intervene in Syrian politics and as marking a division in the ranks of 'Aflaq's supporters. 'Aflaq indeed did not hide his displeasure with Razzaz, and the latter noted that "after being elected Secretary-General I felt a coolness coming over our relations and mutual understanding".[6] For about seven months the angry 'Aflaq refrained from attending National Command meetings and in his speech of February 18, 1966, he did not spare Razzaz who had come to think he knew better than his mentor. A veteran leader's resignation is often an ambivalent step and when it is accepted he might frown upon a close associate who tries to take his place. Speaking in February 1966, almost ten months later, 'Aflaq would claim that events had vindicated his position.

THE MILITARY CONGRESSES AND THE HAFIZ-J'DID DISPUTE

The Eighth National Congress altered the Syrian political scene by restoring the National Command's active role in it and by placing Munif ar-Razzaz at the head of that Command. The new national secretary (or secretary-general, as he was often called) displayed a fresh and more dynamic approach clearly borne out not only by his memoirs but also by the chronology of the period. Razzaz started with a broad plan for reinvigorating the party, but he soon became engrossed in the part he came to play in the conflict which surfaced again within the ranks of the Military Organization.

When the National Command reached a compromise with the

[5] This description of the congress is based on *ibid.*, pp. 119–123, a bulletin of the National Command from April 21, and 'Aflaq's speech of February 18, 1966 (*al-Wathā'iq al-'arabiyya,* 1966), pp. 62–63.

[6] Razzaz, *op. cit.*, p. 145.

leaders of the Military Committee during the Eighth National Congress it was probably unaware of the seriousness of the opposition to the Committee in the ranks of the Ba'thi military. The members of the National Command did not attach any particular significance to the petition presented to the Syrian Regional Congress by a group of officers.[7] But as soon as the congress was over Razzaz was told that the Military Committee no longer represented the Military Organization, that Salah J'did, the chief of staff, had offered his resignation following an acrimonious argument with Major Salim Hatum, and that it had then been decided that the resignation be retracted pending a general Military Congress (of the party's Military Organization). The congress took place in Kisweh late in April (or early in May) and was hence referred to in Ba'thi literature as "the Kisweh Congress". For the first time a high military forum was attended by three civilians—Razzaz, Shibli al-'Aisamī (his deputy), and Muhammad az-Zu'bi (deputy regional secretary). Again, divisions among the military proved to be an important asset for the civilians.

Razzaz was amazed by the strong opposition to the Military Committee displayed by most delegates from the party's military branches. The delegates read the recommendations approved by their respective branches, which called for the deposition of the Military Committee and accused it of "domineering, opportunism, arbitrary conduct, and shirking of responsibility by refusing to hold the Military Congress despite repeated requests".[8] The congress then decided to dissolve the Committee, charge the military members of the National and Regional Commands (Hafiz, J'did, Asad, and Hamad 'Ubaid) with temporarily directing the Military Organization, and appoint a committee composed of these officers, three members of the Syrian Regional Command, and the party's secretary-general, whose task it would be to prepare a new Internal Regulation for the Military Organization.[9]

This committee deliberated for about five weeks and then

[7] Explaining its endorsement of the compromise achieved at the Eighth National Congress, the National Command in a bulletin issued on December 22, 1965, would claim that it had been unaware of the strong opposition to its rivals.

[8] Razzaz, *op. cit.*, p. 142. His description is corroborated by several Ba'thi documents of the period.

[9] *Ibid.*, p. 133.

presented the proposed new Internal Regulation to a second Military Congress early in June. This congress approved the document with minor alterations[10] and by so doing restructured to a degree the political hierarchy of the Ba'thi military.

It will be recalled that according to the compromise reached at the Eighth National Congress (and outlined in the resolutions of the Regional Congress), the direction of the Military Organization was to be entrusted to a Military Bureau pertaining to the Regional Command, while the Military Committee was to continue to exercise the functions of the Officers' Committee over the army as a whole. The new Internal Regulation approved in June abolished the Military Committee altogether as an official organ. It affirmed the role assigned to the Military Bureau with regard to party members in the army and re-established the Officers' Committee. But unlike the Officers' Committees of the UAR and "Separatist" periods, this was to be a Ba'thi organ composed of the military members of the National and Regional Commands, the members of the Military Bureau, and six other officers all of whom had to be registered party members. In this way party control over the army was to be assured. The jurisdiction of the new Officers' Committee over non-Ba'thi officers was to be unlimited, but any action taken by it with regard to Ba'thi officers was to be subject to the Regional Command's approval.[11]

Taken literally, the decisions of the Military Congresses, like those of the then recent Regional and National Congresses, indicated a weakening of the military group that had long dominated the Ba'th regime and a corresponding strengthening of the military rank and file and of the moderate wing of the party's civilian sector. In reality the changes were not as radical—the Regional Command was after all subservient to the defunct Military Committee. By properly manning the Military Bureau and the Officers' Committee, the same military cabal that had previously operated through the Military Committee could continue to dominate the Syrian army, though perhaps more cautiously and with some limitations.

[10] Internal Bulletin from the end of June 1965. The new *Internal Regulation* was published under the title *an-Niẓām ad-Dākhilī li-at-tanẓīm al-'Askarī.*

[11] Razzaz, *op. cit.*, p. 133, and the new *Internal Regulation,* pp. 19–20.

Of much greater consequence was the fact that immediately following the Military Congresses and the establishment of the new organs a long-existing latent tension between Generals Hafiz and J'did developed into a bitter and open conflict that became a governing factor in Syrian politics throughout the rest of 1965 and until the *coup* of February 23, 1966.

It is significant that Razzaz in his account of these months dates the outbreak of the open conflict after the Military Congresses and does not relate it to the "revolt" of the rank and file of the Ba'thi military against their leaders. According to his version, the potential dispute between Hafiz and J'did had long been muffled by the need to close ranks against common rivals, and this no longer was the case once a "truce" had been reached with the National Command.[12] Events as narrated and interpreted above cannot sustain this version. That Razzaz chose to do so can be explained by the role he himself had played in these events. He was later accused by his rivals in the party of exacerbating the conflict by fostering the ambitions of Hafiz, and it was in his interest to show that the conflict had surfaced independently of the events in which he and the National Command had intervened. However, it is difficult to imagine how the rank and file's "revolt" could be divorced from an existing though dormant antagonism between the two foremost leaders of the Military Committee. It is known that the struggle with 'Umran had inflamed the opposition in the Military Organization and it is quite possible that the Hafiz-J'did friction served to bring it into the open. It may very well be that once the "revolt" broke out Hafiz tried to make J'did pay the price deemed necessary to mollify the disaffected officers and perhaps attempted to strengthen his own position at his rival's expense. It is a fact, after all, that the measures advocated by Hafiz to lull the opposition included J'did's ouster from the army and were bound to weaken the stand of his military supporters.

The story of the Hafiz-J'did rivalry is fascinating in view of the striking differences in the personalities of the two protagonists and because of the way in which personal and structural factors were interwoven in it. Each of them brought distinct assets to the alliance

[12] Razzaz, *op. cit.*, p. 139.

Salah J'did

they formed in 1963. The calculating and withdrawn J'did had built the Military Committee's control of the army and its supporters in the party's civilian sector. He accumulated power with little concern for its outward manifestations. The outgoing and impulsive Hafiz broadened the regime's basis of support with the modicum of popularity that he possessed. Together they overcame a series of intra- and extra-party rivals, the last of whom was 'Umran. It may have been the ouster of 'Umran that removed the insulation which until then had prevented their respective interests from clashing. It is impossible to determine exactly when, but sometime in the spring of 1965 the two partners turned into rivals.

While Hafiz enjoyed both popularity and the extensive authority that went with the positions and titles he had accumulated, he did not have sufficient military support to match the power of the officer faction that J'did had patiently built up and placed in key posts. The strong backing J'did had acquired for the Military Committee in the Syrian Regional Command and party hierarchy turned into another source of personal power that Hafiz could not match with a faction of his own.

The developments that had taken place since March 1965 gave Hafiz the opportunity to try to dislodge J'did and some members of his faction from their key positions and consolidate his personal status at the head of the regime. In this he was reportedly assisted (if not encouraged) by another faction of officers headed by Major Salim Hatum. As one of the "Majors" Hatum was a leader of the opposition to the Military Committee which became manifest among the Ba'thi officers, but it seems that his animosity was directed primarily at J'did. Hatum's position in the Ba'th regime derived from the fact that he was one of few Ba'thi officers who had participated in the *coup* of March 8, and he later bolstered it by playing a decisive role in quashing the Nasserite insurgents on July 18, 1963. His commando unit guarded the vital broadcast station and was conducted as a personal unit (it was mainly Hatum and his cohorts that Razzaz had in mind when he spoke of *mulūk aṭ-ṭawā'if*). The origin of the tension between Hatum's faction and that of J'did is attributed to the fact that during the UAR period members of the former group had stayed in Syria so that they did not belong to the original Military Committee and were probably never fully integrated into it.[13] In this particular respect the Ba'thi Military Organization did not differ essentially from other cabals and military coalitions in which primary groups have had considerable import. Factions based on friendships which originated in the Syrian and Egyptian officers' academies and divisions in the ranks of the Algerian FLN are other cases in point.

Following the second Military Congress, Hafiz suggested that both he and J'did leave the army and content themselves with respectively the positions of chairman and deputy chairman of the Presidency Council. As such, he proposed, he himself would be like every other head of state the commander-in-chief of the armed forces, and J'did would serve as his deputy in the latter capacity as well.[14] The obvious catch was that Hafiz intended to retain the powers he had held as the army's "Supreme Commander" by transferring them to the chairmanship of the Presidency Council, while J'did was to lose his specific authority as chief of staff. In a related move the new Officers' Committee established by the second Military Congress transferred Ahmad Swaidani from the post of director of military intelligence to that of director of personnel. This was explained as a measure designed to appease the military opposition, but Swaidani happened to be a supporter of J'did's and both resigned accusing Hafiz of exerting pressure on the Committee.[15]

This was not a mere resignation. J'did was the leader of a strong military faction and his move was a clear threat to resort to violence. Indeed, an Internal Bulletin issued late in June noted in a vague and prudent style that "his resignation caused confusion among part of the military". To avert the danger the Regional Command, reinforced by two members of the National Command, invited J'did to present his position and point of view. J'did attacked Hafiz vehemently, accusing him of "dictatorship", "personal rule", "directing the affairs of the state in a capricious and tribal manner", and charged him with responsibility for the deterioration of the country's economy.[16] J'did

[13] *Ibid.*, pp. 137, 139.

[14] *Ibid.*, p. 136. Razzaz reports the proposal without commenting on it.

[15] *Ibid.*, p. 137. Swaidani, it should be noted, was not transferred to an insignificant post. There seems to have been a determined effort not to push things too far so as to avert a crisis.

[16] *Ibid.*, p. 137 n. 1. "Personal rule" stands for *fardiyya*, which had already been

then proposed the abolition of the Presidency Council (thus ruling out the possibility of his being transferred to it) and the separation of the role and powers of the supreme commander from the office of the president.

Following that meeting the National and Regional Commands began, in the last week of June, to hold a series of joint sessions in an attempt to work out a compromise between the two dissident military factions. The formula on which they finally agreed was to retain the Presidency Council for the time being, to forbid its chairman to hold any other state office, and to leave the title of commander-in-chief with him but to divide the powers of supreme commander among him, the minister of defence, and the chief of staff.[17] In practical terms it meant that Hafiz had to give up the premiership and at least part of his military authority and he refused to abide by the decision unless J'did relinquished his post of chief of staff. The National Command played an active role in mediating between the two protagonists, and it is evident from Razzaz' narrative that he tried to exploit their rivalry in order to bolster the political power of the National Command and to strengthen the civilian element in the regime by reducing the number of the military in the party Commands and by involving the party's civilian leaders in the affairs of its Military Organization.[18]

Attempts to convince Hafiz and J'did to implement the compromise solution were continued throughout the month of July until finally the Regional Command, unable to break the deadlock, submitted its resignation. The crisis thus created restored a measure of fluidity to the situation.

mentioned above as a derogatory term in Ba'thi parlance deploring deviation from the idea of collective rule. It had often been employed against President Nasser. "Tribalism" (*'ashā'iriyya*) refers to Hafiz' traditional manner of speech and behaviour.

[17] Bulletin of late June 1965 (Razzaz, *op. cit.*, pp. 141–142, gives a slightly different account). As this episode clearly indicates, the function of the supreme commander was distinct from that of commander-in-chief. The latter seems to have had a more ceremonial role.

[18] This is put quite explicitly by Razzaz, *op. cit.*, p. 142.

THE EXTRAORDINARY REGIONAL CONGRESS OF AUGUST 1965

The resignation of the Regional Command meant that a Regional Congress had to be summoned. According to the party's Internal Regulation, the membership of an Extraordinary Congress consisted of the delegates to the preceding Regular Congress. In preparation for the session the National Command immediately decided to raise the number of the Regional Command's members to 16. In so doing it prepared the ground for adding some of its Syrian protégés to the Regional Command without having to reduce the number of the old Regional Command's supporters. Again, the overriding consideration was not to hurt the other side in such a manner that he would see no alternative but to resort to violence.[19]

The Extraordinary Regional Congress took place in the second week of August. According to Razzaz, there was a good chance that owing to the crisis in the ranks of the military a number of the National Command's candidates could have been elected to the new Regional Command. His scheme was aborted, however, by 'Aflaq and Bitar's insistence that nine out of the Command's 16 members be from among their supporters and that Bitar himself be one of them (Bitar was not a member of the congress and could not be legally elected to the Command). These demands proved unacceptable to the congress and all 16 members of the new Command were elected from the supporters of the old Regional Command, seven of them army officers. Owing to the division in the National Command the expansion of the Regional Command on the eve of the congress proved to be self-defeating, by increasing the numerical strength of the formers' rivals in joint sessions of the National and Regional Commands.[20]

The import of this episode is not only in its influence on later developments but also in bringing out Razzaz' reaction to 'Aflaq and Bitar's refusal to cooperate with him, which in his opinion had

[19] The story is recounted by Razzaz, *op. cit.*, p. 143.

[20] *Ibid.*, pp. 143–145. The Command's 16 members were evenly divided between supporters of Hafiz and J'did. Six of the seven military members had belonged to the old Military Committee. Another interesting statistic regarding this Command was supplied by 'Aflaq and mentioned above, namely that seven of the nine civilian members in it joined the party after March 8, 1963.

grave consequences for their common cause. "I felt", he writes, "that maître Salah (al-Bitar) was exaggerating in linking the Party to his own personality".[21] Razzaz may have been wrong in his policy judgment,[22] but the feelings of this veteran associate of 'Aflaq and Bitar are indicative of the resentment long felt by more distant party members towards what they termed the tutelage exercised by the two veteran leaders over the party.

The main issue at the congress was naturally the attempt to settle the Hafiz-J'did conflict. Some of the regime's major problems seem to have been discussed with exceptional frankness, but the solution arrived at was not essentially different from the one advocated by the National and Regional Commands in June. Hafiz and J'did both left the army and Hafiz was also to resign from the premiership. The powers of supreme commander were taken from the chairman of the Presidency Council and vested in the minister of defence's office.[23] The expansion of the NCRC, long promised to the Syrian public,[24] was to be completed by September 1. Hafiz was re-elected chairman of the Presidency Council with Nur ad-Din al-Atasi as his deputy. Colonels Hamad 'Ubaid and Muhammad Shnewi were respectively chosen as the new minister of defence and chief of staff, and Colonel Fahd ash-Sha'ir, by then a member of the Ba'th, was made deputy chief of staff.[25]

The appointment of the highly unpopular 'Ubaid and Shnewi to the two highest military positions aroused a wave of criticism among Ba'thi and neutral officers. A Regional Command Bulletin of September 11 responded to that criticism by polemicizing against the "Party's enemies" who raised such hostile questions as "Why

[21] Razzaz, *op. cit.*, p. 146.

[22] Whether the National Command should have confronted the military and the Regional Command at that stage (as 'Aflaq and Bitar demanded) or have reached an understanding with the "positive" elements among them (as Razzaz tried to do) is a debatable point. Razzaz, however, tries to show in his account that the National Command's ultimate failure was not his fault.

[23] A decree to that effect was published on September 12 (*Chronology of Arab Politics,* 1965), p. 299.

[24] On August 3, 1965, *al-Ḥayāt,* being unsympathetic to the regime, could note that two weeks had passed since the Council was to have been convened.

[25] Bulletin of the Regional Command from September 11. The new appointments were soon reported in the Lebanese press.

were unsuitable persons chosen to certain positions?".[26] The incident revealed the degree to which the professional standards of the Syrian army were damaged by excessive politicization but it was also a peculiar testimony to Salah J'did's methods and adroitness. As told by Razzaz, it was J'did who advanced the names of these two Hafiz supporters precisely because they were notoriously incompetent. As he had expected, Hafiz, being a more responsible officer who at least tried to distinguish politics from military affairs, hesitated to endorse these two clients of his, and J'did won a tactical victory by demonstrating to the adherents of his rival that their patron could not be relied upon for unconditional backing. Similarly, Colonel Mustafa Tlas switched his loyalty from Hafiz to J'did following his entanglement in a night-club brawl. Hafiz initiated a disciplinary action against his supporter Tlas while J'did helped him out and won him over to his side.[27] Razzaz does not hide his admiration for J'did's tactical genius which he repeatedly compares to that of Stalin: "I had always thought he was an asset to the Party", says Razzaz, "but an asset that had taken the wrong track and instead of placing his ability and talents at the Party's service put them at the disposal of a distorted version of the Party". As for the episodes described by Razzaz, he may have attributed too much to their consequences. There were also other, more profound, reasons for the desertion of several Hafiz supporters.[28]

The personal struggle between the two foremost military leaders of the regime could not be divorced from the other political issues of the day. Tension between Syria and Egypt had surfaced again in the spring and, as had been the case in December 1963, the question of Syria's role in the Arab Summit Conferences and of its relations with Egypt was further complicated by the internal strife within the Ba'th.

SYRIA AND THE THIRD ARAB SUMMIT CONFERENCE

The Ba'th regime's relations with Nasserite Egypt, that had somewhat improved at the end 1964, began to deteriorate again in the spring

[26] For a journalistic version of this episode see *al-Ḥayāt*, August 31, 1965.

[27] Razzaz, *op. cit.*, p. 150. The incident with Mustafa Tlas was described in detail in an interview given to N. Van Dam; see Van Dam, *op. cit.*, p. 1920.

[28] See Razzaz, *op. cit.*, p. 149 and below pp. 181–182.

of 1965. The deterioration was mainly caused, it seems, by the fact that the contradiction which had been inherent in the "Summit Policy"[29] came into the open on May 13 through the Israeli destruction of Syrian equipment employed in the project of diverting the tributaries of the Jordan River in Syrian territory. The Syrian authorities realized that once Israel decided to use military force to stop the diversion works in their territory they could not prevent it by themselves. This left them with a choice between stopping the work or demanding Arab support, which in practical terms meant Egyptian backing. Egypt was not ready to go to war over the waters of the Jordan River and its stand was that each member of the Unified Arab Command (established after the First Summit Conference) was responsible for its own defence in case of minor incidents like that of May 13, 1965.[30]

The deadlock seemed complete. The Ba'this, who had held a series of meetings following the May 13 incident, did not think they wanted or could afford to stop the diversion works. At odds with most other Arab states, they probably feared that their failure to complete their share of the project would be exposed by rival regimes and contrasted with their earlier vociferous demands addressed to other Arab states. On the other hand, a public demand of Egypt to come to Syria's aid (when that country's unwillingness to do so was known to them) was likely to place Egypt in a most embarrassing position. The Ba'this chose to make their disagreement with Nasser public.

Syria presented its case to the Conference of Arab Premiers held in Cairo between May 26 and 30 and its line was rejected. The Syrian government then launched a full-fledged propaganda campaign directed mainly at Egypt. Pressed by the Syrians, Nasser surveyed the issue at length in a speech he delivered on May 31 to the Palestine National Congress. He announced his readiness to send his planes to Syria but demanded that they be defended by Egyptian ground

[29] See above, p. 102.

[30] The Egyptian position was most clearly explained by President Nasser in his famous speech of May 31, 1965 (*Arab Political Documents* [1965], pp. 220–229, offers an abridged text) and in the speech he delivered on July 22, 1965 (see *ibid.*, pp. 262, 280 and especially pp. 274–275).

forces, a condition the Ba'this would not accept. He also declared that Egypt would choose the time for fighting and would not let Israel determine it. He then hinted that the Ba'this were trying to use the issue to extract concessions from him.[31]

The speech drew a sharp response from Damascus culminating in a declaration by the Regional Command on June 15, which explained why Syria saw itself obliged to continue the diversion works. The growing tension soon manifested itself in other spheres of friction. The Syrian Nasserites intensified their activity and the Ba'th regime was most notably alarmed by the activities of 'Abd al-Hamid Sarraj and Jasim 'Alwan. On June 7 Razzaz publicly protested the latter's assignment to Baghdad. In turn, Syria denounced Egyptian attempts to reach a compromise with Saudi Arabia over the Yemenite question. As a pan-Arab party with branches in the Yemen and Aden, the Ba'th even earlier had pursued an intransigent line with regard to the war in the Yemen, but this was nothing compared with the campaign of the spring and early summer of 1965.[32] The concessions that Nasser had to make in order to secure a respectable withdrawal of his forces from the Yemen were embarrassing in themselves and their denunciation by the Ba'this in the name of pure revolutionism made them even more so.

The Egyptians tried to hit back. The denationalization of 26 workshops and 15 commercial firms in Syria late in June and early in July was presented by Cairo as a retreat from the implementation of socialism and as a proof of managerial failures which resulted from the lack of proper planning.[33] In his traditional speech of July 22, President Nasser vehemently attacked the Ba'th in a manner resembling his anti-Ba'th polemics of 1963, labelling it a fascist party.

[31] *Arab Political Documents* (1965), p. 227.

[32] The intensity of the campaign is illustrated by the frequency of Syrian attacks on Egyptian policy in the Yemen since early June. See for instance *ath-Thaura,* June 2, Amin al-Hafiz' comments in a press conference on July 24 (*Chronology of Arab Politics* [1965], p. 291), editorial of *al-Ba'th* of July 27, 1965, comments by an official spokesman on the Jeddah Agreement on August 24 (in *Chronology of Arab Politics* [1965], p. 295), and Radio Damascus, August 25, 1965, 1:30 p.m.

[33] On the denationalization see Radio London, July 3, 1965, 10:45 p.m., and *Chronology of Arab Politics* (1965), p. 179. For the Egyptian denunciation see Radio Cairo, July 4, 1965, 7:00 p.m.

Finally, during his visit to Moscow in August on the eve of the Third Arab Summit Conference, in a speech addressed to Arab students, Nasser warned that Egypt would withdraw from the Summit Conferences if Syria continued its policies.[34]

In so doing Nasser was again able to call the Ba'thi bluff. It was evident that he would be supported by most Arab states who were interested in the continuation of these conferences and that Syria would find itself totally isolated in the Arab world. This the regime could not afford and a Syrian delegation came to the Summit Conference in Casablanca on Nasser's terms. It had to acquiesce in all the conference's decisions, including the so-called Arab Solidarity Pact which banned all propaganda attacks on other Arab states and was construed as an achievement for the conservative Arab regimes.

The concessions which the Syrian delegation to Casablanca (led by Hafiz and Razzaz) had to make were seized by J'did and used in an attempt to discredit Hafiz and the National Command. The Syrian policy at the conference had been approved beforehand by the Political Bureau but J'did, not wishing to commit himself, did not take part in these meetings.[35] Having led the anti-Egyptian campaign of the previous months, Hafiz (and Razzaz) found it difficult to explain their retreat and their readiness to acknowledge (even temporarily) the right of the "reactionary" Arab regimes to immunity from attacks by the "revolutionary" states. Razzaz in his memoirs tried to use this episode to demonstrate the cynicism of J'did and his civilian allies who would themselves pursue similar policies a little later; but more significant in this context perhaps is his acknowledgment of the fact that the anti-Hafiz campaign of September 1965 rested on a strong anti-Nasserite feeling among the rank and file in the party branches.[36] As this episode indicated, the Syrian Ba'th of late 1965 was an entity completely different from that of 1963, but subsequent events would show that 'Aflaq and Bitar were not sufficiently aware of the change when they planned their political strategy in the summer of 1965. The two leaders, it seems, were still

[34] Radio Cairo, August 30, 1965, 6:00 a.m.

[35] Razzaz, *op. cit.*, p. 152. On the formation and composition of the Political Bureau see above p. 156.

[36] *Ibid.*, pp. 100 and 152–155.

convinced that they commanded respect and support among the party membership. Razzaz appears to have been more realistic but he too tends to fall back on a populistic theme—the "uncorrupted" rank and file as the last resort the party can turn to.

During these tense weeks the Ba'th regime in Syria was still able to complete two long-delayed projects—the setting up of a legislative council and the issuing of a programme of action. These two projects implemented at the height of an internecine contest were naturally affected by it. Their significance, however, is not in constituting another manifestation of that struggle but rather in indicating the relative stability achieved by the regime and in bringing into sharper focus several trends that had been evident before.

THE BROADENING OF THE NCRC

The NCRC was originally conceived of in 1963, and indeed served for some time, as the supreme authority in the state. Its power and authority declined as the regime came to be dominated by the Ba'th and it was replaced in that capacity by the Regional Command (and in certain respects by the Military Committee). Late in 1963 and early in 1964 the NCRC was still reported to have voted on several crucial matters, but this was no longer the case in the latter half of 1964. The constitution of 1964 had envisaged the NCRC as a broadened quasi-parliamentary body, and during 1964 and 1965 the expansion of the NCRC had been repeatedly promised. Judging by Ba'thi pronouncements of the time the new body was originally planned to consist of about 150 members representing mainly professional and and sectoral front organizations.[37] It was to give the regime a more positive image, to demonstrate the wide support it commanded, and to implement the much spoken of "Popular Democracy". Amin al-Hafiz had explained all this at a news conference on January 12, 1965:

> The National Assembly [namely the broadened NCRC] will draw together all classes of the population. It will not be like earlier parliaments which in the past included political groups

[37] *Al-Ba'th,* February 15, 1965.

> of professional politicians and others who acquired power by one way or another. . . . We shall achieve true popular representation. This nation is sixty percent peasants and there is also a large proportion of workers. By workers I do not simply mean factory workers, but artisans and labourers as well. There are also the other unions of doctors, engineers and teachers and the small businessmen, salesmen, etc. In addition there are other socially active groups. The women will also be represented in this assembly. We shall also select members from other political groups, but not on a political basis. . . . We accept only honest individuals who believe in our policy.[38]

Carrying out such a project proved to be an arduous task. Within the Ba'th itself there were those who feared the results of even that limited relaxation of political control it involved. In due course there arose also the need to maintain a balance between the rival factions within the Ba'th. It was difficult to find those reliable "progressive" individuals who were to be added to the Council as participants in a "unionist progressive front". The most complex problem, however, proved to be the establishment of reliable "front organizations" and the reorganization of existing professional associations. When the broadened NCRC was finally inaugurated on September 1, 1965, it was composed of only 95 instead of the 150 or so originally planned. Some of the members, like 'Aflaq and Bitar, were actually boycotting the Council's meetings, probably in protest over the high representation of the supporters of their rivals. Still, Mansur al-Atrash, considered an associate of 'Aflaq and designated by the Regional Command as chairman, attended the first meeting and indeed was elected to that position.

The Council's 95 members belonged to 11 different categories: six Syrian members of the National Command, 14 members of the Syrian Regional Command,[39] five members of the old NCRC,[40] five representatives of the military sector,[41] 14 members of the General

[38] *Arab Political Documents* (1965), pp. 9–10.

[39] Two other members of the Command were included in other categories.

[40] They included Bitar, three Ba'thi officers, and General Ghassan Haddad, the only non-Ba'thi member of the original NCRC to survive all purges.

[41] They were the five members of the defunct Military Committee who did not belong in any of the three former categories.

Federation of Trade Unions, seven women's representatives, five representatives of the liberal professions, seven representatives of the Teachers' Union, two university professors, and 17 "progressive citizens". An analysis of the non-Ba'thi constituents of the Council will indicate both the difficulties inherent in the mobilization process in a country like Syria and the degree of progress the regime had made in expanding its basis of support.

The representatives of the workers and peasants were described in the scheme drawn by Hafiz as the backbone of the regime's popular support in the planned Council in which they would jointly command 80 out of 150 seats. In reality, however, it proved quite difficult to mobilize the workers and (for different reasons) the peasants into active and sustained support of the regime.

The Ba'th's influence among the Trade Unionists dates back to the mid-1950s. Then it had to contend against Communist and right-wing labour organizers, but since 1958 the Ba'th had the Nasserites as its chief rivals among the workers. The Ba'th upon coming to power had to rig elections in the Unions to guarantee the success of its candidates against Nasserite and (to a lesser extent) Communist challengers.[42] Many of the Ba'thi Trade Unionists were, moreover, leftist and even those among them who did not split off with Shufi were hard to control. Thus, in 1965 the Ba'th regime was not able to persuade the radical labour leader Khalid al-Jundi to participate in a workers' congress in Cairo, which he considered a Nasserite forum. In another instance the Regional Command decided on June 29, 1965, to expel from the party a member who in the elections to his Union was a candidate in a list defined as "hostile to the Party and the Revolution".[43]

After it had purged Shufi's staunchest supporters in the Trade Unions during the summer of 1964, the Regional Command set out to reorganize the Unions on the basis of a law enacted on February 29, 1964, which abolished the conservative legislation enacted under the Separatist Regime and established the structure of the General Federation of Trade Unions.[44] A meeting of incumbent Trade Union

[42] Razzaz, *op. cit.*, pp. 191, 230, Salibi, *op. cit.*, and E. Rouleau in *Le Monde*, October 14, 1966.

[43] See Razzaz, *op. cit.*, p. 227.

[44] 'Indani, *op. cit.*, pp. 194–195, and Radio Damascus, March 1, 1965, 7:15 p.m.

leaders was held in October 1964 in Homs in preparation for a general congress. Elections were held during December 1964 and January 1965[45] and the general congress that was originally scheduled for March 7, 1965, was finally convened on April 23. In August the Ba'th had a reliable leadership of the Trade Unions from which it could choose 14 delegates to the broadened NCRC, but it still did not have a solid Trade Union movement at its disposal.

Attempts to organize a previously nonexistent peasants union began late in 1963. These initial efforts were ineffective but the approach of the Regional Command, as reflected in its directive on this issue, is most interesting.[46] The party branches were ordered to organize local peasant unions based on the participation of those peasants who would benefit from the Agrarian Reform laws. With the help of the local government officials (especially the teachers), the party was to organize village committees and to manipulate them directly. A hierarchy of local and provincial committees was to culminate in a General Peasants Union.

Little was achieved in this sphere during 1964 and when on December 17 of that year the formation of such a General Union was decreed it had to be built from scratch. A week earlier the Regional Command had ordered the branches to present a list of candidates from which it would pick its nominees for the provincial unions and General Union. As in 1963, the Regional Command wanted most of the candidates to be reliable but not identified as party members, realizing that an obviously Ba'thi organization could scare away many suspicious peasants, who traditionally do not wish to tie themselves too closely even to a party in power. They and their forbears had seen governments come and go.

Those who were chosen through these procedures were appointed to represent the peasants in the broadened NCRC, but the General Peasants Union itself had not yet come into being when the new Council was inaugurated. It took another month to organize the first Peasants' Congress (on September 20) which was defined as

[45] See, for instance, *al-Ba'th,* January 22, 1965.

[46] Internal Bulletin distributed by the Regional Command sometime at the end of 1963.

designed for "training purposes" rather than for legislation.[47] Before achieving that, the Ba'th had to abandon even the semblance of peasant control of the union and late in August it imposed its trusted men and the governmental bureaucracy on the provincial unions, giving them their actual leadership.[48] This was explained (then and later) by the "objective" inability of the peasants to direct their own affairs and by the party's realization that late in 1965 their union was still built on the traditional *mukhtārs* (headmen) or on the local strongman "who brought his supporters into the organization and retained his old position under a new guise".[49]

The 27 representatives of workers and peasants in the broadened NCRC, then, represented neither these sectors of the population nor, especially in the case of the peasants, a very effective party organization among them. The Ba'this were aware of these shortcomings but they could also claim with a considerable element of truth that in relative terms the Council represented the progress of a regime that a year earlier could not achieve even that much.[50]

Of the other professional groups represented in the Council, a special importance was attached to the teachers who formed a large union of educated persons and were scattered throughout the country. Controlling their union was important for a regime wishing to pervade Syrian society. While many of the Ba'thi militants seem to have been former teachers, the regime's control of their union had not been secured until well into 1964. The regime's efforts to attract the teachers included a plan to furnish them with interest-free loans for housing.[51]

[47] Circular sent by the Peasants Bureau of the Regional Command on September 5, 1965.

[48] Circular sent by the Peasants Bureau on August 29, 1965.

[49] Quoted from the *Detailed Programme of the Peasants Bureau* approved by the Regional Command on November 3, 1965.

[50] The Regional Command in a report it presented to the National Consultative Council (*al-majlis al-istishārī al-qaumī*) on August 8, 1965, stated that "The circumstances of defending the Revolution did not divert us from the determination to build the revolutionary Party and of building the popular organizations around it, and we were able to a certain extent to build an organizational framework for the Party and to build the basic nuclei for the peasant organizations and to direct the Workers and Students Unions in the right direction . . ." (*The Party's Crisis*, p. 45).

[51] *Arab Political Documents*, (1965), pp. 10, 20.

The 17 "progressive citizens" in the Council included some mild unionists, independent leftists, and at least one registered Communist—Samih 'Aṭiyya, who in March 1966 would become the first Communist cabinet member in Syria. At the time the presence of a Communist member in the NCRC was yet another symptom of a growing rapprochement between the radical wing of the Ba'th and the Syrian Communist Party.[52]

The inauguration of the new legislative body was an important achievement in the midst of a grave internal crisis for a regime which until then had not been able to muster even that measure of public support. Though the new Council was carefully chosen and closely controlled there was some free discussion and even mild criticism at its meetings as the minutes of its sessions disclose. The new Presidency Council and cabinet nominated in September would be confirmed by the Council. The decisions were still made behind the scenes but there was a definite attempt to soften the regime's rigidly secretive image.

THE STATE AND PARTY PROGRAMMES OF ACTION

The preparation and publication of a temporary comprehensive programme of action for the Ba'th regime (*minhāj* or *barnāmaj marḥalī*) had been advocated by various Ba'thi forums since the end of 1963 and throughout 1964.[53] It seems that what the advocates had in mind was a Syrian equivalent of the Egyptian National Charter of 1962. The *Points of Departure* of 1963 could be regarded as an ideological counterpart to the Egyptian document but it was theoretical and rather vague and at that stage was considered an internal party document that could not serve as an official policy statement. The Regional Congress of March-April 1965 decided to reconvene later that year to approve the text prepared by the Regional Command.

[52] Other manifestations of the same process were the publication of the resolutions adopted by the Central Committee of the Syrian Communist Party, which were quite favourable to the regime in June 1965 (*Chronology of Arab Politics* [1965], p. 291), and the inclusion of a Communist member in a Syrian delegation to the Three Continents Conference in Havana.

[53] The first documented call for the publication of such a programme is included in a report by the Regional Command from September or October 1963.

By the time the Regional Congress was assembled for that purpose in June the National Command had resumed an active role in Syrian politics and wanted to have a say in the Programme. The text of the Programme could not be compared with earlier drafts and it is not known what changes were introduced at the insistence of the National Command, but the moderating influence of that Command seems to make itself felt at several points. ʻAflaq and Bitar's anti-Marxist bias is thus clearly echoed in the introduction: ". . . we as Arabs have to consider the realities that prevail in the Arab society as a source of theory on the Arab revival . . . and to look with doubt on the necessity of accepting ready-made solutions and theories". The Programme was finally approved at a joint session of the National and Regional Commands and was published on July 22.[54] The date may have been chosen in anticipation of Nasser's attack on the Baʻth in his traditional speech of July 22. A complementary *Party Programme* (*al-minhāj al-ḥizbī*) was issued by the National Command on August 2.[55]

The *Temporary Programme* is the more important document of the two but it, too, contains little that was new as compared with the resolutions of the Regional and National Congresses of 1965. The Programme, however, was not designed to innovate but rather to integrate piecemeal resolutions into a comprehensive platform and to issue it to the public as a state programme couched in practical terms. The section dealing with "Popular Democracy" was barely related to the realities of government and power in Baʻthi Syria, but those covering Arab and foreign policy and social and economic policies were matter of fact and informative.

The Programme took an evasive, cautious stand on the question of Arab unity and provided a theoretical justification for cooperation with conservative Arab regimes in the framework of the Summit Conferences—"Syria considers the Palestine Problem a national

[54] *The Temporary* [or Present Phase] *Programme (al-minhāj al-marḥalī) of the March 8 Revolution in the Syrian Arab Region* (Damascus, July 1965, 130 pp.). An inadequate English translation was published by the Syrian ministry of information. Excerpts from the text were published in *Arab Political Documents* (1965), pp. 256–261.

[55] Published in Damascus, 48 pp. A better English translation of this document was published by the Syrian ministry of information and excerpts are available in *Arab Political Documents* (1965), pp. 286–290.

problem the treatment of which should rise above all other considerations including narrow regional interests and the political and ideological differences between the Arab states".[56] As on earlier occasions, to speak in the name of the state rather than of the party apparently made the ideological concession easier. Even the apparently radical call to nationalize Arab oil was presented in the Programme as "an ultimate goal".[57]

Syria's foreign policy was defined, according to the line approved at the Second Regular Regional and Eighth National Congresses, as one of nonalignment but with a clear bias towards the socialist states and "the states of the third world". Cooperation with the Western states was approved "on the basis of the implementation of national interests and the honouring of our sovereignty and freedom of action".[58] This formulation covered such contracts as were signed in June 1965 with a British firm that was to finance and lay a pipeline connecting the oil fields at Kratchuk to the port of Tartus.

The sections on economic and social policies and planning were the lengthiest and most detailed. Perhaps most important was the statement that the state regarded the nationalization laws which had already been enacted as sufficient "and that it therefore announces that the nationalization measures had by now assumed the form and reached the line desired by the state; it especially considers the spheres of contracting and tourism as open for the activity of the private sector".[59] But at the same time it was emphasized that the private sector was to play but a minor role as compared with the other three sectors of the Syrian economy: the public, public and private combined, and cooperative. The public sector created through the nationalization measures and developed through further investments was to remain the backbone of the national economy.[60]

These statements reflected the progress the regime had made since the spring of 1964. It had achieved a greater measure of political and economic control and it now was offering a *modus vivendi* to those

[56] Pp. 14–17 (all references are to the original).
[57] P. 17.
[58] Pp. 22–23.
[59] P. 59.
[60] Pp. 53–55 and 61.

segments of the middle classes who were ready to reconcile themselves to the regime's hegemony. However, the regime's attitude towards these classes was again to change during the ensuing phases of the intra-Baʿthi struggle.

8 THE COUP D'ÉTAT OF FEBRUARY 23, 1966

> Casting the slogan of returning the army to its camps, all should know, is a rightist slogan which is unacceptable in form and content. No ideological army can accept it under any circumstances. It means leaving the cause to persons other than its owners. . . . (Colonel Mustafa Tlas, then commander of the Central Region, in a speech delivered on Army Day, August 1, 1966).

During the months of August and September 1965 several supporters of Amin al-Hafiz transferred their allegiance to Salah J'did thus making his military and civilian faction clearly predominant. General Hamad 'Ubaid, the new minister of defence, Colonel Mustafa Tlas, of the armoured brigade in Homs, Jamil Shiyya, member of the Regional Command, and Major Salim Hatum were some of those who had been counted on the side of Hafiz and during these weeks were lured away by J'did.[1] Not only did J'did adroitly exploit personal weaknesses and ambitions but he very astutely profited by bringing some essential features of the Ba'thi political system into play.

A major factor determining the political alliances of the period was confessional solidarity (and confessional distrust). It was specifically 'Umran who, until his deposition late in 1964, was identified with the policy of building a large bloc of 'Alawi officers and placing them in key positions as described by Razzaz:

> And it seemed that there was discrimination in discharging those reserve officers summoned to service immediately following the *coup*, and discrimination in the admission (procedures) to the Officers' Academy and in the admission of officers and noncommissioned officers to the ranks of the Party. Then there appeared new symptoms concerning the transfer of officers as the "reliable ones" were concentrated in units stationed near

[1] There is little concrete evidence available on these matters. The accounts in the Lebanese press are mostly unreliable and Razzaz, *op. cit.*, pp. 150–151, gives a seemingly true but not very detailed version.

Damascus while the "unreliable ones" were sent away to the (Israeli) Front or to Aleppo or Ladhiqiyya. The same thing happened with the armoured forces.[2]

J'did was among those who (for political reasons) denounced 'Umran for promoting "sectarianism" (*ṭā'ifiyya*) but ironically he inherited the support of many 'Alawi officers who had been advanced by 'Umran. Once "confessionalism" had been introduced into the Syrian Ba'thi political system it acquired dynamics of its own. The 'Alawi officers promoted by 'Umran realized that their overrepresentation in the upper echelons of the army was resented by the majority, and they seem to have rallied around J'did, by then the most prominent 'Alawi officer in the Syrian army and the person deemed most likely to preserve their high but precarious position. It was also quite natural for Hafiz, after his conflict with J'did had come out into the open and he had encountered the political might of this grouping, to try to gather Sunni officers around himself by accusing J'did of engaging in "sectarian" politics.[3] But resentful as Sunni officers may have been, their motivation was not as strong as 'Alawi solidarity and apprehension. While J'did's Sunni backers stayed with him, the solidarity of his 'Alawi supporters seems to have been further cemented by the feeling that the issue had assumed a confessional character and that their collective and personal positions were at stake.

It is also significant that three of the four supporters of Hafiz who went over to the other side were Druses, Tlas being the only Sunni among them. There had been no traditional proximity or affinity between 'Alawis and Druses in Syria, but it is easy to see why many Druse officers tended late in 1965 to identify with a largely 'Alawi faction once the conflict seemed to develop along confessional lines. Though smaller and not as coherent, the group of Ba'thi Druse officers attained power through procedures similar to those employed by the 'Alawis, and if these procedures as well as the overrepresen-

[2] Quoted from Razzaz, *op. cit.*, pp. 159–160.

[3] *Ibid.*, and *Documentary Report*, pp. 88–96. The latter source consists of the "proofs" assembled by the group victorious on February 23, 1966, in an attempt to discredit rivals. The quotations and reports assembled seem to be authentic but they are often taken out of context and blown up out of their true proportions.

tation of the minorities in the Syrian officer corps were becoming major issues of Ba'thi politics, then they and the 'Alawi officers shared a common cause.[4]

J'did and the military and civilian faction around him, moreover, represented the original orientation and tendencies of the military group that had carried out the *coup d'état* of March 8, while Hafiz seemed to have deviated from them by allying himself with 'Aflaq and Bitar. Razzaz tries to place the beginning of this alliance as late as possible in 1965,[5] but it is quite evident that cooperation began early in the summer of that year and perhaps even in the spring. Aware of J'did's supremacy in the Syrian party organization, Hafiz tended to lean towards the rival party faction. 'Aflaq and Bitar on the other hand coveted the military power possessed by Hafiz without which, they realized, little could be done against the opposition. The bitter feuds of the past were temporarily set aside and so were the ideological differences—Hafiz was never much of an ideologue and he and Razzaz could, for instance, support the same line towards Egypt in September 1965.

But this rapprochement with the party's moderate wing was objectionable to several less confident supporters of Hafiz. Bitar in particular was known to stand firmly for civilian control, for closer relations with Egypt, and for mending fences with the Syrian urban middle classes. One can see how easy it was for J'did to convince several of Hafiz' allies that they would have to pay the price if 'Aflaq and Bitar returned to power. The misgivings felt by military and radical civilian party members towards Bitar and his policies, as well as the causes of their apprehension, are illuminated by the reply that Razzaz gave to a question addressed to him by the Hama Branch, which he then distributed to all party members:

[4] It should be stressed that not all Druse officers were on J'did's side; a few of them (and an even smaller number of 'Alawis) backed Hafiz and the National Command. There were also some high-ranking Isma'ili officers (such as 'Abd al-Karim al-Jundi and Ahmad al-Mir) but they seem to have been loyal to J'did all along.

[5] According to Razzaz (*op. cit.*, p. 164), Bitar negotiated with Hafiz during the summer without the knowledge of the National Command after he had started negotiations with 'Umran. Razzaz wrote nothing about the role he himself may have played in the bargaining with Hafiz, probably because he did not want to support the accusation that the National Command (and its secretary-general) encouraged Hafiz and thus served to bring about the *coup d'état*.

> Each of us, including Comrade Bitar, is not free from mistakes. But Comrade Bitar's mistakes were blown out of proportion . . . because of his position regarding military domineering, opening to the masses and the unionist trend and because of his belief that the Party's composition following the *coup* brought about a considerable measure of artificiality. . . .

As a result of these developments there emerged during the summer of 1965 two broad rival coalitions within the Ba'th regime in Syria, whose struggle governed the last phase of our period and epitomized the major issues of Ba'thi politics. One coalition was composed of J'did's military faction and its supporters in the Syrian Regional Command and party hierarchy, and the other was based at that stage on the tenuous alliance between Hafiz and the 'Aflaq-Bitar wing of the party. J'did's group initially had the upper hand in the army and in the Syrian party organization and its first moves were calculated to consolidate its superior position.

As had been the case in earlier phases of the regime's history, actual power shifted in September 1965 to those institutions which the dominant faction found easiest to manipulate. J'did, who had been elected in August as deputy regional secretary of the Ba'th, chose to operate through the Regional Command. With 'Ubaid, Hatum, Tlas, and Shiyya on his side, J'did could claim the unquestioned leadership of the Command whose membership included also several of his civilian and military backers such as Yusuf Z'ayyin, Muhammad 'Id 'Ashawi, and Marwan Habash. The Regional Command then decided on its own to implement the decisions of the Extraordinary Regional Congress, withdrew its confidence from the cabinet headed by Hafiz, and nominated Yusuf Z'ayyin as premier. According to the arrangements devised by the Eighth National Congress, such decisions ought to have been in the realm of the Political Bureau but they were taken by the Regional Command on its own.

The new cabinet was formed on September 23 and not confirmed by the broadened NCRC until October 17. The delay was probably caused by the expected opposition from the supporters of the National Command in the Council; presumably it was considered less harmful to delay the vote than to encounter an unpleasantly noticeable opposition. The core of the new cabinet was made up of J'did's supporters. Dr. Ibrahim Makhus, a physician like Atasi and Z'ayyin, and at that time the only prominent 'Alawi among the party's civilian leaders, was made deputy premier and minister of foreign affairs. Muhammad 'Id 'Ashawi from Deir az-Zor was entrusted with the important ministry of the interior and 'Abd al-Karim al-Jundi was made minister of agrarian reform. A leftist former schoolteacher, Suleiman al-Khish, was chosen as minister of information, culture, and national guidance.[6]

The formation of a new cabinet was supplemented on October 20 by a reshuffling of provincial governors. The provincial governors in Syria hold considerable local power and occupy an important position in the governmental hierarchy, and the Regional Command wanted to assure its complete control over them.[7]

Control of the army remained the most crucial issue. By winning over some of his rival's military supporters, J'did gained the majority in the Officers' Committee and he initiated extensive transfers in the army designed to remove unreliable officers from sensitive positions. But Hafiz still had some backing in that Committee and he headed the Military Bureau pertaining to the Regional Command, which enabled him to obstruct such action. To circumvent Hafiz an old law was reactivated which vested authority in these matters in the hands of the minister of defence. This post in the new cabinet was held by Hamad 'Ubaid, by then sympathetic with J'did.[8]

Another decision taken by the Regional Command was to arrest Akram Haurani and several of his close associates on October 25, accusing them of being "tools of imperialism and reaction". The arrests followed a press campaign in which the government's organs refuted charges levelled by Haurani to the effect that the regime's oil policy was pro-Western. These accusations referred to the agreement with a British consortium on the financing and building of a pipeline, and their effectiveness showed how difficult it had

[6] For the full composition of the cabinet see Appendix A.

[7] Details of the changes were announced by Radio Damascus on October 20, 1965, 2:15 p.m. Razzaz (*op. cit.*, p. 156) says that the new provincial governors were all supporters of the Regional Command.

[8] Razzaz, *op. cit.*, and *Documentary Report*, pp. 48–49. Razzaz notes that 'Ubaid was hardly more than a tool manipulated by J'did and Suwaidani.

become for the regime to detach one sphere of interests from the general context of its foreign policy.[9] The Regional Command was also alarmed by other moves of the Haurani group and by the prospect of opposition movements exploiting the intra-Ba'thi crisis to resume their activity.[10] But the arrest of a group considered sympathetic to Hafiz could not be divorced from that crisis and was bound to be interpreted as a challenge to him. Hafiz, for one, accepted it; he refused to abide by the Regional Command's decision and displayed his displeasure by visiting Haurani in prison. It was probably the pressure exerted by Hafiz that brought about Haurani's release on "medical grounds" in December.[11]

The rivalry and diffusion of power within the Ba'th regime were also manifested in the differences between *ath-Thaura,* the government's newspaper controlled by and expressing the views of the Regional Command,[12] and the party's organ, *al-Ba'th,* the mouthpiece of the National Command. The duel between these two newspapers had been going on for some time and reached its peak when *al-Ba'th* published a series of six articles by Bitar between October 26 and November 2 (carried simultaneously by *al-Aḥrār,* the party's unofficial organ in Beirut which was controlled by the National Command).

In these articles Bitar sought publicly to invest the conflict between his group and the rival party faction with the proper ideolo-

[9] On the agreement, see above p. 178. For the accusation and press campaign, see *ath-Thaura,* October 2, 1965, *al-Ba'th,* October 6, 1965, and Radio Damascus, October 14, 1965, 7:45 a.m.

[10] The bulletin issued by the Regional Command on October 26, 1965, explaining Haurani's arrest to the party members, cited other instances of revived political activity by Haurani's "Temporary Organization of Arab Socialists" and related it also to a communiqué published by the former Ba'thi leader Jallal as-Sayyid (reported also by *al-Ḥayāt*). Another Ba'thi source (*The Party Crisis,* p. 47) defined Haurani's activity at that period as posing "an alternative to the Party". These sources failed to mention an alarming revolt against the party leadership in the Deir az-Zōr Branch by apparent sympathizers of Haurani, which ended in the expulsion of 14 of them from the party (Bulletin of the Regional Command, October 15, 1965, and *Chronology of Arab Politics* [1965], p. 409).

[11] *Documentary Report*, p. 31. Hafiz' rivals used this incident for documenting their charge that he was guilty of *fardiyya.* See also Radio Damascus, December 2, 1965, 9:15 p.m., and Radio London, December 18, 1965, 10:45 p.m.

[12] It is interesting to note that Zaki al-Arsuzi had a column of his own in *ath-Thaura.*

gical significance. To achieve this he reiterated the basic principles of the Ba'th as conceived by 'Aflaq and himself. To the extent that they could be distinguished from one another, Bitar wrote, nationalism had a priority over socialism. But this socialism was not to be confused with Marxism—Bitar revived the old argument used by the Ba'th against the Communists and stated that one could not be a Marxist and a true Arab nationalist. Socialism (properly defined) and Arab unity were two facets of the same issue, but striving for unity was more revolutionary and should constantly be stressed.[13] He reminded his readers that the problem of Arab unity could not be evaded, that for the time being at least an "encounter" (*iltiqā'*) with the Egyptian Revolution should be accomplished and he implied that it was Ba'thi Syria that had to take the initiative.[14] Bitar denounced the Regional Command and its supporters, accusing them of deception (*taḍlīl*) and of being "opportunistic leftists"—"The sick men of the Left who in search of power used nominal and demagogic revolutionism to leap to the ranks of leadership".[15]

Such phrases were an explicit challenge to Bitar's rivals and the reactions of the Regional Command and its mouthpiece, *ath-Thaura*, indeed indicated that they were accepted as such. But the acrimonious tone of the articles and the resort to traditional slogans that no longer seemed relevant were frowned upon by several party members, including some of Bitar's associates in the National Command.[16] What was not so evident to outside observers at the time was the fact that Bitar's articles also reflected the hard line that he was advocating within the National Command, calling for a showdown with the Regional Command. The muscle behind that hard line was the reinforcement of the alliance between the 'Aflaq-Bitar wing and Hafiz by 'Umran. Contacts with 'Umran established through Lebanese supporters of Bitar had already been reported in June,[17]

[13] "Al-Wahda al-'arabiyya", *al-Ba'th*, October 28, 1965.

[14] "Talāqī ath-thaurāt al-'arabiyya", *al-Ba'th*, November 2, 1965.

[15] "Ath-Thaura wa-ath-thauriyya", *āl-Ba'th*, October 26, 1965.

[16] Razzaz, *op. cit.*, pp. 179–180. He also offers a short criticism of the contents of these articles. On December 28, when Razzaz would have to answer publicly to several questions repeatedly addressed to the National Command by dissatisfied party members, his published reply would refer also to criticism of Bitar's articles.

[17] See *al-Anwār* (Beirut), August 20, 1965.

and he had been in Syria since October 4 on leave from his ambassadorial post in Spain, but it must have taken some time to reconcile Hafiz and 'Umran.

Bringing 'Umran into the coalition seemed to have clear advantages. He still had some backing in the army and the presence of the 'Alawi military leader in the ranks of the National Command's sympathizers could be expected to split the solid 'Alawi support behind J'did.[18] But there was also a group within the National Command which opposed the "showdown policy" and some of Bitar's moves. The views of this group (composed of Razzaz, Mansur al-Atrash, and the Lebanese Jubran Majdalani and Dr. 'Ali al-Khalil) are recorded, perhaps with a measure of hindsight, in the memoirs of Razzaz. At that point the members of the group claimed that the National Command did not possess sufficient military and political might to carry through a confrontation with the Regional Command, and they pointed to the inherent weaknesses of an alliance with both Hafiz and 'Umran.

These two approaches were being debated in a lengthy session held by the National Command between December 8 and 20. Such sessions were not an internal affair of the party's moderate wing, but owing to the presence of General Hafiz al-Asad and Ibrahim Makhus, members of the National Command and supporters of J'did, they also provided a channel of communication with the rival coalition. Suddenly, on December 19, J'did's supporters in the armoured brigade stationed in Homs headed by Mustafa Tlas, chief of staff of that brigade, forcibly arrested Colonel Salah Namur, the brigade's commander, and another officer.[19] That episode, whose true significance seems to be somewhat misinterpreted in Razzaz'

[18] Razzaz, *op. cit.*, p. 164, refers to Bitar's contacts with "a group of officers from among 'Umran's supporters". On p. 160 he offers the unacceptable explanation that the National Command later chose 'Umran as minister of defence because, among other reasons, it did not want the struggle to appear as one between 'Alawis and non-'Alawis. The implication, however, is that the decisive consideration was the hope to divide the 'Alawis by having one of them on the side of the National Command. J'did's supporters later claimed that Hafiz had told a presumed ally that this ('Umran's joining the coalition) would generate conflicts among his rivals and split them (*Documentary Report*, p. 37).

[19] A detailed and most interesting version of this story is given by Razzaz, *op. cit.*, pp. 165–167. *An-Nahār* (Beirut) December 28, 1965, rendered a most detailed

account, was the culmination of a long struggle over a key unit so situated as to affect both Damascus and Aleppo in case of a *coup*.

Owing to its location, Homs had traditionally played a crucial role in those cases when the loyalty of the army was divided between warring factions. J'did, aware of the negotiations with 'Umran, apparently wanted to secure his hold over a vital brigade before a confrontation occurred. This appeared to be such an important advantage that he sanctioned resorting to violence even though it seems that at that stage he wanted to complete his control of the regime without a major confrontation.[20] This time he miscalculated. The rude action antagonized numerous officers and seemed to vindicate the position held by the hard-liners in the National Command. Following a dramatic speech by 'Aflaq,[21] the National Command decided on December 19 to dissolve the Regional Command and to take all military and civil powers into its hands. Realizing that the bulk of the Syrian officer corps, shocked by the "Homs Incident", supported the National Command, the Regional Command complied with a decision that it had rejected a year earlier.[22]

account of the episode which is entirely compatible with that of Razzaz. This is one of the few cases in which a report on internal Ba'thi affairs appearing in the Beirut press proved to be perfectly correct.

[20] Since Razzaz plays down the role of the National Command in recruiting military support (and in particular the alliance with 'Umran), J'did's actions on December 19, as they appear in Razzaz' account, seem out of proportion and uncalculated. But Razzaz himself writes elsewhere that on December 20 Salim Hatum wanted to storm the National Command and was only restrained from doing so by J'did who had not yet completed his preparations (*op. cit.*, p. 196). These preparations were not military; J'did had enough military support and it was not merely a successful *coup* that he was after. If one correctly interprets J'did's character and position as well as the essence of Ba'thi military politics, it seems that he was seeking rather for a quiet, nonviolent victory over the rival faction. Control of the brigade stationed in Homs could have given him such a victory, but to achieve this he had to resort to the "minor violence" involved in the "Homs Incident".

[21] The full text of the speech was published in *al-Jarīda* (Beirut), January 9, 1966.

[22] It seems that a decisive factor in the Regional Command's decision to comply with the resolutions of the National Command was the realization that many of the neutral officers in the army supported the position of the latter because the actions of the Regional Command seemed to lead towards a violent confrontation and to ruin the basis of military hierarchy and discipline. This is clearly alluded to in the memorandum by Bitar published in *al-Muḥarrir* immediately following

A new situation was thus created in the Syrian political scene and the stage was set for the final confrontation.

THE "WHITE COUP" OF DECEMBER 19 AND THE RESTORATION OF BITAR

The decisions taken by the National Command on December 19 were not made public until December 21, by which date they were supplemented by a series of resolutions that aimed at consolidating the hold of the National Command and its allies over the army and the party machinery. These steps were sufficiently far-reaching to reintroduce a fresh ruling group and to indicate its different orientation. At the same time the fact that the balance of power within the regime was not substantially altered, that the bases of power of the group ousted from its leadership were not undermined, served to postpone the final confrontation between the two contending coalitions.

The dissolved Syrian Regional Command was temporarily replaced by a Supreme Party Command (*al-qiyāda al-ḥizbiyya al-ʿulya*), a forum made up of the National Command reinforced by Bitar and four of his Syrian supporters. The composition of the new forum guaranteed a majority in it for ʿAflaq and Bitar's hard line.[23]

The Officers' Committee and the Military Bureau were placed squarely under the authority of the new Supreme Party Command. The Committee and the Bureau were to be completely separated and the latter, unlike its predecessors, was to include both military

the *coup* of February 23 (*al-Wathāʾiq al-ʿarabiyya* [1966], p. 114). The Regional Command was aware of the dangers to its position posed by a resurgence of the feeling of a general nonpartisan sense of military solidarity. See for instance *The Party Crisis*, p. 25.

[23] Razzaz, *op. cit.*, p. 176, writes that he stood for giving all viewpoints a representation in the new Command. This was, indeed, in line with his broader outlook on a solution for the conflict, namely that it had to be based on some form of compromise and not on the eviction of the rival faction. Bitar's opposition to his position is corroborated by the details given in *Documentary Report*, pp. 12 and 55. As a compromise five vacant seats were left in the new Command (Razzaz, *op. cit.*, p. 182).

and civilian party members. By the same token the resolutions of the National Command asserted that, except for the minister of defence, army officers could no longer hold simultaneously military and senior government or party offices, namely membership in the National or Regional Command. (This would have enabled the military still to play an active role in the branches of the Military Organization but not on the regional level.) In order further to discourage active military participation in politics, the same resolutions implied also that an army officer might not be allowed to return to service once he chose to fill a senior government or party office.[24]

As for the party organization, it was decided to re-evaluate the status of both the active membership and of those members who had been ousted during previous periods. The Supreme Party Command was to establish its centralized authority over the propaganda machinery and to launch an "enlightenment campaign" among party members and the "masses" designed to bring the party out of its "isolation".

These resolutions reflected the policy that Bitar had unsuccessfully advocated or tried to implement for almost three years. Not only was there an intention to gain control over the Syrian army but also to minimize or at least conceal the political role of the military. Breaking out of "isolation" meant, in Bitar's terminology, relinquishing the notion of exclusive Ba'thi control through the party organization and its affiliated subservient "popular organizations" in favour of cooperation with other political and social forces.

Through a review of the membership status in the party the National Command sought to re-transform the composition of the party, using the same method that had been employed by the Regional Command to undo what the Regionalists had accomplished during that period. Razzaz seems to have been the most insistent member of the National Command in his belief that through a careful and patient process of re-evaluation of the party's membership the balance of power in the party could be changed again. The party hierarchy and to a considerable extent the branch commands as they were constituted in December 1965 were loyal to the ousted

[24] These resolutions were described in a bulletin distributed by the National Command on December 20.

Regional Command and this state of affairs had to be altered if the new ruling group wanted to remain in power. Razzaz kept telling his colleagues that this was an artificial situation, that 150 *Qaumiyyūn* (namely supporters of 'Aflaq) had been ousted in the Der'a Branch and 70 in the Deir az-Zor Branch, and that this situation could still be reversed.[25] Beyond its immediate political repercussions the issue threw an interesting light on the Syrian political system as it developed under the Ba'th. Political participation was limited to a group of military and civilian party militants and, consequently, even relatively moderate changes in the composition of that group affected the political process in a very significant way.

The line pursued by the National Command, perhaps with some reservations regarding the political role of the military and his own position, was for the time being acceptable to Hafiz. But to the military and civilian group that had gathered around J'did it meant an eventual termination of at least their political careers. This would be very bluntly expressed by Bitar when later demanding a purge of the broadened NCRC: "There is no need for all the military and we'll have half of them resign as well as such a Marwan Habash or Muhammad az-Zu'bi; as for the military, if they don't like it they are welcome to go to their units".[26]

Still, although J'did and his supporters had enough military and political strength at that stage to topple the new Party Command, they chose to comply with the decisions of the National Command for the very reason that the latter had not as yet struck at the root of their power. They could, therefore, follow the rule that had governed intra-party rivalries throughout the history of the Ba'th regime in Syria—violent clashes likely to endanger the very existence of the regime should be avoided. In more specific terms, an armed *coup* against the National Command (which commanded the support of most of the party's branches abroad) and against a significant portion of the army's leadership would surely have a disastrous political outcome and was therefore undesirable. Thus, as long as

[25] Razzaz, *op. cit.*, p. 176, and *Documentary Report*, p. 45.

[26] Quoted from *Documentary Report*, p. 60. Habash and Zu'bi were both members of the Regional Command and supporters of J'did. The quotation seems to convey Bitar's disrespect for J'did's military and civilian protégés of which they were probably aware.

their predominance in the army and their control of the party's hierarchy in Syria were not seriously menaced, J'did and his group could opt for conducting a peaceful political struggle.

The initial objective of their efforts was to embarrass the new party leadership. On December 22, Z'ayyin's cabinet and three of the five members of the Presidency Council tendered their resignations. This created a constitutional crisis of sorts for according to the constitution it was the Presidency Council that had to accept the resignation of the cabinet. The difficulty was resolved on December 27 when the NCRC elected three new members to fill the vacancies in the Presidency Council and Z'ayyin's resignation was formally accepted.[27] Bitar was asked to form the new cabinet.

The formation of Bitar's cabinet and its make-up revealed some of the obstacles that the National Command had to face as well as the forces on which it could or hoped to rely. Bitar's nomination as premier was not unanimously approved by the National Command. Not only were Asad and Makhus members of that Command, but the moderate wing of 'Aflaq's supporters, most notably Razzaz and Jubran Majdalani, was reluctant to have Bitar as a premier. The moderates in the National Command believed that the only way out of the crisis was through some compromise with the rival coalition, which they realized could not be evicted. They feared that Bitar's personality and the hard line he represented might hinder such a compromise.[28] These objections were overruled and Bitar was nominated, indeed drawing criticism from the party in Syria and even from some branches abroad.

Another important decision had to be taken with regard to the ministry of defence. Following the changes of August and September 1965, the minister of defence became the army's supreme commander and the import of the authority vested in that position

[27] The three members of the Presidency Council who resigned were Nur ad-Din al-Atasi, Jamil Shiyya, and Fa'iz al-Jasim (from the Hassakkeh region). They were replaced by Shibli al-'Aisami, 'Abd al-Fattah Bushi, and Ahmad al-Khatib (who at some later point switched to the other side to become secretary-general of the Teachers Union and, in 1970, temporarily, president of the Syrian Arab Republic).

[28] Razzaz, *op. cit.*, pp. 180–181, and *Documentary Report*, p. 27. The latter source quotes a letter sent to Bitar by his staunch Lebanese supporter, Dr. 'Ali Jabir, in which he strongly condemned Majdalani for opposing Bitar's candidacy.

was fully demonstrated by the events which led to the "Incident of December 19". 'Umran was 'Aflaq and Bitar's candidate for this office; not only did he demand it as a price for the military support he brought into the alliance, but it also seems that 'Aflaq and Bitar wanted to use 'Umran for neutralizing Hafiz.[29] The alliance with both Hafiz and 'Umran was after all temporary and tenuous, and from the experience they had gained during the previous three years the veteran leaders surely realized that in case of victory they should not be left alone to contend with the unchecked powers of a military partner. In other words, they seem to have already been preparing for the aftermath of an expected victory over J'did and his group. But all this was probably being considered by Hafiz and 'Umran as well. Hafiz, therefore, made a last-minute attempt to regain part of his former military authority. He did not object to 'Umran's becoming minister of defence but he proposed in the Supreme Party Command that the powers of the army's supreme commander be restored to himself. The significance of his proposal was all too obvious to his colleagues and one of them is quoted as saying: "The old picture will be restored and we'll all go back to where we came from".[30] Hafiz was outvoted and 'Umran was made minister of defence with full powers, to the vexation not only of Hafiz but also of several neutral officers who resented 'Umran's personality and methods (he had been associated in the minds of many with sly schemes and sectarian politics). 'Aflaq and Bitar had their way again but there would be a price to be paid.

With the exception of 'Umran the members of the new cabinet formed by Bitar on January 2 represented two major tendencies. The hard core of the cabinet was composed of such veteran close associates of Bitar as the Ba'thi ideologist 'Abdallah 'Abd ad-Da'im (minister of culture), Shaker Mustafa (minister of information), and Bashir al-Qutb (minister of state for foreign affairs). These were members of what can be called Bitar's faction, rising and falling according to the fluctuations of their leader's political fortunes.[31]

[29] Razzaz, *op. cit.*, p. 181, presents 'Umran as a neutral candidate, but this explanation is unacceptable and is indeed contradicted by his own account in other contexts.

[30] *Documentary Report*, pp. 38–39.

[31] Razzaz, *op. cit.*, p. 175, calls them *jamā'at al-bīṭār* but their rivals accused them of presenting themselves as "the Party's vanguard" (*Documentary Report*, p. 22).

The other group in the cabinet was made up of non-Ba'thi ministers. As he had done in May 1964, Bitar included among them at least two who were known unionists—Muhammad 'Arab Sa'id and 'Abd al-Wahhab Khayyata.[32] This gesture was one of several made towards Egypt and its supporters, indicating that Bitar was seeking a détente. Another such gesture was included in Bitar's policy statement broadcast on January 4.[33] It called for "an encounter of Revolutions" with Egypt, Algeria, and the Yemen, and for "a sound adhesion" to the "Arab liberation movements". This referred in Ba'thi parlance to closer relations with Egypt and with the movements pertaining to its orbit.

But that was not the major theme of the statement, the significance of which lay rather in Bitar's bold treatment of the political role of the Syrian army.[34] The issue had been in the centre of Ba'thi politics for three years and had often been discussed *in camera*. Under the formula of the "ideological army" (as distinct from the "political army") the Ba'th had in fact sanctioned the army's dominant role within the regime. In his statement Bitar for the first time brought the matter into the open and tried to indicate that an essential change had taken place in this respect. "This Cabinet came [to power]", he said, "only after it had been convinced that the army had adhered to its mission and tasks on the frontiers and kept clear of the government". Bitar had presented some preconditions on which he had insisted before accepting the premiership and two of them are mentioned in the sources: a stipulation that his cabinet could be deposed only by a two-thirds majority in the Supreme Party Command, and the ouster of several hostile officers from their key positions, most notably Colonel 'Izzat J'did (an armoured forces officer and apparently a relative of Salah) and Major Salim Hatum.[35] The paragraph from the policy statement

[32] *Al-Ḥayāt*, January 4, 1966.

[33] The text was reproduced in *al-Wathā'iq al-'arabiyya* (1966), pp. 6–9.

[34] The sections of the statement dealing with this issue were indeed the ones that the state radio saw fit to emphasize (Radio Damascus, January 4, 1966, 10:15 p.m.). It is on such occasions that the political importance of the position of the minister of information is underscored.

[35] On Bitar's preconditions see Razzaz, *op. cit.*, pp. 186 and 193, Cairo Radio, December 25, 1966, 9:00 a.m.

quoted above alluded to these preconditions by way of reminding Bitar's rivals that he took power in order to carry out a definite policy. He went on to say that "the long experience and the lessons learned by our military comrades over the years have given them sufficient resistance to seeking power . . . the army can intervene in politics to protect the Revolution but not to threaten it".[36]

This was quite a sweeping statement, but in reality it was obvious that such an extensive wave of transfers as alluded to in the bulletin would be considered a *casus belli* by those concerned and could very well induce them to stage a *coup d'état*. On the other hand, as long as such transfers were not carried out the new ruling group was to remain seriously handicapped by the ever-present threat posed by a hostile military faction in command of most of the army's key posts and the Syrian party machinery. Here was the gist of the dilemma produced by the "white *coup*" of December 19, and the statement quoted above reflected Bitar's unequivocal and unrealistic approach to its solution. It was the attempt and the inability to find a way out of this predicament which underlay the events of the following seven weeks and finally led to the *coup* of February 23, 1966.

THE COUP

The peculiar arrangement devised in 1963 between 'Aflaq and the Military Committee led to a very close mutual involvement of the military and civilian sectors of the regime, so that by the end of 1965 the politics of the Syrian army had become almost indistinguishable from the politics of the Ba'th Party. The principal military protagonists of the period—Hafiz, J'did, and 'Umran—were no longer on military service and their power depended on their intermediary

[36] The problem of the army's political role became a cardinal issue during the period that preceded the *coup* of February 23, 1966, and remained so for some time afterwards as reflected in the speech by Mustafa Tlas quoted at the head of this chapter. Before the *coup*, however, J'did's group did not bring its position into the open. But by March the victorious Regional Command could explain to the party members that keeping the army away from politics ("the army's return to its barracks") was one of the devices employed by "world imperialism and its agents" (*The Party's Crisis*, pp. 15–16). The speech by Tlas, it seems, draws heavily on this source.

supporters in the army and in the party. The military elements had all along remained dominant, but in the Ba'thi political system as it had evolved a military faction would find it difficult to exercise its power without simultaneously gaining ascendency in the party. Consequently, while in January 1966 control of the army was at the core of the struggle, there developed a hardly less vital contest for the domination of the party organization.

J'did and his group had some important initial advantages in the contest. They controlled the party's machinery and the leadership of most branches and they therefore demanded that the Regional Command be summoned to an emergency session as stipulated by the party's Internal Regulation. Article 61 in the new Internal Regulation approved by the Eighth National Congress indeed stated that a Regional Congress ought to be convened following the dissolution of the Regional Command by the National Command.[37] Under the conditions prevailing late in 1965 and early in 1966, the delegates to a Regional Congress were likely to vindicate the ousted Regional Command, and the new party leadership could not afford to abide by the Internal Regulation. Nor could it safely summon the National Congress to an emergency session since the Syrian delegation to that Congress, which had been elected in April 1965, was dominated by J'did's supporters. The solution to the problem, as envisaged by 'Aflaq and Bitar, was to purge the party and hold elections to a new Regional (and eventually National) Congress. This explains why the minister of information, when questioned on January 11, 1966, on the legal aspects of the situation, chose to speak about the Ninth National Congress. The implication of his statement was that the National Command did not intend to summon the Eighth National Congress to an emergency session but rather to conduct new elections.[38]

But this was a lengthy process and in the meanwhile their rivals were chiding 'Aflaq and Bitar for breaking the party's by-laws. Convinced of their own rightfulness and regarding the ousted Region-

[37] The bulletin issued by the Temporary Regional Command on March 1, 1966, boasted (justly, it seems) of the foresight shown by its members when they had insisted on inserting this stipulation.

[38] Radio Damascus, January 11, 1966, 5:15 p.m.

al Command as the product of an illegal conspiracy against the party,[39] 'Aflaq and Bitar were not so much bothered by moral scruples as they were troubled by the accumulating political effect that such accusations seemed to have. It was the levelling of such charges against him that 'Aflaq had in mind when he complained of "the weapon of legality and the Internal Regulation" employed by his rivals.[40]

The National Command had already indicated on December 20 that it intended to remedy the weakness of its position in the Syrian party organization through a re-evaluation of the membership rolls. It soon began its preparations by temporarily banning advancement to higher ranks of membership. This meant in practical terms that whatever potential supporters the ousted Regional Command had as nonvoting members were not to be enfranchised by the branches. But this too was a long and slow process and there was strong pressure for a more rapid solution. 'Aflaq and Bitar wanted to purge the commands of several branches which were particularly loyal to the ousted Regional Command. The command of the Aleppo Branch is known to have been deposed by the Supreme Party Command on January 26,[41] but it appears that little else was accomplished.

Spokesmen for the National Command visited the party's branches in an attempt to win the support of the rank and file. But they usually met with audiences that had been well prepared by their rivals, and even the questions addressed to them tended to be repetitious. They ranged from a general inquiry about the "ideological vacuum" represented by the party's moderate wing to a specific challenge: was not the "white *coup*"of December 19 connected with the visit of the American Sixth Fleet to Beirut, and what, in

[39] In his speech of February 18, 1966, 'Aflaq said: "the form of this Party had been altered and so had been the mentality of its membership . . . moreover, they had been altered according to plans, through resolute and persistent action . . ." (*al-Wathā'iq al-'arabiyya* [1966], p. 60).

[40] "Silāḥ ash-shar'iyya wa-an-niẓām ad-dākhilī," from 'Aflaq's speech at the National Command's decisive session on December 19, 1965. The speech was reproduced in *al-Jarīda* (Beirut), January 9, 1966.

[41] According to the February 1966 issue of *al-Ḥizb*, the Ba'th Party's central organ, p. 90.

that context, did Bitar's meeting with the American Ambassador signify? The leadership of the Quneitra Branch, for instance, had been held by J'did's confidants for quite some time before the crisis and most of its leaders remained firmly loyal to him. The branch's command summoned the commands of the subbranches (*shu'ab*) to prepare a memorandum to be submitted to the Supreme Party Command. On January 29 it reprimanded party members who had met with representatives of the National Command. Although such detailed information on the struggle in other branches is not available, the complaints by Razzaz and Bitar about organized rumours and questions which they seemed to encounter everywhere appear to be warranted.

'Aflaq, Bitar, and their supporters met with similar difficulties in the "front organizations" pertaining to the party. These, most notably the General Federation of Workers and the Student Union, had been built by the ousted Regional Command and remained loyal to it. The minister of labour in Bitar's cabinet, Jamil Thabit, was a veteran Trade Unionist but his support could not guarantee the loyalty of the Trade Unions to the new Party Command. New elections were held in the Unions but the old leaders were returned.[42] On February 9 the Supreme Party Command decided to expel several steadfast opponents from various branches. Among them were Husain Rizq and Fayyad Mustafa, two prominent leaders of the General Federation of Workers. Similarly, the party's Student Union continued to support the Regional Command, and on February 12 a four-member committee was formed by the Supreme Party Command to deal with the "lack of discipline" in that Union.

Perhaps most embarrassing for the new party leadership were the repeated demands by the backers of the dissolved Regional Command to summon the NCRC to vote on the new cabinet and their call to hold a Regional Congress on February 25.

In view of these difficulties and in line with their basic outlook, Bitar and 'Aflaq called for a policy of "opening" (*infitāḥ*). The term "opening" seems to have been construed in two ways. In more general terms it signified Bitar's belief in the need to soften the rigid concept of party exclusivity advocated by the Regional Command.

[42] *An-Nahār*, January 16, 1966.

He thus told a delegation from Damascus and the provinces on January 8: "The Party shall labour to liberate itself from the isolation into which it has fallen and shall emphasize its popular quality".[43] But in a more specific sense "opening" meant opening the ranks of the party to mild unionists such as the Socialist Unionists, who like the *Quṭriyyūn* were former party members. This could change the balance of power in the party and restore it to the course from which, according to 'Aflaq and Bitar, it had been deflected.[44]

The National Command did not have the time to introduce these changes in the party, but unionist elements were readmitted to a minor role on the Syrian political scene through a restructuring of the NCRC. The NCRC as constituted in August 1965 was controlled by the Regional Command, and the Supreme Party Command could not afford to summon it to give Bitar's new cabinet a vote of confidence and clear it from the shadow of unconstitutionality. It took some time until the categories of membership had been altered and the membership expanded from 95 to 134 on February 15.[45] Thirty members of the old NCRC were ousted and 69 new members were added to change the balance of power in the assembly. The Presidency Council, moreover, was empowered to add ten more members "representing liberation movements in the Arab homeland".[46] This probably referred to non-Syrian branches of the Ba'th but the vague wording gave rise to speculation that the Ba'th considered inviting non-Ba'thi delegates from other Arab countries.[47]

[43] *Al-Waqā'i' al-'arabiyya* (1966), p. 38.

[44] It is not known whether members of the Socialist Unionist Movement did actually return to the party at that period; if they did, their number could not have been large. The Temporary Regional Leadership, however, in the bulletin it sent to party members on March 1, 1966, claimed that a number of Socialist Unionists known for their connection with the Egyptians returned, by a pre-arrangement with Bitar, to the party in order to convert it from the inside. Similarly, the ar-Raqqa Branch of the Ba'th was quoted (by *Documentary Report*, p. 72) to complain of Bitar's admission of members of "malevolent factions" (*fi'āt ḥāqida*, namely Nasserites) to the cabinet and to positions in the domain of propaganda.

[45] Details and the composition of the new Council were given by *al-Ba'th*, February 15, 1966.

[46] *Al-Waqā'i' al-'arabiyya* (1966), p. 43.

[47] *Ibid.*, p. 45 (quoting *al-Ḥayāt* of February 22, 1966).

The new delegates to the NCRC included some well-known unionists like the two Socialist Unionist leaders Sami Sufan and Mustafa al-Hallaj. The significance of this change was spelled out by *al-Baʻth* of February 15, which explained the nature of the new policy "the essence of which is to stress the national identity of the Revolution, to open up to the masses, and to bolster the socialist revolutionary orientation".

Adding the unionists to the NCRC was a far-reaching measure and it was followed by a number of other steps which indicated that the National Command had decided to break the deadlock by trying to change the balance of power in the party and in the army. It first decided to summon the Ninth National Congress and to hold preparatory elections in the Syrian party branches. These measures, if carried through, could have meant the loss of J'did's political footing.[48] The threat to him and to his followers was made all the more serious by the Supreme Party Command's decision on February 21 to transfer Ahmad Swaidani from his position as director of personnel and to dismiss ʻIzzat J'did and Salim Hatum from their sensitive command posts near Damascus.

These were three of J'did's best-known and best-placed supporters and their ouster had been demanded by Bitar upon assuming the premiership. It will be recalled that following the formation of the cabinet it was announced that military transfers were to take place within a month. Later in January a new Military Bureau was formed and a number of officers were transferred, though none of those whose removal was desired by Bitar.[49] If the new party leadership wanted to move these officers from their positions it had to be ready to defend itself against the *coup* which they were most likely to stage in reaction; its failure to do so proved the shortsightedness of the attempt to rely on both Hafiz and ʻUmran.

As minister of defence for the new leadership it was ʻUmran's task to discipline the army and to assure it of the necessary support. But he was already thinking about the new conflicts, which he knew from experience were bound to emerge in the event of victory over the rival coalition. In January and February 1966 ʻUmran refrained

[48] Razzaz, *op. cit.*, p. 196, and *Cahiers*, No. 60 (1966).

[49] Circular of the National Command from January 20, 1966.

The residence of Amin al-Hafiz after the *coup* of February 23, 1966

Ba'thi militants forcing open struck shops in Damascus

from flagrantly challenging J'did and his group, and was at least as preoccupied with neutralizing Hafiz as he was with combatting them. It is a moot question whether the combined efforts of Hafiz and 'Umran could have sufficed to overcome the supporters of J'did, but the fact of the matter is that they devoted their energy and most of their time to fighting one another. In his capacity as minister of defence, for example, 'Umran tried to keep army units loyal to Hafiz away from Damascus and to cashier several of the latter's followers.[50] He tried in fact to replace J'did as leader of those officers whose allegiance he had once claimed and he is reported to have employed the same tactics which had then made him unpopular with the ranks of the army, namely to have evoked feelings of communal solidarity and distrust, to have given contradictory promises, and so forth. There are also indications that 'Umran's conduct (and possibly the squabbling between Hafiz and himself) antagonized those independent officers who, following the "Homs Incident", had sided with the National Command whose leaders they regarded as more staid and less likely to endanger the army.[51]

When the National Command decided to transfer Salim Hatum, 'Izzat J'did and Ahmad Swaidani to "innocuous" posts it did not, therefore, possess sufficient military strength to contend with the anticipated reaction. J'did and his group indeed considered the order issued by the National Command a grave threat to their position and decided to stage a *coup d'état*.

The *coup* was carried out early in the morning of February 23. The forces loyal to Hafiz could offer only scattered local resistance and in any case the support of Hafiz al-Asad and the air force served as an ultimate guarantee of the rebels' victory. Fighting took place in Damascus, in the Israeli Front area, and near Homs. Most dramatic was the battle in front of Hafiz' residence in Damascus. At the head of his personal guard he fought for hours against Salim Hatum's commando troops who a few months before had been considered among his supporters. Hafiz was wounded and then captured with his family. The bloodshed and violence, manifested for the first

[50] Razzaz, *op. cit.*, pp. 185 ff., and *Documentary Report*, pp. 32–42 (where many lively details of the Hafiz-'Umran rivalry are furnished).

[51] *The Party Crisis*, pp. 22 ff., and Razzaz, *op. cit.*

time in an internecine Ba'thi struggle, underscored the sharp break with the past that the *coup* signified.

The nature of the political conflict that preceded the *coup* of February 23, 1966, determined two of its essential features. The crystallization of the rival factions into two broad military and civilian coalitions resulted in a situation where a full-fledged ruling group was ready to take power once the military phase of the *coup* was over. Second, the struggle between these two rival coalitions had become so bitter that there was no question of a settlement with the defeated group or part of it. Some of the defeated leaders, among them Hafiz, Bitar, and Jubran Majdalani, were arrested; others, including 'Aflaq and Razzaz, escaped and hid themselves in Syria. All were eventually expelled from the party according to the procedures stipulated in its Internal Regulation. The shelter given to 'Aflaq and Razzaz by party members in Syria was an indication of the opposition still awaiting the new regime, which at that stage, however, remained latent.

Formation of the new ruling institutions was completed in a relatively short time. On the day of the *coup* a so-called Temporary Regional Command was set up as the supreme political authority and it published its first communiqué over Radio Damascus at 6:20 a.m. It immediately appointed Major-General Hafiz al-Asad as acting minister of defence and promoted Colonel Ahmad Suwaidani to the rank of major-general to make him the new chief of staff. On February 25 Nur ad-Din al-Atasi was named president of the state and Yusuf Z'ayyin prime minister. The NCRC was dissolved and legislative authority was vested in the president's office and in the cabinet. The Temporary Regional Command announced on February 24 that a National Liaison Office had been formed whose task it would be to establish contacts with the party's branches abroad.[52] The next day the secretaries of the party's branches in Syria were summoned to a conference in Damascus, which all but two of them attended. Reportedly they gave their confidence to the Temporary Regional Command and decided to convene an Extraordinary Regional Congress on March 10.[53]

[52] Radio Damascus, February 24, 1966, 10:30 p.m.

[53] Radio Damascus, February 27, 1966, 2:15 p.m., and *The Party Crisis*. Only two branches—Homs and Damascus—failed to send representatives to the meeting.

Z'ayyin formed his new cabinet on March 1. It largely resembled his previous cabinet, the one important innovation being the addition of a registered member of the Syrian Communist Party, Samih 'Atiyya, as the minister of communications. The Extraordinary Regional Congress met on March 10 and terminated its work on March 27. Of the 124 original members of the Regional Congress 21 had been expelled, 103 were invited, and 93 attended. The congress formulated the broad lines of the regime's policies and elected a new Regional Command composed of 16 members. It decided to retain the constitutional framework envisaged by the constitution of May 1964.[54]

Thus, about a month after the *coup* the installation of a new regime in Syria was formally completed. But the smoothness of the transition did not conceal the significance of the change and the problems it created. The history of the Ba'th regime in Syria following the *coup* of February 23, 1966, lies outside the scope of this work but it was largely shaped by these problems and the attempts to solve them. The *coup* also marked a definite turning point in the history of the Ba'th Party and as such again affected the political process in Syria. It is in this context that the immediate results and significance of the *coup* are examined.

IMMEDIATE RESULTS AND SIGNIFICANCE OF THE COUP

The events of February 23, 1966, produced the deepest and most important schism in the history of the Ba'th Party. Earlier splits and dissensions had been painful and politically harmful but 'Aflaq and Bitar had emerged from them as the recognized leaders of a party whose historical continuity and essential features had been preserved. But the *coup d'état* of February 23, 1966, brought to power in Syria a new group which claimed to represent the true Ba'th Party, in composition and orientation different from that of 'Aflaq and Bitar, and, owing to a combination of factors, widely

[54] The details concerning the organizational aspects of the congress were taken from *The Party Crisis*, pp. 32–37.

recognized as a legitimate new leadership. ʻAflaq and Bitar and some of their principal supporters were detained in Syria and their adherents abroad were hampered by lack of financial means and the loss of the political backing of the Syrian government which they had enjoyed since 1963. Other Arab governments (in particular the Lebanese) were at that time reluctant to tolerate open opposition to the Syrian government. On the other hand, their party rivals, who had previously played but a marginal role in national (all-Arab) Baʻthi politics, now had the resources of the Syrian state at their disposal. They could contact elements hostile to ʻAflaq in non-Syrian Baʻthi organizations and promise them positions of leadership, or they could build alternative organizations from Arab students in Damascus. During 1966 they were able to establish a national organization of their own, to hold the Ninth National Congress, and to elect a National Command subservient to them.[55] ʻAflaq and Bitar's wing of the party continued to exist and to command the support of several branches outside Syria, but in political terms it was overshadowed by the organization affiliated with the Syrian Regional Command.

These developments served to make the new Baʻth Party more distinctively Syrian than it had been prior to the *coup*. Syria's new leaders wanted to maintain the party's pan-Arab character since it was an essential feature of the Baʻth in whose name they ruled Syria and on whose prestige the legitimacy of their government was partly based. Also, that posture ought to have prevented them from becoming a mere provincial government and it certainly furnished them with an instrument of intervention in neighbouring Iraq, Lebanon, and Jordan. Nevertheless, their pan-Arab aspirations could hardly be compared with those of the old National Command even after the decline of the party's position as an all-Arab force in November 1963. From November 1963 to February 1966 the notion of an all-Arab Baʻth Party organization, illusory as it often was, still sufficed to introduce an extraneous element into Syrian politics and to enable ʻAflaq and Bitar to maintain a political foothold in Syria through their position in the National Command. This

[55] The methods employed by the Regional Command resemble those which had been used on the eve of the Seventh National Congress. See above p. 106.

was changed in February 1966 and the National Command became subservient to the Syrian Regional Command, an instrument of the Syrian government rather than one of its moulders.

The leaders brought to power by the February *coup* had all played important, often dominant, roles in Syrian and Ba'thi politics in the preceding three years, but during that period their impact had been cushioned by the participation of rival factions in directing the regime and its policies. The elimination of these rivals gave them full power and pinpointed the issues involved in the social background and political orientation of Syria's new rulers.

A number of attributes distinguished Salah J'did and his partners and adherents from their defeated party rivals. They were generally younger and tended to come from minority communities, from the "remote and poor provinces", from small towns and from the countryside. In the political struggles that preceded the *coup* they appeared as the party's left wing, identified with radical economic and social policies, dominated by the military, and harbouring a reserved attitude towards Egypt and Arab unity. As the following quotation indicates they were aware that this was their public image: "describing the latest crisis as the overcoming of the Party's civilian sector by the military sector, itself of rural origins . . . and tending to regional seclusion . . . is an entirely false description based on an unwillingness to see the truth or on insistence to regard it from a certain angle".[56]

The Ba'th regime was hardly acceptable to large segments of Syria's urban population prior to the *coup*, and the public image of the new ruling group made it even less so. Hafiz, after all, enjoyed a measure of popularity and Bitar was known to advocate a more benign attitude towards the urban middle classes. Their dislodgment seemed to have further estranged these strata from the regime whose leaders were acutely aware of the political danger to which such a gap, and especially the majority's resentment of their minoritarian background, exposed them. The Extraordinary Regional Congress of March 1966 warned that:

> It is necessary to acknowledge that Reaction in the Syrian region still possesses a large measure of power. It has waged

[56] Quoted from the appendix to the June 1966 issue of *al-Munadil*.

an unrestricted vicious campaign against the Party and the Revolution based on plots and conspiracies and the generation of an artificial atmosphere of spreading doubts and rumours and the rousing of communal, regional, and racial fanaticism; one must indicate here that certain Party members in both the military and civilian sectors were voluntarily and involuntarily trapped in these reactionary schemes and participated in arousing communal fanaticism.[57]

The widened gap between government and populace was to remain an important trait of Syrian politics but it also had more immediate repercussions. The *coup d'état* of February 23, 1966, narrowed the political basis of the regime by ousting an important segment of the party and turning it into an active opposition group. The new ruling group itself was an incoherent alliance temporarily united by a common opposition to the coalition defeated in the *coup*; and indeed tensions within it soon became apparent. Under these circumstances the hostility of the urban population became all the more significant. The feeling of weakness bred by these developments as well as the proclivities of Syria's new rulers led to the adoption of radical measures in an attempt to consolidate their position and remain in power.

This intensified radicalism which characterized the Syrian political scene following the *coup* of February 23 was confined mostly to the political sphere. The social and economic policies of late 1964 and early 1965 were essentially reaffirmed by the Extraordinary Regional Congress of March 1966, though it decided to apply them with more rigour and consistency. Potilical radicalism manifested itself in the general political climate generated by the *coup* and more specifically in the regime's resorting to novel political strategies. Prominent among these were the interrelated decisions to cooperate with the Syrian Communist Party and to expand considerably cooperation with the Soviet Union, and the resolution to embark on

[57] Quoted from the report on internal politics submitted to the Extraordinary Regional Congress in March 1966 and reproduced in *Decisions of the Extraordinary Regional Congress*, p. 63.

a more radical and active policy in the Arab-Israeli conflict, probably in an attempt to embarrass foreign and domestic foes alike.[58] These changes were all based on earlier developments and were also related to broader developments in the area, but they were most intimately linked to the repercussions on Syrian politics of the *coup*. In turn, the role played by the new Syrian regime in the genesis of the Middle East crisis of May 1967 may prove to have been the most significant outcome of the *coup d'état* of February 23, 1966.

[58] The (well-controlled) cooperation with the Syrian Communist Party was symbolized by their representation in the new cabinet. The closer relations with the Soviet Union would become apparent early in 1966 after a short period of uncertainty, and the decision to develop such relations was clearly alluded to in the report on foreign policy submitted to the congress. The resolutions and recommendations approved by the congress included the following: " . . . The Congress recommends cooperation with all socialist states and strengthening relations with them and opening towards them and guaranteeing their assistance, backing and support" (*ibid.*, p. 34). The recommendations of the congress in the sphere of internal politics included one calling for "considering the Palestine problem the fundamental pivot (*al-miḥwar al-asāsī*) of our internal, Arab and international policies" (*ibid.*, p. 66).

CONCLUSIONS

The last chapter of this study ended with an evaluation of the political consequences of a *coup d'état* in which all the elements and issues of the Ba'thi political system were involved. But important as these consequences were, they still did not convey the full significance of the events and changes which took place in Syria from March 1963 to March 1966. Thus, seen against the background of earlier periods, the very fact that the Ba'th regime could be engrossed in a sustained internecine struggle without facing a serious threat by another political power to exploit the crisis was one index of a substantial change in Syrian politics. That one could explain that struggle in terms of internal Syrian politics almost without reference to the impact of outside forces is another measure of such a change.

Perhaps the most important development in Syria during these years was the reaffirmation of her existence as a sovereign independent state. This the Separatist Regime had failed to achieve from September 1961 to March 1963, and when the Ba'th came to power it still had to contend with the problem for several months. Like its predecessor, the Ba'th regime failed to obtain President Nasser's endorsement, but unlike it, it became sufficiently strong to withstand the pressures he exerted. It is difficult to assess how effective was the attempt by the Ba'th to acquire legitimacy in Syria by posing as an at least equivalent alternative to Nasserism, but the party's success in controlling the army and in suppressing the Nasserites proved sufficient to maintain it in power despite Nasser's hostility. In time, the appeal of the unionist idea and of Nasser's leadership weakened in the Arab world, so that while Egypt's ill will remained a source of embarrassment for the Ba'th it no longer posed a grave threat to its rule.

This process was matched and furthered by developments within the Ba'th Party. 'Aflaq and Bitar and their group never really reconciled themselves to the notion of a Ba'thi regime whose scope and impact were to be virtually limited to Syria. But the Ba'thi officers and party militants who finally triumphed over the "founding fathers" in February 1966 were quite content to rule undisturbed in Syria. Formally they still subscribed to the party's unionist ideology and they maintained its pan-Arab organization, but this they did for political rather than ideological reasons. The change within the Ba'th facilitated the normalization of Syria's relations with Egypt. It appeared ironic, as Munif ar-Razzaz would bitterly point out in his memoirs, that when President Nasser finally acknowledged Syria's renewed sovereignty by re-establishing diplomatic relations with her in November 1966, he benefited the so-called anti-unionist wing of the Ba'th. His move is to be explained primarily by the problems of inter-Arab relations he faced at that stage, but it seems quite safe to say that it was easier for him to recognize a Ba'th regime with a pronounced local bias.

Inside Syria the establishment of the Ba'th regime and the subsequent supremacy of the party's radical wing resulted in profound social and political changes. Most visible was the installation of a new ruling elite. The traditional Syrian ruling group, whose hold was being steadily weakened since independence, enjoyed a brief and partial restoration after September 1961, but under the Ba'th its political power was finally broken and it lost much of its social and economic power as well. The break with the past became all the more pronounced as the new Ba'thi ruling elite achieved by 1965 a practical monopoly of meaningful political activity in the state and established its presence in numerous spheres of social and economic activity.

The Ba'th's success was made possible by the exhaustion of the traditional right wing and of the unionist parties and by the political skill of its own military leaders. By effectively controlling the army the Ba'thi military leaders guaranteed the survival of the regime when it was fragile and then, together with the party's civilian leaders, they performed a still limited function of government. The broadening of the scope of government and of the party's capabilities, which became evident in 1965, is one of the important consequences of Ba'thi rule in Syria. The Ba'th failed to become the mass party it aspired to be—penetrating Syrian society with a network of party members, sympathizers, and members of affiliated "popular" and professional organizations; it did, however, succeed in subordinating to its control almost all spheres of public activity and expression—voluntary and professional associations, the press, the universities. Implementation of the Agrarian Reform and the nationalization of the main branches of industry and commerce gave the party, through the government, much of the power that had previously been in private hands.

It is easier to discern what sectors of Syrian society were disaffected with these social and political changes than to determine which social classes benefited from them. The new ruling group, Ba'thi officers and party militants, were largely recruited from traditionally deprived or marginal segments of Syrian society—minority communities, remote provinces, rural areas. This quality became even more pronounced as a result of the *coup* of February 23, 1966. In a sense, they represented these segments (and their grievances), and this indeed seems to have been the complaint of many middle-class Sunnis from the cities. The radical wing of the Ba'th, which emerged victorious from the *coup* of February 23, 1966, reconciled itself to the hostility of the upper-middle classes whose political and economic power it set out to destroy, but it did try to appeal to the lower-middle classes—a large and important sector of the urban population. It seems, however, that the traditional and conservative elements of that class were deterred by the radical image of the new ruling group as well as by the social origins of its members. The dissatisfaction of large segments of the urban population with the regime that surfaced forcefully in the spring of 1964 did not evoke the same acute or overt political expression in the next two years but it was to remain a significant trait of the Syrian political scene.[1]

On the other hand, it is difficult to examine what measure of support the Ba'th acquired among the urban lower classes, in the minority communities, and in the countryside (including the small towns and large villages in the provinces). Too little is known about the changes that occurred within these sectors but evidently they were, to some degree at least, beneficiaries of the reforms carried out by the Ba'thi regime from 1963 to 1966. Unlike the urban Sunnis, members

[1] The Ba'this own awareness of the importance of this weakness was clearly expressed in the resolutions of the Regional Congress they held in March 1966. An outburst similar to that of 1966 would only take place again in May 1967.

of minority communities and residents of "remote provinces" did not resent the social origins of the new ruling group. It seems rather that, in addition to the satisfaction of having one of their number in a position of power, several of them enjoyed material benefits, most notably new opportunities in the expanded governmental bureaucracy.[2] All this, however, did not mean real participation in ruling the country. Power remained in the hands of a small group of officers and party leaders who tried to manipulate the so-called popular classes but did not intend to share power with them. The attempt to mobilize these classes in active support of the regime met with little success, but the Ba'th seems to have enjoyed among them a modicum of passive support (difficult to measure).

More crucial politically was the regime's control of the Syrian army. The regime's most distinctive feature and one of the most absorbing facets of Syrian political history between 1963 and 1966 was the symbiosis, exceptional in the Arab world,[3] of a relatively vigorous ideological party and a military cabal (which gradually developed into a rather elaborate Military Organization). While the military set the regime up and guaranteed its existence, the party provided it with a legitimizing ideology, with a cadre of activists and loyal bureaucrats, and with a framework for institutionalized political activity. The military's alliance with the civilian Ba'th accounted also for much of the internecine squabbling that plagued the regime during these years, as the party's founders would not reconcile themselves to the role of mere lay figures assigned to them by the army officers. Their close involvement and the divisions among the military enabled the civilian leaders to meddle at times in military politics, but the significant fact was that the military were and remained unquestionably paramount. Ba'thi rule depended on military support and the army officers who provided it had the final say in the party's inner councils and in the state. In due course they gained complete control over the party, remoulded it, and fashioned it into an obedient instrument. The party's leaders had been aware of the dangers inherent in an alliance with the

[2] This is indicated in several sources. Perhaps the most vivid is Jundi's description (*op. cit.*, p. 136) of the "caravans of rustics" leaving villages and coming "from the coasts and from the mountains" to Damascus.

[3] A most interesting similar symbiosis exists at present in the Iraqi Ba'thi regime that came to power in July 1968.

military but they had also realized that there was no alternative road to power open before them. Their tragedy (and that of other Arab ideologists and political reformers) was that cooperation with the military was at one and the same time indispensable and self-defeating.

The political supremacy of the military and their factionalism, which had been prominent features of Syrian politics since 1949, have continued to be so under Ba'thi rule, but the symbiosis with the Ba'th Party served to modify the pattern of Syrian military politics. For one thing, political activity in the Syrian army became confined almost exclusively to the ranks of the Ba'thi officers who achieved effective control of the Syrian army and did not lose it even in times of crisis. Only by joining the party's Military Organization could an army officer attain the privileges (and incur the risks) of a political position. What had not been solved, and this had important consequences, was the problem of factionalism and personal rivalry even within the relatively small group that emerged victorious in February 1966.

It seems that the predominance of the military in Syrian politics accounted also to a large extent for the turn taken by the issue of inter-communal relations in Syria between 1963 and 1966. It was primarily through the army that members of minority communities, which in the early 1950s had yet to be fully integrated into the Syrian state, came to occupy (the) central positions in Ba'thi Syria. How this came about and what its political impact has been are quite well documented, but several questions remain to be answered, such as from what segments of the 'Alawi (and other minority) communities did the Ba'thi officers and party militants come?; what has been their relationship with their communities' traditional leadership?; what changes took place in the social and political structure of the 'Alawi, Druse, and Isma'ili communities?

It is curious that the years 1963–6 which saw profound social and political changes take place in Syria witnessed also the emergence there of a relatively solid (or at least durable) political structure. One observer of Syrian affairs in the late 1960s[4] even went so far as to justify the record of the ruling Ba'thi group on the ground of the stability created by its long tenure of power. That stability ought to be seen in relative terms. However, when viewed against the background of

[4] Kamal Salibi in an unpublished paper as quoted by Seymour, *op. cit.*, pp. 45, 47.

Syrian political history since 1945, the fact that one party has held power for over nine years looms as an achievement. This was made possible by the effective control exercised over the Syrian army by the dominant Ba'thi military group, the absence of serious rivals, and by the transformation that the Ba'th had undergone during the years 1963–6. Until 1963 the party had been a definite entity closely identified with the specific leadership of 'Aflaq and Bitar, but after that year it had gradually been "depersonalized" and "institutionalized". The party was now more amenable to change from within and a party faction that took control could claim and maintain continuity without serious opposition. This was clearly demonstrated by events in 1966 and later years.

POSTSCRIPT

The history of the Ba'th regime in Syria since 1966 can be conveniently divided into two major periods: March 1966 to November 1970, and November 1970 to the present. During the first period Syrian (and Ba'thi) politics were governed by the political structure that had taken shape during the years 1963–6 and was finally moulded by the *coup d'état* of February 23, 1966. Since November 1970 some substantial changes have been introduced in that structure.

During 1966 the dynamics of the new political order in Syria gradually came into play. The regime at that stage was dominated by Salah J'did who chose to build his authority on and exercise his power through the Syrian party organization. He himself served as the assistant secretary of the Regional Command of the Syrian Ba'th, a post he had held for a while in 1965 but that now became the focal point of Syrian politics. Besides suiting J'did's proclivity for discreet, almost anonymous, use of power, this arrangement had the advantage of rendering the 'Alawi element in the regime somewhat less conspicuous. Through the Regional Command's Military Bureau and the party's Military Organization the assistant secretary was also to maintain direct contact with the politicized section of the Syrian army. His hold on the military was, however, to be maintained primarily by further cultivation of his personal faction, the real basis of his power.

Those members of the heterogeneous military coalition which emerged victorious in February 1966 who were dissatisfied with the supremacy of J'did and his faction rallied around Salim Hatum. Hatum and his partners finally staged an abortive *coup* in September 1966. Politically the *coup*-makers were linked to the ousted National Command of the Ba'th, while militarily they relied mostly on Druse officers who felt they were being deprived or threatened by the 'Alawis. The events of the *coup* centered on Sweida and Jabal ad-Duruz and, as had happened in similar instances in the past, the revolting Druse officers fled across the border to Jordan where Salim Hatum publicly denounced the regime he had helped to mould. The whole episode heightened tensions between Druse and 'Alawi and further underscored the role of confessional loyalties in Ba'thi politics.

Friction among the Ba'this continued. The party's radicals became unruly late in 1966 and, more significantly, a latent conflict seemed to develop between Salah J'did and Hafiz Asad, commander of the air force and acting minister of defence. This conflict pointed to to the complexity of the confessional issue as the two protagonists were 'Alawis. But these frictions were soon overshadowed for a while by the outbreak of serious anti-government demonstrations in several Syrian cities and then by the Six-Day War.

The demonstrations of May 1967 were triggered by an atheistic article published in the Syrian army's weekly magazine. That the incident assumed such proportions was a testimony to the hostility of the urban middle classes to the Ba'th regime. No new significant nationalization measures were enacted after 1967, but the social composition of the Ba'thi ruling group and the radical mood of the majority of its members continued to frighten and alienate the urban middle classes. The Ba'thi leaders were perturbed by this hostility which they constantly sought to neutralize, but they were not confronted with a serious challenge to their rule.

The absence of serious rivals to the Ba'th was fully revealed during the aftermath of the Six-Day War. The Ba'this were discredited and confused but no real contender for power appeared on the scene. A few weeks later the regime had regrouped and was ready to ward off criticism with an elaborate explanation of its past record and a programme of action for the future.

Of greater political significance were the intra-Ba'thi altercations which followed the war. It seems that Salah J'did and his associates sought to weaken the position of Hafiz al-Asad by blaming him for the poor performance of the Syrian army during the war. Asad, however, was too strongly entrenched to be dislodged. The rivalry between him and J'did became now the cardinal issue of Syrian politics. Asad held sway in the Syrian army and he gradually assumed the role of the military's representative, while J'did's influence was being confined to the civilian party organization and to a dwindling faction of his military followers. As a rule, J'did was supported by the party's radicals but the struggle between him and Asad was not an ideological but rather a personal conflict.

By 1969 (and perhaps earlier) Asad possessed sufficient military support to oust his rivals and take power into his hands. But it seems that Asad preferred to avoid a violent confrontation as long as this was possible. Also, he did not as yet command sufficient support in the party's civilian branches to ensure a smooth transition of power. The decision was, however, forced on him by his rivals in November 1970 as they assailed him at the Syrian party congress, charging him with responsibility for the abortive, half-hearted Syrian intervention in the Jordanian civil war. As it happened, Asad won an easy victory and encountered no real difficulty in purging the party hierarchy and staffing it with new personnel.

Since assuming power in November 1970, Asad has considerably altered the nature of the Ba'th regime. After a short period of transition, it has become a presidential regime based on the personal leadership of Asad and on the entourage of his associates who control and operate the army, the party, and the security apparatus. The regime acquired a heavier military accent and the Ba'th Party's role in it seems to have declined.

Having secured his position, Asad set forth to eliminate the antagonism between the regime and the urban middle classes. A policy of relative liberalization was launched which indeed terminated the austere atmosphere which characterized Syrian public life between 1966 and 1970. This was accompanied by a more pragmatic attitude to issues of internal politics and foreign policy. An attempt was made to base the regime on firmer constitutional foundations. A "progressive front" was formed in which the Ba'th has cooperated with other parties in an effort to mellow the rigid and exclusivist concept of Ba'thi domination in Syria and to make the regime more acceptable.

While all key positions were carefully retained by his loyal supporters, Asad came in the spring of 1972 to the point where he tried to experiment with relatively free local elections. The outcome was disappointing for the regime but the fact that such an experiment could take place was a measure of the regime's success.

APPENDIX A

SYRIAN CABINETS, MARCH 1963–MARCH 1966

1. March 9, 1963–May 11, 1963

Ṣalāḥ al-Bīṭār premier and minister of foreign affairs
Nihād al-Qāsim deputy premier and minister of justice
Dr. ʻAbd al-Wahhāb Ḥaumad minister of finance
General Muḥammad aṣ-Ṣūfī minister of defence
Brigadier-Gen. Amīn al-Ḥāfiz minister of the interior
Manṣūr al-Aṭrash minister of labour and social affairs
Dr. ʻAbd al-Ḥalīm Swaidān minister of agriculture
Dr. Sāmī ad-Durūbī minister of education and culture
ʻAbd al-Karīm Zuhūr minister of the economy
Dr. Jamāl al-Atāsī minister of information
Darwīsh ʻAlwānī minister of state for religious endowments
Hānī al-Hindī minister of planning
Al-Walīd Ṭālib minister for municipal and rural affairs
Sāmī Ṣufān minister of supply
Jihād Ḍāhī minister of communications
Aḥmad Abū Ṣāliḥ minister of public works
Shiblī al-ʻAisamī minister of agrarian reform
Dr. Ibrāhīm Mākhūs minister of health
Ṭālib Ḍamād minister of industry
Dr. Sāmī al-Jundī minister of guidance

2. May 13, 1963–August 4, 1963

Ṣalāḥ al-Bīṭār premier and minister of foreign affairs
Amīn al-Ḥāfiẓ deputy premier and minister of the interior
Dr. Sāmi al-Jundī minister of information, culture, and national guidance
Manṣūr al-Aṭrash minister of labour and social affairs and acting minister of industry

Al-Walīd Ṭālib minister of municipal and rural affairs

Aḥmad Abū Ṣāliḥ minister of communications and acting minister of public works

Shiblī al-'Aisamī minister of agrarian reform and acting minister of education

Muṣṭafa ash-Shammā' minister of finance

'Abd ar-Raḥmān at-Ṭabbā' minister of religious endowments

Dr. 'Abd al-Khāliq an-Naqshbandī minister of state for the affairs of the chairmanship of the NCRC

Maẓhar ash-Shurbajī minister of justice and acting minister of state for the affairs of the union

Brigadier-Gen. Ghassān Ḥaddād minister of planning

George To'meh minister of the economy

Dr. 'Ādil Ṭarabīn minister of agriculture and acting minister of supply

Abd ar-Raḥmān ash-Shaqafī minister of health

Major-Gen. Ziyād al-Ḥarīrī charged with the functions of the minister of defence

3. August 4, 1963–November 11, 1963

Ṣalāḥ al-Bīṭār premier and minister of foreign affairs

Dr. Sāmī al-Jundī minister of information, culture, and national guidance

Manṣūr al-Aṭrash minister of labour and social affairs

Aḥmad Abū Ṣāliḥ minister of communications and public works

Shiblī al-'Aisamī minister of agrarian reform

Muṣṭafā ash-Shammā' minister of finance

Dr. 'Abd al-Khāliq an-Naqshbandī minister of state for the affairs of the chairmanship of the NCRC

Brigadier-Gen. Ghassān Ḥaddād minister of planning

George To'meh minister of the economy

Dr. 'Ādil Ṭarabīn minister of agriculture

Dr. Ibrāhīm Mākhūs minister of health

Dr. Shāker Faḥḥām minister of education and culture

Maẓhar al-'Anbarī minister of justice and religious endowments

Dr. Nūr ad-Dīn Rifā'ī minister of industry

Ṣāliḥ Maḥāmīd minister of municipal and rural affairs

Nūr ad-Dīn al-Atāsī minister of the interior
Maḥmūd Juyūsh minister of supply
Brigadier-Gen. 'Abdallāh Ziyādeh minister of defence

4. November 12, 1963–May 13, 1964

Major-Gen. Amīn al-Ḥāfiẓ premier
Major-Gen. Muḥammad 'Umrān deputy premier
Dr. Sāmī al-Jundī minister of information
Brigadier-Gen. Ghassān Ḥaddād minister of planning
Brigadier-Gen. 'Abdallāh Ziyādeh minister of defence
Dr. Ibrāhīm Mākhūs minister of health
Dr. 'Abd al-Khāliq an-Naqshbandī minister for the affairs of the NCRC and the affairs of the union
Dr. George To'meh minister of the economy
Dr. 'Ādil Ṭarabīn minister of agriculture
Dr. Nūr ad-Dīn ar-Rifā'i minister of public works
Dr. Nūr ad-Dīn al-Atāsī minister of the interior
Dr. Ḥasān Mureiwed minister of foreign affairs
Dr. Yūsuf Z'ayyīn minister of agrarian reform
Dr. Muṣṭafa Ḥaddād minister of education
Manṣūr al-Aṭrash minister of labour and social affairs
Aḥmad Abū Ṣāliḥ minister of communications
Shiblī al-'Aisamī minister of culture and national guidance
Al-Walīd Ṭālib minister of state
Muṣṭafa ash-Shammā' minister of finance
Maẓhar al-'Anbarī minister of justice
Sāliḥ al-Maḥāmīd minister of municipal and rural affairs
Maḥmūd Juyūsh minister of supply
Khair ad-Dīn al-Ḥaqqī minister of industry
Aḥmad Mahdī al-Khaḍr minister of religious endowments

5. May 14, 1964–November 3, 1964

Ṣalāḥ al-Bīṭar premier
Thābit al-'Arīs minister of state
Dr. 'Abdallāh 'Abd ad-Dā'im minister of information
Major-Gen. Ghassān Ḥaddād minister of planning

Muṣṭafa ash-Shammā' minister of finance
Dr. 'Abd al-Khāliq an-Naqshbandī minister for the affairs of the NCRC and the affairs of the union
Dr. 'Ādil Ṭarabīn minister of agriculture
Maẓhar al-'Anbarī minister of justice and health
Dr. Nūr ad-Dīn ar-Rifā'ī minister of communications and public works
Dr. Ḥasan Mureiwed minister of foreign affairs
Dr. Muṣṭafa Ḥaddād minister of education
As'ad Maḥāfil minister of culture and national guidance
'Ādil Sa'dī minister of industry
Dr. Kamāl Ḥusnī minister of the economy
Major-Gen. Mamdūḥ Jābir minister of the interior
Fahmī al-'Āshūrī minister of labour and social affairs and of municipal and rural affairs
Dr. Ṣalāḥ Wazzān minister of agrarian reform
'Abd ar-Raḥmān al-Kawākibī minister of religious endowments

6. October 4, 1964–September 22, 1965

Major-Gen. Amīn al-Ḥāfiẓ premier
Dr. Nūr ad-Dīn al-Atāsī deputy premier
Major-Gen. Ghassān Ḥaddād minister of planning
Al-Walīd Ṭālib minister for presidential affairs
Dr. 'Ādil Ṭarabīn minister of agriculture
Sāliḥ al-Maḥāmid minister for municipal and rural affairs
Dr. Ḥasān Mureiwed minister of foreign affairs
Dr. Muṣṭafa Ḥaddād minister of education
Dr. 'Abd ar-Raḥmān al-Kawākibī minister of religious endowments
Major-Gen. Mamdūḥ Jābir minister of defence
'Abd al-Fattāḥ Būshī minister of the economy
Suleimān al-Khish minister of culture and national guidance
Husein Muhanna minister of justice
Lt.-Colonel 'Abd al-Karīm al-Jundī minister of agrarian reform
Jamīl Shiyya minister of supply
Muṣṭafa 'Izzat Naṣṣār minister of health
Mashhūr Zaitūn minister of information

Samīḥ Fakhūrī minister of communications
Maḥmūd Najjār minister of public works
Hishām al-'Āss minister of industry
Col. Maḥmūd Badawī minister of the interior

7. September 22, 1965–December 21, 1965

Dr. Yūsuf Z'ayyīn premier
Dr. Ibrāhīm Mākhūs deputy premier and minister of foreign affairs
'Abd al-Fattāh Būshī deputy premier and minister of finance
Al-Walīd Ṭālib minister for the affairs of the Presidency Council
Dr. 'Ādil Ṭarabīn minister of agriculture
Sāliḥ Maḥāmīd minister of municipal and rural affairs
Dr. Muṣṭafa Ḥaddād minister of education
Dr. 'Abd ar-Raḥmān al-Kawākibī minister of religious endowments
Major-Gen. Mamdūḥ Jābir minister of public works
'Alī Taljibīnī minister of labour
Ibrāhīm Bīṭār minister of the economy
Suleimān Khish minister of information, culture, and national guidance
Major-Gen. Ḥamad 'Ubaid minister of defence
Husain Muhanna minister of justice
Lt.-Colonel 'Abd al-Karīm al-Jundī minister of agrarian reform
Mas̲h̲hūr Zaitūn minister of supply
Samīḥ Fakhūrī minister of communications
Hishām al-'Āss minister of industry
Col. Muḥammad Khair Badawī minister of planning
Dr. Ṣādiq Far'ūn minister of health
Muḥammad 'Īd 'Ashāwī minister of the interior
Dr. 'Adnān Shumān deputy minister of labour

8. January 1, 1966–February 22, 1966

Salāḥ al-Bīṭār premier and minister of foreign affairs
Major-Gen. Muḥammad 'Umrān minister of defence
Dr. 'Abdallāh 'Abd ad-Dā'im minister of education

Fahmī al-'Āshūrī minister of the interior
Dr. Ṣalāḥ Wazzān minister of agriculture
Kamāl Ḥusnī minister of the economy
Major-Gen. Mamdūḥ Jābir minister for the affairs of the Presidency Council
Hishām al-'Āss minister of industry
Samīḥ Fakhūrī minister of communications
Maḥmūd Najjār minister of municipal and rural affairs
Muwaffaq Shurbajī minister of finance
Yūsuf Khabbāz minister of tourism and government affairs
Dr. Ḥunain Sayaj minister of health
Dr. Muḥammad Fāḍil minister of justice
Dr. Aḥmad Badr ad-Dīn minister of communications
Jamīl Thābit minister of labour and social affairs
Jamīl Ḥaddād minister of agrarian reform
Dr. 'Abd al-Wahhāb Khayyāṭa minister of planning
Bashīr Quṭb minister of state for foreign affairs
Kamāl Shahādeh minister of supply
Nizāl Deirī minister of state for the affairs of the Euphrates and the Jazira
Dr. As'ad Darqāwī minister of culture and national guidance
Maḥmūd 'Arab Sa'īd minister of state for religious endowments
Dr. 'Adnān Shumān deputy minister of labour
Ra'īs al-Farḥān aṣ-Ṣayyād deputy minister of state for the affairs of the Euphrates and the Jazira

9. March 1, 1966–October 15, 1966

Dr. Yūsuf Z'ayyīn premier
Dr. Ibrāhīm Mākhūs deputy premier and minister of information, tourism, and national guidance
Ṣāliḥ Maḥāmīd minister of municipal and rural affairs
Major-Gen. Mamdūḥ Jābir minister of public works
Dr. Muṣṭafa Ḥaddād minister of education
Lt.-Colonel 'Abd al-Karīm al-Jundī minister of agrarian reform
Mashhūr Zaitūn minister of supply
Muḥammad 'Īd 'Ashāwī minister of the interior
Muwaffaq Shurbajī minister of finance

‘Abd as-Salām Ḥaidar minister of justice

Ghālib ‘Abdūn minister of religious endowments

‘Abd al-Ḥamīd Ḥasan minister of planning

Samīḥ ‘Atiyya minister of communications

Dr. ‘Abd al-Raḥmān al-Akta‘ minister of health

Colonel Muḥammad Rabāh aṭ-Ṭawīl minister of labour and social affairs

Dr. Aḥmad Murād minister of the economy

Dr. As‘ad Taqla minister of industry

‘Abdallāh Wāthiq Shahīd deputy minister for higher education

Major-Gen. Ḥāfiẓ al-Asad exercising the functions of the minister of defence

APPENDIX B

COMPOSITION OF REGIONAL AND NATIONAL COMMANDS 1963–66

1. Regional Command Chosen by the Syrian Regional Congress in September 1963[1]

Ḥamūd ash-Shūfī (secretary-general), Dr. Nūr ad-Dīn al-Atāsī, Khālid al-Ḥakīm, Dr. Maḥmūd Naufal, Aḥmad Abū Ṣāliḥ, Colonel Ḥamad 'Ubaid, Colonel Ḥāfiẓ al-Asad, Captain Muḥammad Rabāḥ aṭ-Ṭawīl.

2. Regional Command Chosen by the Extraordinary Syrian Regional Congress in February 1964

General Amīn al-Ḥāfiẓ, Colonel Ṣalāḥ J'did, Colonel Muḥammad 'Umrān, Colonel Ḥamad 'Ubaid, Colonel Ḥāfiẓ al-Asad, Colonel 'Abd al-Karīm al-Jundī, Fahmī al-'Āshūrī, Suleiman al-'Alī, Muḥammad az-Zu'bī, Sāmī al-Jundī, Jamīl Shiyya, Dr. Nūr ad-Dīn al-Atāsī.

3. Regional Command Chosen by the Second Regional Congress in April 1965

General Amīn al-Ḥāfiẓ, General Salāḥ J'dīd, Colonel Ḥamad 'Ubaid, Jamīl Shiyya, Dr. Nūr ad-Dīn al-Atāsī, Dr. Yūsuf Z'ayyīn, Ḥabīb Ḥaddād, Muḥammad az-Zu'bī, Muṣṭafa Rustum, 'Adnān Shumān. Al-Walīd Ṭālib.

4. Regional Command Elected by the Extraordinary Regional Congress in August 1965

General Amīn al-Ḥāfiẓ, General Ṣalāḥ J'dīd, Colonel Ḥamad 'Ubaid,

[1] Unless otherwise indicated, the composition of the Commands is taken from Ba'thī sources. This is based on *an-Nahār*, February 9, 1964.

Colonel ʻAbd al-Karīm al-Jundī, Colonel Muṣṭafa Ṭlās, Major Salīm Ḥaṭūm, Major Muḥammad Rabāḥ at-Ṭawīl, Dr. Nūr ad-Dīn al-Atāsī, Dr. Yūsuf Zʻayyīn, Jamīl Shiyya, Muḥammad az-Zuʻbī, Muṣṭafa Rustum, Muḥammad ʻĪd ʻAshāwī, Marwān Ḥabash, Fā'iz al-Jāsim, Ḥisām Ḥaiza.

5. Regional Command Chosen by the Extraordinary Regional Congress in March 1966

General Ḥāfiẓ al-Asad, General Aḥmad Suwaidānī, Colonel ʻAbd al-Karīm al-Jundī, Major Muḥammad Rabāh aṭ-Ṭawīl, Ṣalāḥ J'dīd, Nur ad-Dīn al-Atāsī, Fā'iz al-Jāsim, Marwān Ḥabash, Kāmil al-Ḥusein, Ḥabīb Ḥaddād, Muṣṭafa Rustum, Muḥammad az-Zuʻbī, Dr. Yūsuf Zʻayyīn, Jamīl Shiyya, Muḥammad ʻId ʻAshāwī, Dr. Ibrāhīm Mākhūs.

6. National Command Elected by the Sixth National Congress in October 1963[2]

From Iraq: Aḥmad Ḥasan al-Bakr, Mahdī ʻAmmāsh, ʻAlī Ṣāliḥ as-Saʻdī, Muḥsin ash-Shaikh Rādī, Ḥamdī ʻAbd al-Majīd. *From Syria:* Michel ʻAflaq, Amīn al-Ḥāfiẓ, Ṣalāḥ J'dīd. *From Lebanon:* Jubrān Majdalānī, Khālid al-ʻAlī. *From Jordan:* Dr. Munīf ar-Razzāz (?).

7. National Command Elected by the Seventh National Congress in February 1964

From Syria: Michel ʻAflaq, Amīn al-Ḥāfiẓ, Ṣalāḥ J'did, Muḥammad ʻUmrān, Shiblī al-ʻAisamī, Manṣur al-Aṭrash. *From Lebanon:* Jubrān Majdalānī, ʻAbd al-Majīd ar-Rafiʻī, ʻAli al-Khalīl. *From Iraq:* Aḥmad Ḥasan al-Bakr. *From Jordan:* Dr. Munīf ar-Razzāz. *From Saudi Arabia:* ʻAli Ghannām.

2 Only the partial composition of the two National Commands is known. The Baʻthi sources did not disclose the names of the Jordanian delegates.

3 Taken from *al-Anwār* (Beirut), February 28, 1964, where an apparently reliable report on the congress was published.

APPENDIX C

NATIONAL CONGRESSES OF THE BA'TH PARTY 1947–66 AND REGIONAL CONGRESSES OF THE SYRIAN PARTY ORGANIZATION 1963–66

National Congresses

1. First National Congress, 1947. Formal foundation of the party as a pan-Arab political movement; held in Damascus, Michel 'Aflaq chosen as the party's secretary-general.

2. Second National Congress, 1954. Held in the wake of the union with Akram Haurānī's party and the Ba'th Party's emergence as an important political force after the fall of Shishakli.

3. Third National Congress, 1959. Held in Lebanon after the party's formal dissolution in the UAR. The congress confirmed the dissolution but expelled the extremist Nasserites headed by Rimāwī and Rikābī.

4. Fourth National Congress, 1960. Held in Lebanon when the party's quarrel with Nasser came to the open. The congress denounced the UAR regime and the party's dissolution, and for the first time in the party's history was dominated by the leftist wing.

5. Fifth National Congress, May 1962. Held in Homs and was dominated by 'Aflaq and his Iraqi supporters. It laid the foundations for the re-establishment of the party in Syria.

6. Sixth National Congress, October 1963. Again held in Damascus and sought to formulate policies for the party's regimes in Syria and Iraq. The opposition to 'Aflaq predominated at this congress and the party's doctrine was altered by it.

7. Seventh National Congress, February 1964. Held in Damascus and resulted in the elimination of the leftist faction headed by 'Ali Ṣāliḥ as-Sa'dī.

8. Eighth National Congress, April 1965. Its central theme was the attempt to reach a compromise between the National Command and the Syrian Regional Command. 'Aflaq, who resented this attempt,

refused to be re-elected as secretary-general and was replaced by Munīf ar-Razzāz.

9. Ninth National Congress, September 1966. Held in Damascus following a successful effort by the group that had emerged victorious from the *coup d'état* of February 23, 1966, to build an all-Arab party organization subservient to it.

Regional Congresses

1. Extraordinary Regional Congress, April 1963. Held in anticipation of the Sixth National Congress, which originally was to be held in May 1963. The congress did not follow prescribed procedures.

2 First Regular Regional Congress, September 1963. Held in anticipation of the Sixth National Congress. The domination of the Syrian party organization by the military and their radical civilian allies was revealed at this congress.

3. Extraordinary Regional Congress, February 1964. Summoned by ʿAflaq and the military in order to eliminate the influence of the radical left on the Syrian party.

4. Second Regular Regional Congress, March/April 1965. It marked the hegemony of the military and their new, more disciplined, civilian partners. On the other hand, it witnessed the surfacing of opposition among the Baʿthi military to their leaders.

5. Extraordinary Regional Congress, August 1965. Summoned in an attempt to break the deadlock that resulted from the Ḥāfiẓ-J'dīd crisis.

6. Extraordinary Regional Congress, March 1966. Organized by the military-civilian coalition that emerged victorious from the party crisis. It formulated the policies of the new regime.

APPENDIX D

THE BA'TH PARTY: AN ORGANIZATIONAL SCHEME

The following scheme of the organization of the Ba'th Party is based on the Internal Regulation of the Ba'th Party, approved by the Eighth National Congress, and on the Internal Regulation of the party's Military Organization in Syria, issued several weeks later. The scheme describes the party as it should have been late in 1965, disregarding its development and deviations from these rules in the actual operation of the party.

Membership

There are three categories of membership in the Ba'th Party: Active Member (*'uḍw 'āmil*), Apprentice Member (*'uḍw mutadarrib*), and Supporter (*naṣīr*). An Active Member participates in all formal meetings of his unit and has the right to vote in all party elections and, depending on the duration of his active membership, to run for party offices. In Syria a new recruit must spend 18 months as a Supporter and 18 more months as an Apprentice Member before he becomes an Active Member.

The Syrian Regional Organization

The smallest unit in the party's hierarchy is the Cell (*ḥalqa*) which includes three to five members. Three to five Cells constitute a Section (*firqa*), defined by the party as "the elementary unit of the organization". The Section elects its own Command (*qiyāda*), composed of five members, but its Secretary (*amīn sirr*) is appointed by the Command of the superior Subbranch (*shu'ba*). The Subbranch is made up of three to five Sections and is the lowest level in the party to hold a periodical Congress (*mu'tamar*). Certain Subbranches are independent and they elect their own Commands and Secretaries, but in those Subbranches that are incorporated in Branches (*far‘u*, pl. *furū‘*) the Secretary is appointed by the superior Branch. The party's 13 Branches in Syria are each composed of two to five Subbranches and are structured according to the administrative division of the state. The Branch's Congress elects both a Command and a Secretary. The Command operates through Bureaus (*maktab*, pl. *makātib*) such as The Workers Bureau (*maktab al-‘ummāl*), The Bureau of the Secretariat (*maktab al-imāna*), and so on.

The Military Organization (*at-tanẓīm al-‘askarī*) is made up of Branches modeled after the civilian ones. Unlike the civilian sector of the Syrian Ba‘th, the Military Organization is run by a separate Military Bureau (*maktab ‘askarī*) and holds periodical Military

The Military Organization and the civilian sector converge in the Regional Congress (*mu'tamar quṭrī*). The active membership of the Congress is made up of representatives from the Branches while other party functionaries participate as observers. The Congress elects a Regional Command, a Regional Secretary, and a Regional Tribunal. It evaluates the party's performance since the previous Congress and formulates its broad policies for the coming period. The length of that period is determined by the incumbent Regional Command. The Regional Command operates through Bureaus and meets for regular weekly sessions.

The National Organizations

The National Organization (*at-tanẓīm al-qaumī*) is made up of the party's regional organizations. The party's organization in most Regions (*aqṭār*) reaches only the level of a Branch or a Subbranch. The National Congress attended by their representatives is the highest authority in the party. It elects the National Command, the party's secretary-general, and the National Tribunal, and determines the party's policies and procedures. The National Command, too, operates through Bureaus and its regular sessions are monthly. Between National Congresses the National Command is accountable to the National Consultative Council (*al-majlis al-istishāri al-qaumī*), a forum composed of delegates representing the party's Regions according to size.

APPENDIX E

SYRIAN AND BA'THI PERSONALITIES APPEARING IN THE TEXT

'Abd ad-Dā'im, 'Abdallāh Ba'thi ideologist and one of Bīṭār's close confidents; he was born to a Sunnī family in Damascus in 1924 and holds a doctorate from the Sorbonne. Since 1962 he has served in various Syrian cabinets.

'Abd al-Karīm, Aḥmad A leftist army officer and politician; he was born in 1926 in the Ḥaurān and played a major role in Syrian military politics in the late 1950s and in the politics of the Separatist Regime.

Al-'Abdallah, Munīr 'Alawī lawyer from Lādhiqiyya; a leader of the *Quṭriyyūn* faction.

'Abd al-Majīd, Ḥamdī A radical member of the Iraqi Ba'th.

Abū Ṣāliḥ, Aḥmad A Sunnī lawyer from Aleppo who has been active in the Ba'th since the late 1950s and emerged as a leader of the party's radical wing in 1963.

'Aflaq, Michel Leader of the Ba'th until 1966.

'Aisamī, Shibblī A moderate Ba'thi Druse leader; former schoolteacher who in 1963 appeared on the scene as a member of the Syrian cabinet and of the National Command.

Al-'Alī, Ibrāhīm Ba'thi officer, supporter of Ṣalāḥ J'dīd.

Al-'Alwān, Jāsim A native of Deir az-Zōr (1926); a prominent leader of the Syrian Nasserite Officers, he finally settled in Egypt.

'Ammāsh, Mahdī Iraqi Ba'thi leader.

'Arab Sa'īd, Muḥammad A Sunnī lawyer from Aleppo and a moderate Nasserite.

Arsūzī, Zākī 'Alawī refugee from Alexandretta, co-founder of the Ba'th and rival of 'Aflaq.

Al-Asad, Ḥāfiẓ 'Alawī founding member of the Military Committee, commander of the Syrian air force, and presently Syrian president and virtual ruler.

Al-A'sar, Badr An independent Syrian officer who played an important role in the *coup* of March 28, 1962.

'Ashāwī, Muḥammad 'Īd A Sunnī lawyer from Deir az-Zōr and a leader of the *Quṭriyyūn*. He began his career under the Ba'th regime as a provincial governor and then served as member of Syrian Regional Commands and cabinets. He was ousted from power after November 1970.

Al-Atāsī, Hāshim A leader of the nationalist movement in Syria and Syrian president.

Al-Atāsī, Jamāl A native of Ḥoms (1910) and a psychiatrist by profession; a veteran leader of the Ba'th who in the late 1950s published its organ *al-Jamāhīr*. In the early 1960s Atāsī emerged as a Marxist ideologist but since 1963 he has been close to the Nasserites.

Al-Atāsī, Lu'ayy An independent unionist officer. In 1963 served as chairman of the NCRC.

Al-Atāsī, Nūr ad-Dīn A leader of the radical wing of the Syrian Ba'th; a native of Ḥomṣ (1924?) and a physician by profession. Between 1963–70 he served in several capacities including Syrian president and premier.

'Aṭiyya, Samīḥ A Christian lawyer from the Tel al-Kalaḥ region, who in February 1966 became the first Communist cabinet member in Syria.

Al-Aṭrash, Manṣūr Son of the Druse leader Sulṭān al-Aṭrash (b. 1925), a veteran member of the Ba'th, and a notable supporter of 'Aflaq. He served as member of the National Command and chairman of the Broadened National Council of the Revolutionary Command.

Al-'Aṭṭār, 'Iṣām Leader of the Muslim Brethren in Syria who presently lives in Europe.

Al-'Auda, Maḥmūd An independent Syrian army officer who cooperated with the Ba'th on March 8.

Al-'Aẓm, Khālid Prominent politician during the 1950s and during the Separatist Period.

Al-'Azmeh, Bashīr Syrian premier in 1962. A physician by profession and member of an eminent Damascene family, he had been close to the moderate wing of the Ba'th.

Bakdash, Khālid Leader of the Syrian Communists.

Al-Bakr, Ḥasan Iraqi president and a leader of the Iraqi Ba'th.

Al-Bīṭār, Ṣalāḥ Co-founder of the Ba'th and 'Aflaq's associate.

Al-Būshī, 'Abd al-Fattāḥ A Sunnī lawyer from Ḥamā (b. 1923) who began his career in the Ba'th as a supporter of Ḥaurānī. He served as Syrian deputy-premier and member of the Presidency Council.

Ad-Dairī, Akram An officer-politician, native of the Ḥauran region and a leader of the Nasserite military.

Dawālibī, Ma'rūf A leader of the People's Party and Syrian premier during much of the Separatist Period.

Aḍ-Ḍullī, Ṣalāḥ A Ba'thi officer, supporter of Amīn al-Ḥāfiẓ.

Durūbī, Sāmī A veteran Ba'thi who was born in Ḥomṣ (1920) and graduated from the Sorbonne. An essayist, translator, professor of philosophy in Damascus, and diplomat. Under the Ba'th regime he served as a cabinet member and ambassador.

Al-Fakīkī, Hānī A radical member of the Iraqi Ba'th.

Al-Ghānim, Wahīb 'Alawī, early member of the Ba'th Party.

Ḥabash, Marwān A native of Jubata az-Zait in the Quneitra region and a graduate of Damascus University, who rose rapidly in the Syrian Ba'th as a protégé of Ṣalāḥ J'dīd. He became a member of the Syrian Regional Command until he fell from power together with his patron in November 1970.

Ḥaddād, Ghassān An independent officer who cooperated with the Ba'th and was rewarded with promotions and ministerial rank.

Ḥaddād, Ḥabīd A supporter of Ṣalāḥ J'dīd and the *Quṭriyyūn*. Greek Orthodox, native of the Haurān region, and a physician by profession.

Ḥaddād, Muṣṭafa A Ba'thi militant who appeared on the political scene in 1963. A native (b. 1930) of Salakīn in the Idlib region, who holds a Ph.D. from the Sorbonne.

Al-Ḥāfiẓ, Amīn A central leader of the Ba'thi officers and for a long time the Syrian "strong man" and head of state.

Al-Ḥāfiẓ, Yasīn A leftist ideologist, a former Communist, and until 1964 member of the Ba'th.

Al-Ḥajj 'Alī Muṣṭafa A Ba'thi officer who took part in the March 8 *coup*.

Al-Ḥakīm, Khālid A leftist member of the Syrian Ba'th and a veteran trade unionist.

Al-Ḥallāj, Muṣṭafa A leader of the Socialist Unionists; native of the Ḥamā area.

Ḥamdūn, Muṣṭafa A prominent Druse military supporter of Haurānī in the 1950s. He had played an important role in the overthrow of Shishakli and reached the peak and end of his career as a member of cabinet.

Al-Ḥarīrī, Ziyād The real maker of the *coup d'état* of March 8, 1963; eventually he was deposed by his Ba'thi partners. Ḥarīrī is a Sunnī Muslim from Ḥamā.

Ḥāṭūm, Salīm A Druse Ba'thi officer, commander of a commando unit, who played an important role in Ba'thi politics until September 1966; he was executed following the Six-Day War in 1967.

Ḥaumad, 'Abd al-Wahhāb Syrian politician, native of Aleppo, a lawyer by education who in the 1950s was affiliated with the People's Party. From the time of the Union Period he became a Nasserite.

Al-Ḥaurānī, Akram Since 1953, one of the three main leaders of the Ba'th and an important Syrian leader.

Al-Ḥaurānī, 'Uthmān A relative of Akram al-Haurāni and founder of a local party in Ḥamā that the latter eventually took over.

Al-Hindī, Muhīb A Damascene officer, an associate of Naḥlāwī and one of the leaders of the *coup* of September 22, 1961.

Al-Ḥusainī, Faiṣal Sirrī A leader of the *coup* of September 22, 1961.

Al-Ḥusainī, Ibrāhīm A Syrian officer who collaborated with Shishakli, later settled in Saudi Arabia.

Al-Ḥusāmī, Rātib A Nasserite politician and one of the leaders of the United Arab Front. Born in Ḥomṣ (1920), he served in the fifties as a member of the Syrian parliament; affiliated with the left wing of the People's Party.

Jābir, 'Alī A Lebanese Ba'thi, supporter of Bīṭār.

Jabīr, Mamdūḥ An independent ex-general who collaborated closely with the Ba'th and served in several cabinets. He is a Muslim Sunnī from Ḥamā.

Jadīd (J'dīd), Fu'ād A senior 'Alāwī officer, member of the PPS, brother of Ṣalāḥ J'dīd.

J'dīd, Ghassān Brother of Salāḥ, he was murdered in Beirut for his role in the assassination of 'Adnān al-Mālikī.

J'dīd, 'Izzat An 'Alawī Ba'thi colonel who as commander of a key unit played an important role in the execution of the *coup* of Feb. 23, 1966. Possibly a relative of Salāḥ J'dīd.

J'dīd, Salāḥ The real leader of the Military Committee and from his victory in 1966 up to 1969 the "strong man" of Syria.

Al-Jallād, Hānī A prominent Damascene businessman.

Al-Jāsim, Fā'iz A radical Syrian Ba'thi; Sunnī Muslim from Deir az-Zōr. He is a lawyer who began his career under the Ba'th regime as governor of Hassakeh province and later became a member of the Regional Command and the Presidency Council.

Al-Jawwād, Ḥāzim A moderate Iraqi Ba'thi.

Al-Jundī, 'Abd al-Karīm An Ismā'īli Ba'thi officer, born in Salamiyya in 1930. He was one of the organizers of the *coup d'état* of March 8 and distinguished himself as a leftist officer-politician. He committed suicide (or perhaps was murdered) in 1969 while serving as head of Syria's security services.

Al-Jundī, Khālid Brother of Sāmī al-Jundī and a leftist Ba'thi trade unionist.

Al-Jundī, Sāmī An older cousin of 'Abd al-Karīm al-Jundī (b. 1920 in Salamiyya), an early member of the Ba'th, and a dentist by profession. Having converted to Nasserism he rejoined the Ba'th in 1963 to become a member in several cabinets. He then was removed to Paris as Syria's ambassador and in 1969 was jailed for some time in Syria.

Kaftārū, Aḥmad Syrian grand mufti under the Ba'th regime, who seems to acquiesce with the Ba'th.

Kan'ān, 'Uthmān One of the four Ba'thi officers who actually participated in the *coup d'état* of March 8, 1863.

Kanj, Nūr ad-Dīn An independent Druse officer, native of Majdal Shams in the Golan Heights, who collaborated with the Ba'th in carrying out the *coup* of March 8.

Al-Khalīl, 'Alī A Lebanese Ba'thi.

Al-Khaṭīb, Aḥmad A Ba'thi militant from the Haurān. President of the Teachers' Union in the early years of the Ba'th regime, he would become, temporarily, president of the Republic in 1970.

Khayyāṭa, 'Abd al-Wahhāb A moderate Nasserite who served in Bīṭār's cabinet in 1966.

Al-Khish, Suleimān A leftist leader of the *Quṭriyyūn*. A native of Ṣafita near Ladhiqiyya (b. 1929), a schoolteacher, poet, and journalist. He served as minister of education and as minister of information in several Syrian cabinets.

Al-Kuzbarī, Ḥaydar A Damascene officer, leader of the *coup* of September 22, 1961; a relative of Ma'mūn al-Kuzbarī.

Al-Kuzbarī, Ma'mūn A Damascene politician, a leader of Shishakli's Liberation Rally, and a prominent politician of the Separatist Period.

Al-Mahdāwī, Muḥammad An Iraqi Ba'thi officer.

Majdalānī, Jubrān A Lebanese member of the National Command of the Ba'th and a notable leader of its moderate wing.

Mākhūs, Ibrāhīm Prominent 'Alawī member of the radical wing of the Ba'th and a physician by profession. Between 1963–9 he was a member of several cabinets and party commands. He was then removed from power following Ṣalāḥ J'dīd's political decline.

Al-Mālikī, 'Adnān Leader of the Ba'thi officers who was assassinated in 1955.

Al-Mālikī, Riyād Prominent Ba'thi officer in the 1950s and an important supporter of Haurānī.

Al-Mīr, Aḥmad An Ismā'īlī, Ba'thi officer, member of the Military Committee.

Muḥārib, Fawwāz A Nasserite Syrian officer member of the NCRC after March 8.

Murquṣ, Elyās A Marxist (ex-Communist) ideologist.

Muṣṭafa, Fayyād A radical Ba'thi trade unionist.

Muṣṭafa, Shākir A Damascene supporter of Bīṭār; a publicist and a professional diplomat.

Al-Muzāḥim, Yūsuf A Nasserite politician. Born in a village near Damascus (in 1922), he pursued a normal bureaucratic career and began to rise rapidly under the Union's regime to become a staunch Nasserite.

An-Nāfūrī, Amīn A prominent leftist officer-politician of the late 1950s and early 1960s; a native of Nabak in the Ḥaurān (b. 1921).

Naḥlāwī, 'Abd al-Karīm A Damascene officer (b. 1926 to a traditional Sunnī family); the most notable leader of the military *coup* which resulted in Syria's secession from the Union. Since April 1962 he has been exiled from Syria.

Namūr, Ṣalāḥ A senior 'Alawī officer, supporter of 'Umrān; his arrest resulted in the "white *coup*" of December 19, 1965.

Al-Qaddūr, 'Abd al-Ḥalīm An associate of Haurānī.

Al-Qāsim, Nihād A Nasserite politician who in the 1950s was associated with the People's Party; he was a member of Bīṭār's first cabinet.

Al-Qudsī, Nāẓim A leader of the People's Party and Syrian president during the Separatist Period.

Al-Quṭainī, Rāshid A Nasserite officer and participant in the *coup* of March 8, 1963.

Al-Quṭb, Bashīr A Ba'thi from Damascus, a senior Syrian diplomat, and a confidant of Bīṭār.

Rabāḥ aṭ-Ṭawīl, Muḥammad A Sunnī Ba'thi officer from Lādhiqiyya who served in several Syrian cabinets and Regional Commands and as commander of the Ba'thi militia.

Raslān, Hilāl A Druse supporter of Ḥamūd ash-Shūfī; in 1963 he served as governor of Aleppo.

Ar-Razzāz, Munīf A Jordanian Ba'thi ideologist and leader; from April 1965 to February 1966 he was secretary-general of the Ba'th.

Ar-Rifā'ī, Fā'iz A Damascene associate of Naḥlāwī, believed to be more of a Unionist than the other partners to the *coup* of September 1961.

Ar-Rikābī, Fu'ād An Iraqi Ba'thi who in 1959 became an all-out Nasserite and, together with Rimāwī, led a seceding faction of the Ba'th.

Ar-Rimāwī, 'Abdallāh A Jordanian Ba'thi and most notable among those party members who in 1959 became all-out Nasserites.

Rizq, Ḥusayn A militant of the Ba'thi trade unions.

Rustum, Muṣṭafā A radical Ba'thi, member of several party commands.

As-Sa'dī, 'Alī Ṣāliḥ A leftist leader of the Iraqi Ba'th who, following his expulsion from the party in 1964, founded an insignificant party of his own.

Aṣ-Ṣafadī, Muṭā' A Ba'thi novelist and publicist who became an ardent Nasserite.

Sālim, Muṣlīḥ Ba'thi from Deir az-Zōr who belonged to the *Quṭrīyyūn* faction of the Syrian Ba'th and was director of Dar al-Waḥda, the state publishing house.

As-Sarrāj, 'Abd al-Ḥamīd Nasser's foremost supporter in Syria.

As-Sayyīd, Jallāl A veteran member of the Ba'th (b. 1923 in Deir az-Zōr) who left the party in 1955 but remained active in Syrian politics.

Shabīb, Ṭālib An Iraqi Ba'thi leader.

Shā'ir, Fahd A Druse officer who took part in the *coup* of March 8 as an independent but eventually joined the Ba'th and played an important role in Ba'thi military politics.

Shishaklī, Adīb Syrian dictator, 1949–54.

Shiyya, Jamīl A Druse Ba'thi militant; having been a schoolteacher and director of education in Sweida, he became, after March 1963, member of several cabinets and Regional Commands.

Shnewī, Muḥammad A supporter of Amīn al-Ḥāfiẓ and Syrian chief of staff until the *coup* of February 23, 1966.

Ash-Shūfī, Ḥamūd A leader of the radical Marxist faction that played an important role in Syrian and Ba'thi politics in 1963–4. He is a Druse and a former schoolteacher.

Aṣ-Ṣūfī, Muhammad A Nasserite participant in the *coup* of March 8, 1963.

Suwaidānī, Aḥmad A leftist officer from the Ḥaurān; a supporter of Ṣalāḥ J'dīd, he became chief of staff following the *coup* of February 23, 1966, but eventually quarreled with his partners and fell from power.

At-Takrītī, Ḥardān An Iraqi Ba'thi.

Ṭalās (Ṭlās), Muṣṭafā Sunnī supporter of J'dīd who would later replace Suwaidānī as chief of staff. By switching his loyalty to Ḥāfiẓ al-Asad he has so far retained his power.

Ṭālib, al-Walīd A member of Bīṭār's entourage; native of the Idlib region (b. in the late 1920s). He was elected to the Syrian parliament in December 1961 and later held ministerial and party posts.

Ṭarabīshī, Jurj A radical Nasserite Ba'thi (until his expulsion in 1964).

Thābit, Jamīl A Ba'thi trade unionist and a one-time minister of labour.

Ṭo'meh, George A Greek Orthodox from Damascus (Constantine Zurayyiq's brother-in-law) who has been close to Bīṭār's group and outlook. In 1963–4 he was Syrian minister of the economy and has since been Syria's UN representative.

'Ubaid, Ḥamad A Druse Ba'thi officer who became minister of defence prior to the *coup* of February 23, 1966, and was subsequently removed and jailed.

'Umrān, Muḥammad A central leader of the Ba'thi officers who was removed from Syria after 1966 and assassinated in Lebanon in 1972.

'Urfī, Ismā'īl A leftist Ba'thi journalist from Deir az-Zōr.

Yaḥyā, Ṭāhir A former Iraqi premier and a moderate Ba‘thi.

Zahr ad-Dīn, ‘Abd al-Karīm Commander of the Syrian army during the Separatist Period.

Za‘īm, Ḥusnī Leader of the first Syrian military *coup* in 1949.

Zaitūn, Mashhūr A Ba‘thi of the *Quṭriyyūn* faction. A native of a village in the Haurān (b. 1932), he is a lawyer by education. After pursuing a bureaucratic career he rose under the Ba‘th regime to become a member of the cabinet and the Regional Command.

Zu‘ayyīn (Z‘ayyīn), Yūsuf A leader of the radical wing of the Syrian Ba‘th and several times premier of Syria. A native of Abū Kemal, near Deir az-Zōr, he is a physician by profession and brother-in-law of Nūr ad-Dīn al-Atāsī.

Az-Zu‘bī, Muḥammad A former schoolteacher from the Haurān who rose in the ranks of the Syrian Ba‘th as a supporter of Ṣalāḥ J'dīd to become member of the cabinet and the party commands.

Az-Zu‘bī, Mūsa A Ba‘thi officer, member of the Military Committee, and a supporter of Amīn al-Ḥāfiẓ.

Zuhūr, ‘Abd al-Karīm A moderate Ba‘thi, native of Ḥamā, who had been active in the party and in Syrian politics in the 1950s. After distinguishing himself in the Cairo Unity Talks in 1963, he left the party and became an independent Unionist.

APPENDIX F

EXCERPT FROM "SOME THEORETICAL POINTS OF DEPARTURE"

Freedom: The Exercise of Popular Democracy

The Arab Socialist Ba'th Party emerged in Arab and international conditions dominated by a forceful violation and far-reaching falsification of freedom:

Traditional direct imperialism was still occupying most countries of our Arab homeland, quashing the people's liberty to guarantee the protection of its positions and interests and the continuation of its influence.

And in the Arab countries which achieved a traditional independence, Reaction inherited some of the imperialist centres and deprived the masses of the fruits of their struggle. It turned power into an instrument for exploiting the popular masses and allied itself with imperialism so that each would guarantee the other's influence and interests; when the struggle of the masses intensified, Reaction was forced to exercise direct, overt terror, while in other circumstances it relied on falsifying the slogans of freedom and democracy and emptied them of their true contents, and the democracy of Reaction became a mere facade hiding tyranny, falsification, and exploitation by the reactionary classes.

At the same time the socialist experiences witnessed a tangible considerable aggravation of the dangers of bureaucracy, socialist legitimacy was abused, and socialist democracy in the majority of the socialist camp's states turned into a mummy covering a sanguinary autocratic tyranny. And in a revolutionary confrontation of principle with these conditions the Arab Socialist Ba'th Party raised the slogan of freedom so that it came as a true reliable response to the position of a party believing in socialism as a means of total and radical liberation of the Arab man.

Now then, freedom for the Arab Socialist Ba'th Party means—primarily—a complete political and economic liberation from all forms of imperialist domination. And for that reason the Arab Socialist Ba'th was the first revolutionary Arab movement to place the question of anti-Imperialist struggle on a revolutionary level of principle and for that reason too the Party launched a permanent relentless struggle against all forms of imperialist domination. And in those Arab countries in which the Party struck deep roots and developed its strength among the masses, the Party's struggle was a basic factor in menacing and undermining all forms of imperialist domination, whether political or economic, direct or indirect. And at the same time, the Party's socialist points of departure turned it into the first revolutionary nationalist movement to detect the roots of imperialist influence in the make-up of the reactionary classes and it set out to fight them with force and determination.

The Party's socialist points of departure and its commitment to the interests of the popular masses enabled it to play an active role in exposing the falsification of freedom by the reactionary classes and the distorted false application of bourgeois democracy. And while the objective conditions in the Arab world had prevented the consolidation of a solid, sound basis for a serious permanent exercise of democracy in its bourgeois framework, the Party had also participated —due to the socialist nature of its struggle—in exposing the bourgeois-feudal concept of freedom even if it did not undertake to formulate a new doctrinal basis for a definite tangible concept of freedom and democracy in their socialist framework.

The humanistic character of the Party's socialism had always been prominent and evident, since man's bondage under regimes of exploitation is the gravest form of loss of human freedom. Due to these objective circumstances only toppling and liquidation of the regimes of exploitation and replacing the capitalist relations of production can create the suitable objective conditions for liberating man and saving him from loss and exploitation. And on this basis the Party had always deplored instances of violation of socialist legitimacy and encroachment on the freedom of the popular masses and bureaucratic domination over them—instances which had occurred in some socialist revolutionary experiences in the world. On this basis the Arab Socialist Ba'th Party had always stressed the necessary inseparability of freedom and social justice which alone can deepen the human significance of socialism and turn it into the solid material basis for the development of man's liberty.

The Arab Socialist Ba'th Party had placed the question of the struggle against imperialism in its international and human framework and considered the socialist camp a positive, active force in the struggle against imperialism. And the political and doctrinal submissiveness of the local Communists, their sectarian closed-mindedness and intellectual stagnation, their enmity to the Arab nationalist orientation and to Arab unity, and the fundamental and tactical errors that the Soviet Union had many times committed and is still committing could not obscure from the Arab Socialist Ba'th Party its profound encounter with the fundamental starting points of the socialist camp's policy, nor could they change the Party's independence from this camp and its criticism of its mistakes into an enmity. The Party was the first to propose the slogan of positive neutralism as a broad line for Arab foreign policy and has always stressed the principle of "non-commitment" towards any of the international camps, but this formula meant fundamentally a determined revolutionary struggle of principle against imperialism. Therefore the Party did not regard the two camps equally since the horizon of struggle of a colonized or semicolonized people and of a homeland crushed and exploited by imperialism render the fundamental starting points of the socialist camp more harmonious with the interests of our Arab homeland and more in sympathy with our Arab people.

The policy of non-commitment traced by the Party, while it meant in direct terms avoiding submissiveness and keeping away from entanglement in daily direct and private battles of the two camps, meant at the same time commitment to a principled revolutionary policy on the international level, based on support for the national liberation movements of all peoples struggling against imperialism.

II

The Party's basic points of departure in understanding the problem of political freedom had been correct in their broad lines but the Party did not try to clarify its social and class aspects in a complete concrete fashion. The Party had rejected all forms of distortion and coercion sustained by human freedom in general and the freedom of Arab man in particular.

The Party had denounced personal dictatorship and bureaucratic dictatorship but it did not clearly define its fundamental outlook on bourgeois parliamentary democracy and it did not place the theoretical framework of the problem of freedom within its concrete reality by linking it to the revolutionary phase in which our Arab people is living and to the revolutionary classes in Arab society, and finally it did not search for a model draft of the basis of power . . . revolutionary, radical and popular democratic at the same time.

And because the Party was satisfied with laying the broad bases and lines of its outlook on the problem of political freedom, it tumbled into a certain ambiguity in its daily struggle under some conditions, since it has not adopted a definite opinion with regard to the liberal bourgeois concepts of political liberty.

The Party had operated starting from a militant spontaneity on the level of the military sector and on the parliamentary level:
(1) On the level of the military sector the Party worked to mobilize this sector in a number of countries and endeavoured to convert it from a professional sector operated by the reactionary authority into a revolutionary sector closely united with the Arab masses in their struggle against imperialism, fragmentation, and exploitation.

And in the first phases of the Party's struggle in this sector it managed to recruit it to the struggle against imperialism but it was unable at the outset to transform it completely into a revolutionary instrument at the hand of the masses because it was incapable in the first phases of its struggle of making the revolutionary elements in it an organic part of the Party's structure, and for that reason the accomplishments of the Party's struggle in this domain remained partial. But seen from the angle of the historic development of the popular struggle, this struggle had its positive consequences. It had shared in the weakening of the reactionary classes and exposed the reactionary nature of the reactionary democratic regime and it also had played a decisive role in repelling the imperialist assaults on the independence of some Arab countries.

It would have been possible to follow a complete revolutionary programme in this sector if the Party had followed from the first phase the conscious revolutionary tactic that detonated the glorious revolution of February 8 in the Iraqi region and which from the outset persistently considered the organization of the masses a problem to be treated by the revolution and which believed that the role of this sector is to be merely one of the fronts of revolutionary action and merely a struggle complementing the fundamental struggle whose base the popular masses ought to remain. Only such a mature revolutionary programme can implant the revolutionary roots and deepen the socialist contents of any event in which the revolutionary military element figures as a chief element in the direct battle.

All this explains the failure to transform the military sector into a revolutionary instrument before the revolution of February 8 as it explains the setback of attempted military *coups* and the shift of some of the military into the ranks of opportunism and reaction, since in the conditions of political and social backwardness prevailing in our homeland the possibility of bureaucratic disintegration and installation of a new class over the popular masses exists if the military sector is not organically linked to the Party, and if the organization of this sector does not include the masses of soldiers, NCOs, and officers, and if the masses of workers and peasants are not mobilized in a serious conscious fashion.

The Party had demonstrated a revolutionary firmness when it turned to struggle in the military sector, for on the one hand, the total profound crisis from which our people suffers necessarily affects this sector and, on the other hand, revolutionary action requires mobilization of all the forces for the victory of the national and socialist issues. But this revolutionism was to a large extent spontaneous and it needed a complete awareness of the nature of this sector and its conditions on the one hand and an objective definition of the fundamental forces of revolution on the other.

(2) Even though the Party's points of departure were of a revolutionary fashion in their outlook on social change, the Party in countries which offered a political climate suitable for the (sporadic) existence of a parliamentary front, played "the parliamentary game" in a manner indicating its acceptance of the parliamentary regime in its bourgeois liberal concept as a solid, sufficient framework for political struggle and action.

And though the Party's revolutionism brought it to doubt the merit of bourgeois parliaments as a way to socialist transformation, it became—during some periods—immersed in the domain of parliamentary activity and forgot the fundamental issue, the issue of mass organization, leapfrogging above the objective conditions of the Arab homeland which confirmed that parliamentarianism in its bourgeois liberal concept could not serve as an instrument of radical social transformation, and that it was merely a formal facade covering the influence of feudalism and the grande bourgeoisie.

Mass struggle alone is the way of the revolution and parliamentary struggle can only be one form of struggle, aiming at strengthening and deepening relations with the masses and exposing the policy of the reactionary classes and their complete falsification of democracy.

The slipping of some Party branches during certain periods into the adoption of parliamentarianism had pushed them into attempting to win voters' votes in a traditional fashion, descending to the stagnant state of the masses and to their points of weakness, succumbing to their individual partial and daily problems. This slipping had also reflected in a negative way on the Party's composition in these branches and in its plans of action.

III

(A) The greater part of the Arab homeland is still subject, to varying degrees, to imperialist influence in its old and new form.

And though the course of historic development of the peoples' struggle, including our Arab people, had scored great victories against imperialism, this did not eliminate its plots and manoeuvres to obstruct the liberation of peoples and to preserve its positions and monopolies and the other forms of its influence.

The escalation of the peoples' struggle and its expansion induces world imperialism day after day to liquidate the partial contradictions between its wings and to replace its methods, rendering them more flexible and attentive. And while the feudal classes and the upper groups of monopolistic bureaucracy had played the role of ally to the old imperialism, the bureaucracy and bourgeoisie are playing the role of ally to neo-imperialism and are sharing with it in exploiting the masses of the people.

The conditions of economic backwardness from which our homeland suffers, together with the existence of bourgeois bureaucracy as a political leadership, will lead to consolidation and continuation of the influence of neo-imperialism. Therefore, only an authority representing the interests of the popular masses can stop the new imperialist infiltration and liquidate its interests.

The exploitation of the difficulties of economic construction in our homeland and alliance with the exploiting parasitic groups and support of their control of economic development and encouragement of individual enterprise and the private sector are the new methods employed by the imperialist states for preserving their actual control under new forms. And therefore, it is wishful thinking that the construction of a new socialist society, regarding the interests of the masses as its prime concern, can take place without a permanent harsh struggle against the phenomenon of imperialism. And on this basis it seems irrational to rely on foreign aid but as an additional and secondary factor in the process of our homeland's economic development. Only mobilization of the material and human resources of the Arab people and the pursuit of the scientific method in planning and socialist transformation will enable the achievement of a harmonious and serious development of Arab economy.

Only a fundamental revolutionary policy on the foreign level, a policy originating in the socialist concept which rejects all forms of exploitation whether in or out of the Arab homeland, a policy based on confidence in the power of the Arab masses, can enable the Arab people to join forces—on the international level—with solid allies in the Arab struggle against imperialism. Strengthening the solidarity with the countries of the Third World—to which we belong—that exercise the policy of positive neutralism and deepening relations with them (in a discriminating fashion, according to their conditions of government and the degree of their economic independence) will most certainly contribute to strengthening the front of struggle against imperialism.

Also, strengthening the friendship between the Arab people and all the states whose interests suit the wishes of the Arab people to liberate itself of the remnants of imperialism will create real opportunities for exterminating the imperialist positions and monopolistic economic interests in the Arab homeland and will also lead to strengthening the joint general human struggle against imperialism.

And since the liberation of Palestine basically depends on the unity of Arab progressive forces and their growth, then it is a fundamental flexible and revolutionary policy that will be able to induce the progressive forces in the world to support the case of the Arab people in Palestine in a fashion that will enable the liquidation of this problem, drawing the minimal direct reaction from imperialism which created Israel and supports it now with the means of life and power.

The Arab nationalist movement, being the movement of an oppressed people, must always necessarily regard itself as an inseparable part of the movement of struggle of all peoples against imperialism. The Arab people is therefore always moved by a resolute will for an active positive participation in battling all forms of imperialism all over the world and it will lend support to all peoples struggling against imperialism.

(B) Freedom in its political form is not an abstract absolute term, not even freedom in the bourgeois sense of the term, but it is rather always a concrete freedom with definite social contents given to certain classes and deprived—in this or that form—from other classes. When the bourgeoisie staged its revolution against feudalism it called for ideal absolute freedom in the name of all the people, but once it had taken power freedom for it turned into definite class interests. And the bourgeoisie did not hesitate to trample its idealism for exploiting the democratic state and for striking the popular masses when danger threatened its interests. The bourgeoisie had turned absolute freedom or what is called human rights into class interests. Democracy in its present form in Western Europe is not the bourgeoisie's gift to the popular masses but the fruit of a long stubborn popular struggle.

(C) The parliamentary regime in Western Europe emerged with the rise and development of the bourgeoisie and consequently served as the political cover for the bourgeois economic regime. The parliaments represented at the outset the propertied classes alone and, with the development of the workers' movement and as a result of its long political struggle, franchise spread until it became universal and the influence of the popular forces in the parliaments increased gradually. But the changes which took place in the structure of the capitalist states had led to the concentration of real power in the state's administrative, economic, and military apparatuses. And thus "the laws of arithmetic" fell short of reflecting the will of the masses and of accomplishing their aims, since the bourgeoisie enjoying actual real privileges managed to convert the parliamentary activity into an instrument of the capitalist economy, and the working class' entry into Western Europe's parliaments did not lead to subversion of the bourgeoisie's authority but only forced it to adopt new forms and styles more flexible and better tuned to the demands of the situation, so that the bourgeoisie absorbed some of the workers' demands and froze their revolutionary struggle and remained in power.

The parliamentary regime was tottering and its crisis was aggravated by the victory of the socialist revolution in the Soviet Union, the rise of the Fascist regimes between the two world wars, the victory of the nationalist revolutions in Asia, and the entry of the capitalist industrial countries into the age of the new industrial revolution.

(D) Since the parliamentary regime is the Western bourgeoisie's way of government and part of the superstructure of these societies, the application of parliamentarianism in certain Arab countries was a mere transmission of a Western facade cut off from its political and economic roots and its direct practical needs.

Since Arab societies are not simple bourgeois societies but rather semifeudal tribal bourgeois societies, parliamentarianism in our homeland remained a mere slender cardboard structure and a false copy of Western parliamentarianism. Therefore, it will be incapable of facing the tasks of nationalist socialist struggle or of implanting its roots in political life.

The phenomenon of military *coups* had become closely connected with this regime in our homeland and it is both a result of it and an index of its failure. Parliamentarianism in our homeland had reflected the backward semifeudal tribal and sectarian social situation, and through the contradiction between the expectations of the masses and the reactionary backward state of parliamentarianism and as a negative spontaneous reflection of the anger of the masses the military *coups* broke out and parliamentary democracy and military *coups* succeeded one another, each carrying the seeds of the other only to abort them.

For all these reasons the failure of parliamentarianism in the Arab countries and its fall do not issue simply from its misapplication by evil factions but it was rather determined by the objective concrete reality and the conditions of the development of the social and political struggle in the Arab homeland and in the backward countries in general.

The failure of personal rule exploring "progressive" horizons in search of a successful alternative for parliamentary democracy means no exoneration for that democracy, neither is it an index of its merit even if the bourgeoisie and Reaction regard this symptom as justifying their distorted concept of democracy. Later, the failure of personal bureaucratic rule in totally mobilizing the resources of the masses produces real foundations for a consolidation of the socialist transformation on a democratic basis, which will reconfirm to the toiling popular masses and to their revolutionary vanguards that revolutionary democracy cannot be fully and actively applied unless it is based on a popular vanguard organization that will ensure the broadest and deepest form for the democracy of the masses and will set the stage for an active vanguard rule for the workers and peasants in particular and for the toiling masses in general.

(E) Revolutionary popular democracy is not an ideal scheme for the organization of government independently of the actual concrete conditions of the struggle of the masses and its current phase. Nor is it a subjective wish since it is organically linked to the extent and deepness of the growth of the mass struggle and it is, finally, associated with the revolution's development and the needs of the socialist construction.

And in the present circumstances when the transition from the quasi-feudal capitalist society (in several Arab countries) is taking place, power ought to shift from the feudal bourgeois classes to the toiling classes, and therefore parliamentarianism should be avoided, being as it is one form of the domination of the popular masses by these classes.

Avoiding parliamentarianism does not mean transition to dictatorial, personal bureaucratic or military forms of government, but it rather means the disappearance of the bourgeois quasi-feudal framework of democracy and the transition to a broader, deeper, stronger, and sounder democracy, namely popular democracy, which on the one hand guarantees the curbing of Reaction and on the other hand assures the mobilization of the capacities and potential of the masses in the process of the socialist revolutionary construction of Arab society. It is popular democracy that will permanently develop the government, and the revolution's impulses will strengthen, preserve, and expand the gains of the masses, and will provide the climate for the development of the mass mobilization and the deepening of its roots in terms of consciousness and organization.

(F) The concept of popular democracy involves an extensive measure of democracy for the popular masses but it also stresses at the same time the need to seclude the class and political forces hostile to the socialist revolution. This seclusion ought to take its legal form on the one hand and its popular form on the other. The residues of the notion of "class cooperation" in the minds of the backward section of the masses ought to fall and be liquidated. The battle with the reactionary forces hostile to the revolution requires a long stubborn struggle taking a variety of forms and fought on various levels and in all sectors of life, economic, political, administrative, military, and cultural. The battle with Reaction requires not only suppression and prevention of its sabotage attempts but its eradication, since Reaction had no mercy for the toiling masses for thousands of years. The masses, therefore, must take the question of the class struggle against the reactionary classes in a clear and decisive fashion—either we survive or reaction does so, and any compromise settlement is a lie or deception whose result will be the deliverance of Reaction.

Local Reaction in each Arab country, weakened as it may seem to us, disposes of formidable forces and numerous weapons. It has its material resources, moral and intellectual influence, and its relations and sons in the organs of government; then there are the revolution's mistakes and the shortcomings of its action. These weapons give Reaction long breath in its resistance and provide it with opportunities to regroup its forces and enter the battle against the popular forces once by way of sabotage and obstruction of the socialist transformation and another time by way of devising plots. Therefore, the battle against Reaction is not so much in need of impetuous boldness as it is in need of a conscious, persevering, organized boldness.

(G) Popular democracy will not develop beyond a representative style for the popular masses without a revolutionary political framework and without organized political vanguards that will include the most deeply conscious and the most stable militant elements, who enjoy political farsightedness and practical ability and are filled with the spirit of self-sacrifice and are ultimately devoted to the cause of the masses. It is this revolutionary vanguard that will give popular democracy its revolutionary spirit and will faithfully reflect the wishes of the masses with regard to the nationalist socialist revolution. It is this vanguard alone that will guarantee the balance and harmony between the centralism, effectiveness of the popular organization, the unity of revolutionary struggle, and unity of the constructive work on the one hand and the democracy of organization required by the popular character of the revolution that will guarantee the complete mobilization of the human resources of the masses.

It is only the vanguard revolutionary organization that always preserves deep vital relations with the masses, at once preceding them and tied to them, teaching them and learning from them, living with them in a relationship of interaction, not of patronage, that can assure the centralist and democratic character of the popular democratic authority. Only an authority that meets these requirements can plan, call up, and recruit the popular masses for mobilizing all the human and material resources for accomplishing the socialist transformation and economic growth.

(H) The centralism of the popular democratic authority can only be maintained seriously and effectively through a vanguard revolutionary political organization. But this centralism ought not necessarily to eliminate the principle of election and turn it into a formal act. The basic condition for the democracy and revolutionism of the popular councils is in their formation by direct free election on all levels—village, city, region, and province . . . and then on the country (*quṭrī*) and national (*qawmī*) levels.

The task of the nationalist socialist vanguard is to assure the combination of the principle of popular voting and its freedom in the election of the representative bodies and popular councils. Such a task can only be accomplished if this vanguard can guarantee the gathering of the great majority of the masses around it by regarding the masses as the basis and protector of the revolution and consequently rejecting the principle of patronage over the people or of exercising power by deputation representing the people. There is but a short distance between the fascist concept of the "elite" and the socialist concept of the vanguard. However, the "elite" concept regards the masses as merely a passive flock led by the "elite" to "happiness and justice", which in practice leads to seclusion from the masses and to rising above them so that the "elite" necessarily slips to aloofness from the masses and to exercising a direct dictatorship over them, at one time by way of terror and another time through distortion of public opinion and its moulding according to its will. But the socialist concept of the vanguard regards the masses as the essence of revolution and democracy, and it leads to a conscious humble opening towards them which deepens the living relations with the masses to an organic degree and leads them on the road to maturity and liberation from the moral influences of the feudal bourgeouis situation by way of amiable interaction which regards the people as the source of wisdom and revolution.

The application of popular democracy in a revolutionary fashion will not be accomplished through the vanguard's subjective wishes nor by insisting on repeating the slogans of freedom and democracy; rather, objective foundations ought to be created that will ensure the seriousness and steadfastness of this application. And the decisive objective foundation for the application of democracy is the vanguard's ability to lead the decisive majority of the masses relying on the masses' free, deep confidence, because a party without masses is bound to deteriorate into a gang practicing tyranny over the masses.

The revolutionary socialist vanguard is the instrument of the masses in bringing about a transformation of the social and economic relations, but for this transformation to materialize in a comprehensive radical and human fashion it should be brought about by the masses themselves; as for the socialist vanguard it will play the role of mediator and leader (even if it is in power) who acts to direct the journey of the masses towards the socialist future in a scientific way and in a democratic style.

(I) The political organization of the revolutionary popular authority in the conditions of socialist construction in a backward country ought to be based on foundations enabling a combination of the leadership's unity and power and its democracy and popularity. Therefore, the principle of democratic centralism is the suitable foundation for the existence of such an authority—and the democracy of this authority is assured through the election of the organs of political authority by the people and the ensuring of a permanent and effective supervision of these organs by the people, and through the election of the higher organs by the lower and the periodic convening of congresses of the popular councils and of the organizations. Democracy ought to be hierachical, developing upwards so that the principle of collective leadership becomes the democratic form of the revolutionary authority at the top. But collective leadership does not mean diluting of responsibility and does not have to obstruct the daily initiatives of the revolutionary authority, and it also does not necessarily have to negate the absolutely flexible manoeuvring of this leadership.

As for centralism in the authority's political organization, it is assured through the minority's voluntary candid submission to the majority, and the submission of the lower organs to the higher ones, and the submission of the organs and organizations to the decisions and directives of the central leadership.

(J) For the popular masses to exercise their democratic rights in a conscious, disciplined and responsible fashion, they ought to be mobilized in organizational frameworks that will give them power and will enable their political and social indoctrination. These frameworks are the workers' and peasants' unions, the students' federations, the youth organizations, organizations of officials and employees, women's federations, etc. . . the popular representative councils do not exhaust the forms and dimensions of popular organization and they do not abolish the role of these frameworks but rather complement them. And without the organizational frameworks and the popular councils the masses turn into a haze without power and awareness and without a conscious responsible discipline.

Naturally the party cannot take in all the popular masses, only their vanguard, being as it is the moving force that sets in motion and leads the popular organizations and councils. It is the Party with its deep insight, penetrating the intellectual state of the masses, that crystallizes their aspirations, and in this respect it is the Party which guarantees the revolutionary and popular exercise of democracy.

(K) An abstract, absolute linking of the problem of democracy to the principle of the plurality of parties represents the bourgeois mentality in the conception of democracy. This problem should always be conceived on the basis of the concrete historic conditions of the social and political struggle.

A principal party leading a front of political forces, which exercises the revolutionary authority, does not necessarily lead to a disregarding of democracy.

The principle of "the leading party" was made necessary by the temporary need for a firm central authority leading the operation of socialist construction and it had been confirmed by the revolutionary socialist experiences in the world and particularly by the conditions of the developing countries. But in order to guarantee the exercise of popular democracy, a prerequisite for the success of socialist construction, two conditions should be met: (a) the party's ability to lead the decisive majority of the popular masses and to assure their voluntary conscious rallying around it; (b) the exercise of internal democracy within the leading party.

The exercise of democracy within the leading party does not consist merely in electing, voting and irresponsible mindless debating at meetings. In order for democracy to be an instrument for continuously developing the party and for deepening its relations with the masses and in order to be an instrument for implanting its principled and revolutionary policy and jettisoning all that is opportunistic, unprincipled, and unrevolutionary, it is necessary that in the party there obtain such objective conditions that enable this serious conscious exercise of democracy. Among these conditions:

1) The party's policy should always be clear and defined and in accordance with its ideological points of departure and fundamental goals. Only the continuous clarification of the party's tactical and strategic policy in an analytical fashion tied to the party's theoretical points of departure enables the party's rank and file to comprehend the party's policy on the one hand and to explain it in a clear scientific manner to the non-party masses on the other. And in addition to this, and fundamentally, it will give the rank and file opportunities for a conscious responsible debating of the party's policy that will make possible the improvement and, if necessary, correction of that policy.

Permanent clarity of the party's policy helps to create the

objective conditions for a voluntary enlistment in the party's ranks as well as in isolating the opportunistic and destructive elements in its ranks.

2) The permanent struggle against the symptoms of backwardness and deviation that might spread from the bourgeois-feudal-tribal situation into the party's ranks.

Lack of political culture and scientific criteria for analyzing and thinking is bound to lead to the creation of tribal blocs and factional spirit and feudal mentality within the party's ranks. And in the absence of democratic education in the party's ranks and in case of doctrinal and ideological ambiguity, the fundamental objective relations between the party militants are corrupted and some are led to seek other relationships. And thus the party's rank and file slip into backward anarchic factions, centred on backward concepts, or into circles of personal friendship or groups centred on individuals, and thus it deteriorates into surrendering to the remnants of mental habits left by bygone historic ages.

The psychology and mentality of the petty bourgeoisie always threaten to corrupt democracy within the party and to create a gap between the party and the simple non-partisan masses. The psychology and mentality of the petty bourgeoisie manifest themselves in personal arrogance, and vanity, and frivolousness in struggle, and in formalistic outward behaviour, and in the excitation and haughtiness veiled by revolutionism, and in the race for benefits and positions, in standing above the masses of the people and the ordinary militants, in keeping away from the simple persistent daily work on the minutest facts and problems while uttering "revolutionary" prattle, in being content with preaching without seeking objective instruments of struggle; all these are the attributes of the petty bourgeoisie, which corrupt the party's democracy and lead to the party's isolation from the masses and to its conversion into a closed circle, if it is in the phase of struggling for power, or into a bureaucratic class above the people if it is in power.

3) Exercising democracy's revolutionism requires permanent scientific education in the party's ranks. The revolutionary struggle and the exercise of political responsibility are not merely good sincere intentions towards the masses nor are they mere individual

moral values found among the party's militants; the party militants ought to have such qualities but these alone do not qualify them for a conscious exercise of democracy within the party nor do they suffice for the exercise of a positive revolutionary struggle aiming at the transformation of society.

It is only the scientific logic based on the objective scientific analysis of the conditions of struggle and on the realistic analysis of the concrete situations which continue to develop and change that can raise the intellectual capabilities in the party's ranks. And it is only this logic which excludes all forms of subjective thinking such as improvisation and approximative outlook, mental laziness and sermonizing thinking, and other idealist trends of thinking. This way of thinking corrupts the objective relations within the party and renders the party incapable of producing the objective instruments for its revolutionary struggle.

(L) In the conditions of the transition to socialism most socialist revolutionary experiences witnessed at the stage of state capitalism a grave negative phenomenon, namely the rise of bureaucracy as a new class. The danger of this phenomenon had gotten out of hand and reached alarming proportions in a number of socialist countries and had turned into an obstacle to the development of democracy; it distorted the development of democracy and the natural development of a socialist relationship in society and it became a distinct power occupying a position above the actually productive elements in particular and above the general masses of the people in general.

The regime of state capitalism and the numerical and organizational weakness of the working class produce the objective conditions for the development of bureaucracy. Therefore, the democratic direction of the means of production and the organization of the working class and the preservation of its relative independence from the government will open the road for the development of popular democracy and will contribute to the reduction of the negative symptoms in the state capitalism regime.

The democratic direction of the means of production had become a fundamental condition for the exercise of popular democracy on the political level; therefore, it is necessary that the workers' councils fulfill a fundamental role in directing the productive industrial projects; and while considering the still complicated necessities of socialist construction and the requirements of technical developments, the yoke of directing industry ought to be placed gradually on the shoulders of the working classes until their performance acquires its fundamental active form which guarantees the workers' leadership of production activities and opens the way for initiatives of the masses of workers in improving work and increase of production and organization of the administrative work and ensures correction of manifestations of routinism and impersonality in the direction of factories and projects of production. Finally, it ensures a conscious sincere involvement of the working class in the problems of socialist building and develops in the workers a sensitivity for the morality of human work regarding it as an honour for man rather than a heavy burden.

(M) In the circumstances of a certain class rule the government's administrative apparatus is necessarily a reflection of that rule and one of its instruments. Therefore the party when it holds power ought to develop the state apparatuses to render them capable of active participation in the problems of socialist construction.

The separation of these apparatuses from the people is a concrete matter just as the strong links and complicated ties between the upper groups of these apparatuses and the Reaction render their stay in power in their present form an obstruction to the development of popular democracy. Therefore, the starting point for a socialist and popular development of these apparatuses is the establishment of a strict popular supervision over it. This supervision will refresh the mentality of these apparatuses and their style and mode of operation, will save them from routinism, indifference, and bureaucratic stagnation and it will relieve the employees from a mercantile relationship with the state and turn the employee into a citizen involved in the problems of the people, believing in the aims of the masses.

(N) The actual exercise of popular democracy requires rejection of the principle of keeping the army away from politics—this would render politics incomplete and distorted, depriving an important segment of the citizens of exercising their political rights. The actual outcome of the principle of keeping the army away from politics is domination of the army or at least part of it and its employment as a reserve force at the hands of Reaction; rather, the notion of the professional army is fundamentally the principle relied on by the ruling Reaction and bourgeoisie, since sheer professionalism accompanied by material privileges will render the army an obedient tool for the exploiting classes.

The revolutionary struggle waged by the Arab masses had encountered its reflections and echo in the military sector in a number of Arab countries as there developed in some countries revolutionary armies with the full significance and dimensions of the term. Thus, political activity in the military sector became a fundamental fact of the historic development of the Arab struggle and any attempt to deny it is bound to be destructive for the revolution and an obstruction of the socialist transformation.

The democratic exercise of politics is not only the right of those citizens who work in the military sector but a fundamental necessity of socialist construction. And during the forward march of the socialist revolutionary struggle attention should be permanently paid not only to the uprooting and containment of the remnants of Reaction but also—and fundamentally—to the development of the mediating character of the army units along popular and socialist lines. Such a development seems all the more urgent as the class struggle and social conflict become more acrimonious during the advance towards socialist transformation and its expansion.

The organic fusion of the military and civilian vanguard sectors is an urgent prerequisite for creating an ideological interaction between them that leads to a unity of thinking and to a common, direct, actual and complete confrontation with the problems of socialist construction, preventing a military seclusion and fusing the army and the people in a common revolutionary fate.

The political and ideological indoctrination of the army is under no circumstances of lesser importance than military training; on the contrary, it rather creates a climate suitable for a new revolutionary concept of discipline based on belief in superior ideals and not on fear of coercion. It also terminates the bourgeois professional methods in the relations between superior and subordinate and creates a comradely relationship moved by belief in the cause of the masses and in which the employment of coercion becomes an exceptional means exercised against unsound elements.

The service of the flag is an honour to the citizen and ought to be rendered by everyone; and in a backward county like ours the service of the flag could turn into a school for the socialist revolution and into a means for liquidating illiteracy and intellectual backwardness (thus) mobilizing the countryside in a revolutionary manner that perfects and develops the agricultural socialist revolution and invests it with its human content.

(O) Adherence to the truth is a fundamental factor in the revolutionary exercise of popular democracy. Truth is at once revolutionary and ethical and it is only this adherence that distinguishes revolutionism from opportunism, mission from propaganda, and progressiveness from demagoguery.

Veiling the truth from the masses is a transgression of the simplest requirement of democracy and casts doubt on their wisdom and ability to distinguish between right and wrong. Doubting the sound perception of the masses is the first phase in the slipping into fascist concepts.

Flexibility and realism in political activity require consideration of the result and usefulness of a given position. But a distinction should always be made between an immediate temporary usefulness and one that is far-reaching and permanent. This distinction is one of the fundamental characteristics that sets revolutionism apart from opportunism. The slogan of interests, when perceived correctly and in the long range, cannot conflict with respect for the truth.

Adherence to the truth before the masses will be a means for educating them and a basic factor in perfecting their political maturity. Therefore the revolutionary vanguards and the revolutionary authority are always called upon to frankly inform the people about everything which concerns its political, economic, and social affairs; they are called upon to reveal mistakes whether they are intentional or spontaneous, small or big; they are called upon to reveal the weak aspects of the development and explain the difficulties and obstacles facing socialist construction whether they came by ignorance or opportunism or by way of neglect or sabotage.

The road before the revolutionary government is not smooth and contradictions are liable to obstruct its advance. It may have to agree to a number of temporary concessions or necessary bargaining positions and sometimes it may be forced to retreat. All this can happen in all spheres of revolutionary activity. In such situations the people should be presented with this truth in no uncertain terms, without any ambiguity and with no opportunistic, false justification. The people should know of both victories and setbacks, gains and losses. The people ought to be frankly informed of the true nature of every bargaining and retreat contradicting the fundamental ideological positions, which are made necessary by temporary circumstances and which, in particular, may be dictated by non-fundamental contradictions or by the revolution's inability to confront them in a certain situation.

The frank truth will not weaken the revolutionary determination of the masses when they are led by experienced, conscious revolutionary vanguards; rather it will assure a serious recruitment and a conscious planning for their [the contradictions] liquidation in a different situation and at another phase.

Any attempt to veil the truth is an overt fall from revolutionism to opportunism.

(P) The spread of illiteracy among the popular masses will hamper their exercise of democracy and will keep it incomplete, superficial, and formal unless it is accompanied by political indoctrination supplying the masses with the minimal level of culture that will enable them to grasp the general matters and the broad lines of the problems of politics and socialist construction.

The complete and rapid liquidation of illiteracy seems therefore a matter of necessity and priority and so are the efforts to educate the illiterate citizens, teaching them not only reading and writing but also enabling them to absorb a minimum of knowledge that will allow them a conscious exercise of their democratic rights. The liquidation of illiteracy is an urgent duty for the government and the party and it will bolster [?] the mass organizations.

(Q) The exercise of popular democracy will remain incomplete as long as the woman is removed from society's general life. Therefore, the liberation of the Arab woman has become a democratic necessity in addition to being a human necessity. The disparaging view of the woman is an integral part of the ideology of the feudal-tribal society so that the liberation of the woman is a primary task of the nationalist-socialist revolution and the building of a modern, democratic, liberated society cannot be complete and proper unless it confronts the problem of the woman's liberation, boldly, fundamentally, and comprehensively. Education alone cannot accomplish the task of the woman's liberation in a revolutionary fashion and resignation to the spontaneous development of the problem will bring about incongruity and disharmony between various aspects of Arab development. Socialist construction of society will be distorted and defective unless the problem of the woman's liberation in Arab society is solved radically, since socialism is a solution to the problem of the human being, whether a man or a woman.

The removal of imperialist influence, the disintegration of the feudal-tribal regime, and the spread of education had advanced the problem of the woman's liberation. But it is only socialist society that can furnish objective conditions for a rapid radical liberation of the woman.

The revolutionary party and government should endeavour to combat the negative attitude to women and work to eliminate the effects of reactionary notions. They should turn this struggle into an actual applied style that will make possible for her active participation in general life and in the struggle. It is this active participation that will remove all bonds which hamper the woman's development and will open up her human personality. But the revolutionary party and government are at the same time called upon to resist the superficial, formal, bourgeois concepts of woman's liberation, which contradict the positive sides of the Arab traditions and which, at the same time, obstruct the path of socialist construction.

Woman's true liberty can only be attained in a two-front struggle: against backward frameworks, traditions, and customs and against the bourgeois formal concept of liberty. The new concept of woman's liberty should also be linked to the problem of Arab society's socialist construction.

BIBLIOGRAPHY

Collections of Printed Documents and Primary Source Material

American University of Beirut. *Arab Political Documents.* 1963, 1964, 1965.
———. *Chronology of Arab Politics.* 1963, 1964, 1965.
———. *Al-Wathā'iq al-'arabiyya.* 1963, 1964, 1965, 1966.
———. *Al-Waqā'i' al-'arabiyya,* 1963, 1964, 1965, 1966.

Da'ūq, Bashīr (ed.) *Niḍāl al-Ba'th fī sabīl al-waḥda wa-al-ḥuriyya wa-al-ishtirākiyya* ("The Struggle of the Ba'th for Unity, Freedom, and Socialism"). Vols. IV (Beirut, 1964) and VI (Beirut, 1965).

Haikal, M.H. (ed.) *Maḥāḍir muḥādathāt al-waḥda* ("Protocols of the Unity Talks"). Cairo, 1963.

Itim Mizraḥ News Agency. Monitoring Service. Summary of Arab Broadcasts. Tel Aviv.

Oron Y. (ed.) *Middle East Record: Vol. II, 1961.* Jerusalem, 1966.

Arabic Newspapers Quoted in the Text

Al-Ahrām, Cairo
Al-Aḥrār, Beirut
Al-Anwār, Beirut
Al-Ba'th, Damascus
Ad-Difā' Jerusalem
Al-Ḥayāt, Beirut
Al-Jarīda, Beirut
An-Nahār, Beirut
An-Naṣr, Damascus
Rūz al-Yūsuf, Cairo
Ṣaut al-'Urūba, Beirut
Ath-Thaura, Damascus
Al-Usbū' al-'Arabī, Beirut
Al-Yaum, Beirut

Arabic Books

'Abd ar-Raḥīm, Maḥmūd. *Qiyādat ḥizb al-ba'th al-murtadda* ("The Apostate Leadership of the Ba'th Party"). Cairo, 1964 (?).

———. *Ash Sha'b al-'arabī yudīn al-'Aflaqiyyūn* ("The Arab People Will Convict the 'Aflaqites"). Cairo, n.d.

'Aflaq, Michel. *Fi sabīl al-ba'th* ("For the Ba'th, or On the Road to the Renaissance"). Beirut, 1959.

———. *Ma'rakat al-maṣīr al-wāḥid* ("Battle of the One Destiny"). Beirut, 1958.

'Allūsh, Nājī. *Ath-Thaura wa-al-jamāhīr* ("The Revolution and the Masses"). Beirut, 1962.

Anon. *Dirāsāt fi al-ishtirākiyya li-majmū'a min al-mufakkirīn* ("Studies in Socialism by a Group of Intellectuals"). Beirut, 1960.

———. *Qiṣṣat Ath-thaura fi al-'irāq wa-sūriyya* ("The Story of the Revolution in Iraq and Syria"). Beirut, 1963.

Bahā' ad-Dīn, Aḥmad. *Azmat ittifaqiyyat al-waḥda ath-thulāthiyya* ("The Crisis of the Tripartite Unity Agreement"). Cairo, 1963.

al-Ghādirī, Nihād. *Al-Kitāb al-aswad fi ḥaqīqat 'Abd an-Nāsir wa-mauqifihi min al-waḥda wa-al-ishtirākiyya wa-qaḍiyyat filasṭīn* ("The Black Book of the Truth about Abdel Nasser and His Position towards Unity, Socialism, and the Palestine Problem"). Damascus, 1962.

al-Ḥāfiẓ, Yāsīn (ed.). *Fī al-fikr as-siyāsī* ("On Political Thought"). Damascus, 1963.

———. *Ḥaula ba'ḍ qaḍāya ath-thaura al-'arabiyya* ("On Some Problems of the Arab Revolution"). Beirut, 1965.

Haikal, Muḥammad Ḥasanain. *Ma alladhī jara fi surya?* ("What Happened in Syria?"). Cairo, 1962.

Ḥashshād, 'Adlī, and 'Atiyya 'Abd al-Jawwād. *Suqūṭ al-infiṣāl* ("The Fall of Secessionism"). Cairo, 1963.

al-Ḥuṣrī, Sāṭi'. *Al-Iqlīmiyya judhūruha wa-budhūruha* (Provincial Particularism: Its Roots and Seeds"). Beirut, 1963.

'Indānī, Taufīq. *Al-Ba'th fi durūb an-niḍāl* ("The Ba'th on the Roads of Struggle"). Damascus, 1965.

al-Jundī, Sāmī. *Al-Ba'th*. Beirut, 1969.

al-Munajjid, Ṣalāḥ ad-Dīn. *at-Taḍlīl al-ishtirākī* ("The Socialist Delusion"). Beirut, 1965.

Murquṣ, Elyās. *Ta'rīkh al-aḥzāb ash-shuyū'iyya fi al-waṭan al-'arabi* ("History of the Communist Parties in the Arab Homeland"). Beirut, 1964.

an-Nafūrī, Amīn. *'Abd al-Nāṣir bada'a fi dimashq wa-intaha fi shtūra* ("Abdel Nasser Began in Damascus and Ended Up in Shtura"). Damascus, 1962.

ar-Razzāz, Munīf. *At-Tajriba al-murra* ("The Bitter Experience"). Beirut, 1967.

al-Rimāwī, 'Abdallāh. *Al-Manṭiq ath-thauri li-al-ḥaraka al-qaumiyya al-'arabiyya al-hadītha* ("The Revolutionary Logic of the Modern Arab Nationalist Movement"). Cairo, 1961.

aṣ-Ṣafadī, Muṭā'. *Jil al-qadar* ("The Generation of Fate"). Damascus, 1960.

———. *Ḥizb al-ba'th, ma'sāt al-bidāya wa-ma'sāt al-nihāya* ("The Ba'th Party: The Misfortunes of Its Beginning and of Its End"). Beirut, 1964.

Salāmeh, Ibrāhīm. *Al-Ba'th min al-madāris ilā ath-thakanāt* ("The Ba'th from the School to the Barracks"). Beirut, 1969.

Ṭarābīshī, Jurj. *Sartre wa-al-marxiyya* ("Sartre and Marxism"). Beirut, 1964.

Zahr ad-Dīn, 'Abd al-Karīm. *Mudhakkirāti 'an fatrat al-infiṣāl fi-surya* ("My Memoirs of the Separatist Period in Syria"). Beirut, 1968.

Books and Articles in Languages Other than Arabic

Abu Jaber, Kamel S. *The Arab Ba'th Socialist Party: History, Ideology and Organization*. Syracuse, N.Y., 1966.

Agwani, M.S. "The Ba'th: A Study in Contemporary Arab Politics", *International Studies,* III (1961), pp. 6–24.

Anon. "Soviet Interest in Syria", *Mizan,* VIII(1) (1966), pp. 23–33.

———. "Soviet Opinions on Syria and the Ba'th", *Mizan,* VIII(2) (1966), pp. 73–86.

Avi-Dan (pseud.). "Elites and Centre in Syrian Society" (in Hebrew), *Hamizrah Hehadash,* XVIII (1968), pp. 205–222.

Baer, G. *Population and Society in the Arab World.* New York, 1964.

Baghdache, Khalid, "La Syrie sur une voie nouvelle", *Orient,* IX (1965), pp. 109–128.

Be'eri, E. *Army Officers in Arab Politics and Society.* New York and London, 1970.

Ben-Tsur, A. "Composition and Membership of the Ba'th Party in the Kuneitra Region", *Hamizrah Hehadash,* XVIII (1968), pp. 269–273.

———. "The Neo-Ba'th Party of Syria", *Journal of Contemporary History,* III (1968), pp. 161–181.

Binder, L. *The Ideological Revolution in the Middle East.* New York, 1964.

———. "The Tragedy of Syria", *World Politics,* XIX (1967), pp. 521–549.

Bitar, Salah. "Retour sur le passé", *Orient,* X (1966), pp. 173–210.

Borthwick, B.M. "The Islamic Sermon as a Channel of Political Communication", *Middle East Journal,* XXI (1967), pp. 299–313.

Buck, J. de. "Les nationalisations en Syrie", *Correspondence d'Orient,* VII (1965), pp. 61–67.

Chevallier, D. "De la production lente à l'économie dynamique en Syrie", *Annales* (1966), pp. 59–70.

Chevallier, F. "Forces en présence dans la Syrie d'aujourd'hui", *Orient,* I(4) (1957), pp. 179–185.

Colombe, M. "La nouvelle politique arabe de la Republique Arabe Unie", *Orient,* III(3), 1959), pp. 13–19.

———. "La mission a Damas du Maréchal égyptienne Abd al-Hakim Amer", *Orient,* III(4) (1959), pp. 27–35.

———. "Particularismes et nationalisme arabes à la lumière du coup d'état syrien", *Orient,* V(3) (1961), pp. 15–18.

———. "La Republique Arabe Syrienne à la lumière du coup d'état du 28 mars", *Orient,* VI(1) (1962), pp. 11–17.

———. "Révolutions, socialisme et unité", *Orient,* VII(1) (1963), pp. 7–15.

———. "Remarques sur le Ba'th et les institutions politiques de la Syrie d'aujourd'hui,', *Orient,* X(1) (1966), pp. 57–67.

Dabbagh, S.M. "Agrarian Reform in Syria", *Middle East Economic Papers,* n.v. (1962), pp. 1–15.

Dann, U. *Iraq under Qassem.* London and New York, 1969.

Dawn, C.E. "The Question of Nationalism in Syria and Lebanon". In W. Sands (ed.), *Tensions in the Middle East.* Washington, D.C., 1956, pp. 11–17.

———. "From Ottomanism to Arabism: The Origin of an Ideology", *Review of Politics,* XXIII (1961), pp. 378–400.

Frost, C.R. "The UAR: A Study in Arab Nationalism and Unity" (unpublished Ph.D. dissertation, University of Denver, 1966).

Garzouzi, E. "Land Reform in Syria", *Middle East Journal,* XVII (1963), pp. 83–90.

Grunebaum, G.E. von. *Modern Islam.* New York, 1964.

Haim, S. "The Arab Awakening: A Source for the Historian?", *Die Welt des Islams,* n.s., II (1953), pp. 237–250.

———. *Arab Nationalism: An Anthology.* Berkeley and Los Angeles, 1964.

———. "The Ba'th in Syria". In M. Curtis (ed.), *People and Politics in the Middle East.* New Brunswick, N.J., 1971, pp. 132–143.

Halpern, M. *The Politics of Social Change in the Middle East and North Africa.* Princeton, 1963.

Hansen, B. *Economic Development in Syria.* Santa Monica, Calif.: Rand Corporation, 1969.

Hansen, G.H. "Farewell to Syrian Coups", *Middle East Forum,* XXXIX (1963), pp. 13–14.

Hilan, Rizkallah. *Culture et développement en Syrie et dans les pays retardés.* Paris, 1969.

Horton, A.W. "Syrian Stability and the Ba'th", *American Universities Field Staff, Reports Service, Southwest Asia Series,* n.v. (1) (1965), pp. 1–11.

Hottinger, A. "Syria: War Psychosis as an Instrument of Government", *Swiss Review of World Affairs,* XVII (1967), pp. 3–5.

———. "How the Arab Bourgeoisie Lost Power", *Journal of Contemporary History,* III (1968), pp. 111–128.

Hourani, A.H. *Syria and Lebanon.* London, 1946.

———. *Minorities in the Arab World.* London, 1947.

———. *A Vision of History.* Beirut, 1961.

———. *Arabic Thought in the Liberal Age, 1789–1939.* London, 1962.

Jabale, J. "Dossier des Cahiers de l'Orient Contemporain: La crise du Ba'th", *Cahiers de l'Orient Contemporain,* No. 60 (April, 1966), pp. 6–12.

Jargy, S. "La Syrie à la veille d'une nouvelle expérience", *Orient,* III(2) (1959), pp. 19–31.

———. "Le declin d'un parti", *Orient,* III(3) (1959), pp. 21–39.

———. "La Syrie d'hier et d'aujourd'hui", *Orient,* V(6) (1961), pp. 67–76.

Kerr, M. "The Emergence of a Socialist Ideology in Egypt", *Middle East Journal,* XVI (1962), pp. 127–144.

———. "Arab Radical Notions of Democracy", *St. Antony's Papers,* 16 (1963), pp. 9–40.

———. *The Arab Cold War.* 2d ed. London, 1967.

Khadduri, M. *Republican Iraq.* London, 1969.

———. *Political Trends in the Arab World.* London, 1970.

Khalidi, T. "A Critical Study of the Political Ideas of Michel 'Aflaq", *Middle East Forum,* XL (1966), pp. 55–68.

Lenczowski, G. "Radical Regimes in Egypt, Syria and Iraq: Some Comparative Observations in Ideologies and Practices", *Journal of Politics,* XXVIII (1966), pp. 29–56.

Lerner, D. *The Passing of Traditional Society.* New York, 1964.

Majdalani, Jubran. "The Arab Socialist Movement". In W.Z. Laqueur (ed.), *The Middle East in Transition.* New York, 1958, pp. 337–350.

Mirsky, G. "Troubled Times in Syria", *New Times,* No. 34 (1963), pp. 13–16.

Nabulsi, H. "Labor Organization and Development in Syria: 1946–1958" (unpublished Ph.D. dissertation, Georgetown University, 1960).

Oron, Y. "The Arab Socialist Renaissance Party: Its History and Ideas", *Hamizrah Hehadash,* IX (1959), pp. 241–263.

Palmer, M. "The United Arab Republic: An Assessment of Its Failure", *Middle East Journal,* XX (1966), pp. 50–67.

Pennar, J. "The Soviet Road to Damascus", *Mizan,* IX (1967), pp. 23–29.

Rondot, P. "The Minorities in the Arab Orient Today", *Middle Eastern Affairs,* X (1959), pp. 214–218.

———. "Quelques remarques sur le Ba'th", *Orient,* VIII(3) (1), pp.7–19.

Rouleau, E. "The Syrian Enigma: What Is the Ba'th?", *New Left Review,* No. 45 (1967), pp. 53–65.

Saab, E. *La Syrie ou la révolution dans la rancoeur.* Paris, 1968.

Safran, N. *From War to War.* New York, 1969.

Salibi, Maurice. "Syrian Communists in the Fight for Social Progress", *World Marxist Review,* VIII (1965), pp. 76–78.

Seale, P. "The Ba'th's Role in the Ramadan 14 Revolution", *Middle East Forum,* XXXVII (1963), pp. 17–19.

———. *The Struggle for Syria.* London, 1965.

Seymour, M. "The Dynamics of Power in Syria since the Break with Egypt", *Middle Eastern Studies,* VI (1970), pp. 35–47.

Shimmel, N. "Developments in Syria", *New Times,* 6 (1966), pp. 7–8.

Steppat, F. "Eine Bewegung unter den Notabeln Syriens, 1877–1878: Neues Licht auf die Entstehung des arabischen Nationalismus", *Zeitschrift der Deutschen Morgenlandischen Gesellschaft,* Supplement I, Teil II (1969), pp. 631–649.

Suleiman, M. *Political Parties in Lebanon.* Ithaca, N.Y., 1967.

Tibawi, A.L. *A Modern History of Syria.* London, 1969.

Tibi, B. *Die rabische Linke.* Frankfurt am Main, 1969.

Torrey, G.H. *Syrian Politics and the Military, 1945–1958.* Columbus, Ohio. 1964.

———. "The Ba'th: Ideology and Practice", *Middle East Journal,* XXIII (1969), pp. 445–470.

Van Dam, N. "De Ba'thparty in Syrie (1958–1966)", *Internationale Spectator,* XXV (November 1971), 1889–1933.

Vernier, B. "Le role politique de l'armée en Syrie", *Politique Etrangère,* XXIX (1964), pp. 458–511.

———. *Armée et politique au moyen orient.* Paris, 1966.

Viennot, J.P. "Le Ba'th entre la theorie et la pratique", *Orient,* VIII (1964), pp. 13–27.

———. "Le role du Ba'th dans la genese du nationalisme arabe", *Orient,* IX (1965), pp. 65–80.

Weulersse, J. *Le pays des Alaouites.* Tours, 1940.

———. *Paysans de Syrie et du Proche Orient.* Paris, 1946.

Winder, B. "Syrian Deputies and Cabinet Ministers, 1919–1959", *Middle East Journal,* XVI (1962), pp. 407–429, and XVII (1963), pp. 35–54.

El-Za'im, I. "Le problème agraire syrien: Etapes et bilan de la réforme", *Developpement et Civilisations,* 31 (1967), pp. 68–78.

Zuwiyya-Yamak, L. *The Syrian Social Nationalist Party: An Ideological Analysis.* Cambridge, Mass., 1966.

INDEX